*Enjoyment of life
is not related to the satisfaction
that a career and family provide,
but to the strength
with which they are pursued!*

Walter Schmidt, 2016

Für Lolo mit großem Dank

DR. DR. WALTER SCHMIDT
INTERN. MANAGEMENT AND HUMAN RESSOURCES CONSULTANT

Rush Hour of Life

Managing the Clash between Family and Career

FRIELING

www.rushhour-of-life.com

Bibliographic Information of the German National Library

The German National Library has registered this publication in the German National Bibliography; detailed bibliographic information can be found online at http://dnb.d-nb.de.

© Frieling-Verlag Berlin • www.frieling.de
Rheinstr. 46, D–12161 Berlin, Phone (0 30) 766 999 80

ISBN 978-3-8280-3389-4 · E-Book: ISBN 978-3-8280-3390-0
1st Edition 2017 • Layout: Michael Reichmuth, Berlin
Image verification: © Ursula Deja - Fotolia.com
All rights reserved • Printed in Germany

This book can offer you help in self-help. Almost 250 billion euros, which the state spends directly or indirectly on family support every year, are sufficient. It is time for people like us to learn to lead a good family life with our own strength. This book shows you a possible way.

The economy and the church have discovered how important this way is in balancing family and career. The author wishes to thank the Vereinigung der Bayerischen Wirtschaft *(Bavarian Business Association, VBW)* and the Archdiocese of Munich for the support of the German book publication.

Preface

The topic of this book is a key issue of our time. Combining work and family life is a practical challenge which many people find to be very nerve-consuming every day. Women in particular are often torn between the demands imposed on them as professionals and managers in business life and as mothers, wives and daughters who have parents to care for.

To a significant extent, people label the options which remain available to them in this tense relationship with negative terms. Those who apply the qualifications that they state not only in their workplace, but also want to develop further accordingly, quickly get a reputation as a "bad mother". On the other hand, those who want to spend several years dedicated to the upbringing of their children, are quickly labelled with the term "cricket on the hearth".

Behind these labels are standards which society as a whole applies to individual couples in the "rush hour of life". These standards are undergoing a new kind of sharpening, caused by demographic change. After all, our ageing society requires women to be both professionals and mothers to the young in order to remain sustainable. With this demographic dilemma, we require good solutions and new ideas, and are also developing these at the Bavarian Business Association (vbw).

In his book, Dr Walter Schmidt touches on an aspect which has (surprisingly) hitherto remained fully underexposed in discussion of the question of reconciling work and family. While, according to the State, accompanying financial or structural measures are quickly called for, it is rarer for one to ask how Dr Schmidt is doing, which individual options affected parties actually have and could develop. In this domain, as well, it is worth assessing the logic of the social market economy in a subsidiary fashion i.e. from the smallest unit.

This is proven by the results that are contained in this book, which shows not only feasible methods in the tense arena of work and family life. Major chances and development potentials (both for individual couples and for companies) are also worked out here – assuming the reconciliation of work and family life actually succeeds.

I hope that this extremely exciting book will be read by many, and that many people who play a part in our economy will apply the suggestions in this book in practice.

Professor Randolf Rodenstock

Honorary president of vbw – Bavarian Business Association
Managing partner of Optische Werke
G. Rodenstock GmbH & Co. KG

Inhalt

Preface		7
1 Prologue		13
2 A Complex Net of Conflicts		15
3 Men and Women in the Rush Hour of Life		17
4 The Conflict of Objectives: Professional Success and Creating a Harmonious Family Life		19
	Upheaval of Values and Living Conditions	19
	The Area of Tension between Career and Family	22
	The Conflict of Objectives, its Characteristics, Consequences and Possible Escape Routes	24
	Analysis of the Conflict	27
	• Causes and Motives	27
	• Possible Causes of Conflict	28
	• The Inner Attitude to Family and Marriage	37
	• Career and Character	39
	» Power as an Internal and External Driving Force	40
	» Career as a Personal and Social Challenge	41
	» Character as a System of Value, Measuring and Control	42
	Conclusion: The Conflict can only be resolved by consideration of the other party's motives	44
5 Conflict Resolution based on Salutogenic Model by Antonovsky		45
	The Salutogenic Model	47
	The Sense of Coherence	50
	How the Sense of Coherence changes in Course of Life and how it can be applied to our Target Group	55
	Influencing the Sense of Coherence by psychotherapeutic Measures	58
	Conclusion: The salutogenic model is a promising method to solve the conflict	61
6 Looking for Individual Resources		63
	Control of Emotions	65

- Searching for Meaningfulness — 70
- Self-respect, Identity, Self-protection — 72
- Conclusion: The Sense of Coherence is Decisive — 77

7 Co-evolution of Family and Career by Changing the Sense of Coherence of Interacting Individuals — 79

- Basics of Family Ethics — 83
  - "Person" as a term establishing family ethics — 87
  - Ethical and Sociological Metamorphoses of the Family — 91
- Coping Strategies for the Family — 96
  - Self-realization and variety of roles — 99
  - Open discussion of the Dilemma and sensitive Dealing with the Conflict by Family Members — 104
  - Mutual Evolution of Couples; Personal Resources — 105
    - The partner's map: to know, to recognize, to understand — 111
    - Emotional Attachment, Feelings and Love — 117
    - Emotional Intelligence and Competence — 122
    - Family as a School of Feelings — 129
    - Creating of a Common World — 131
    - Conclusion: Resistance resources can be enlarged — 134
  - Changing Behaviour in the Relationship; Resources Input — 134
    - Founding a Dyadic Construct System — 137
    - Developing of Convergence Controlled by Behaviour — 138
    - Perceiving, accepting, influencing and differentiating the behaviour in partnerships — 140
    - Generation of Common Flow Experience — 145
    - Closeness and Distance — 150
    - Control of Commitment — 152
    - Conclusion: a common inner world should be created — 154
  - Recognizing and Monitoring of Control Mechanisms: Resilience, Transaction, Coherence — 154
  - Development of Culture of Constructive Controversy — 156
- Basics of Corporate Ethics — 159
- Pervasion of the family by the society – a paradigm change — 165
- Coping Strategies at Work — 169
  - Scope of Requirements on Executive Managers and Their Character Properties — 170
  - Servant Leadership – Managers' Development as Personality Development — 176
    - Conceptional Basics of Servant Leadership — 176
    - The Dilemma of Management — 177
    - The New Attitude of Servant Leadership — 178
    - The New Type of Manager – Basic Trust instead of Primal Fear — 182

8 History of the Future: Solution Approaches between Individualizing and Collectivizing — 185

- Searching for Meaning and Identity at Work and in the Family as Holistic Co-Evolution Process — 187
  - The Impatient Society — 187
  - Conflict between Character and Experience — 188
- Developing the Sense of Coherence in Groups — 189
  - Group Consciousness and Group Vibes — 189
  - The Social Setting — 190
- Cooperative Leadership at Work — 191
  - Concept Feasibility Prerequisites — 191
  - The Role of Individual in Cooperative Leadership — 192
- Servant Leadership in Families – a Serving Family Leader — 193
- Salutogenic Work-Life Balance — 195
  - Self-Management and Relationship Management — 195
  - Salutogenic Health Management — 196
  - Conclusion: Future development of the salutogenic model makes the rush hour of life controllable — 197

9 Summary and Forecast — 199

Annex

- Bibliography — 211
- List of tables — 223

Prologue

"A view of societies in other cultures offers no model at all for the struggle for equality of opportunity of men and women in our society. Our model of marriage is actually not the standard for the world. This means that types of life together in other societies can look fundamentally different from here – that is to say, less focused on couples. Our type of relationship, as we know them, is a special case and not the general reality around the world. It's an exception."[1]

Our couple-focused society includes about 800 million people in Europe and North America. The struggle between men and women in particular takes place here. What determines the behaviour of these people, and how do they pass on their behaviour to the next generation?

"There are inevitabilities of cooperation and conflicts, both generally between individuals, genders and generations, but also between genes and cultural behavioural programs. Programs are not only saved and reproduced in the genes, but also in brains. They succeed not only through gametes, but also through tradition in new carrier individuals; these do not expand through reproduction, but through convincing; which also requires a completely different behaviour of individuals than what is required by genetic programs for their expansion. So it's no surprise that culture does not always favour reproduction. Every incorrect behaviour, i.e. one that does not serve the expansion of the program, is automatically eliminated. In evolution, this happens if the successful program can be passed on to future generations and there develops behaviour that promises corresponding success under certain environmental conditions. In principle, it does not matter how the program reaches the next generation. We will have to get used to the image that the individual person displays as an executive body for several behavioural programs that often work against each other, which are still here today because their carriers successfully programmed them in the past. These programs sometimes go against ancient genetic programs. They are "unnatural" like contraception and birth control. The welfare state is also unnatural, which is unstable in its evolution because it almost essentially exploited and undermined by egoistical tendencies of individuals."[2]

The behaviour of the couple-focused society, which we address here, is also passed on through procreation and convincing. We build on the genetic circumstances of humans today and try to find out how we can change the behaviour of people in the relationship between men and women through convincing, training and mutual influence. We are searching for the secret that successful people are influenced by a different behaviour than that of less successful people.

---

1 Laubscher, M., Frau und Mann – Geschlechterdifferenzierung in Natur und Menschenwelt, in Schubert, V (Publisher), Eos Verlag Erzabtei St. Ottilien, pp. 93–94.
2 Wickler, W., extract from the preface to the German edition of "Das egoistische Gen" by Dawkins R., Spektrum Akademischer Verlag, Heidelberg, 2008, pp. 20–21.

"The biographies of successful people often strikingly show that the goal was not career in itself, but that tasks given to somebody were able to be successfully completed. The successful people had a pervasive, lasting, but dynamic feeling of trust that their internal and external environment can be predicted and that there is a high probability that things will develop as you can reasonably expect them to."[3]

---

[3] Antonovsky, A., Health, Stress and Coping, New Perspectives on Mental and Physical Well-Being, Jossey-Bass Publisher, San Francisco, 1985.

A Complex Net of Conflicts

Nowadays, there are two points of orientation in the cohabitation between men and women, which are felt today as equal value: career and family, or, as said in Bründel's words: profession and relationship. Both of these items lead to happiness and satisfaction, provided that they are in a well-balanced correlation to each other. However, social reality reveals an imbalance, since men and women approach these points of orientation very differently. While men primarily tend to think and act job-related, women tend to primarily feel responsible for family and partnership. The number of women working in leading positions is still significantly smaller in comparison to men. In Germany, it varies between 7 and 14 % and in the United States, between 22 and 26 %, depending on the branch, age and level of position.[4] However, women's perception of their role in society is changing. Thus, men's role, which seems to be well-balanced, no longer exists as such. A change in men and women's understanding of their social roles has led to these roles interfering with each other. This trend is partially amplified and accelerated by exogenous transformations in economy and work, i.e. in the fields that men have dominated up until now. Unemployment destabilizes the traditionally organized employment system, in which men work on a regular basis outside of their homes. One's life story and one's organization of individual phases of life have become uncertain. Consequently, a diversity of goal conflicts has arisen. This is no longer a mere one-dimensional conflict between career and family orientation, but a complex multi-dimensional net of conflicts. During different stages of life, this net of conflicts will change its characteristics and coerce men and women to re-structure their relationships.

---

4   Only in the below-30 age class, there is a similar number of men and women in leading positions. On the contrary, women between 30 and 45 years old only make a 14 % share in leading positions. Scientific works are known for verifying more or less abstract theories through empirical investigation and conclusion. Federal Statistical Office, focus on: Frauen in Deutschland, 2006, p. 28.

Men and Women in the Rush Hour of Life

Scientific works commonly have a more or less abstract theory that is verified by empirical investigations and conclusions. In the present lecture, we use a reversed approach: first, empiricism and then, the theory. The author is an international executive search consultant. He and his team interviewed over 15,000 young executives from 1981 to 2009, i.e., a period of 28 years. In such structured interviews, not only the conflict between family and career planning was researched but also, the reasons, characteristics, possible solutions and approaches were discussed and recorded.

Through the transference of three scientifically based theorems, i.e.

- "Salutogenesis" (A. Antonovsky)
- "Servant Leadership" (R. Greenleaf)
- "Co-evolution" (J. Willi)

to the empirical findings, practically usable and secured solutions and approaches were developed. Based on the changes in the behaviour of working and married partners, these approaches may lead to a partnership that is free of conflicts.

Occupation is defined as any type of employment conducing to income and earning money. In this context, there is no difference between being employed and a freelancer. However, earning money does not exclude expressive goals. Being interested in work contents and social contacts are also important in one's occupation, besides the basic instrumental goal of gaining income. Unofficial and gratuitous employment is not considered in this context.

In the sense of Lüscher[5], we do without the nominative use of the family-sociological concept. We consider a broader definition of family, which includes all types of cohabitation in a household comprising adults and children. Thus, it is not limited to a specific type of family, for example, the traditional one (father, mother and child). However, we essentially limit our consideration to the most common and socially focused way of life, which includes two adults and at least one child to care for. The definition of career that this study is based on has a broader sense than a mere employment-related term. The different stages in one's life are the matter of

---

5   Lüscher, K., Die postmoderne Familie: familiale Strategien und Familienpolitik in einer Übergangszeit, Konstanz, 1988, pp. 15–38.

discussion here. Luhmann's[6] definition of career which is used here, allows for the coequal recognition of family careers, in particular, parenthood and employment careers. The focal point of this discussion is "agreement career". This term means the stage in one's career in which gainful employment and parenthood – in particular, the responsibility for children who are not yet independent – overlap and should be matched.

The following sections will address the behaviour of men and women within their families and jobs, and will be geared towards young executives with five to ten years of work experience and children at pre-school and primary school age (core target group). In our context, "executives" means both employees and self-employed people, whose responsibilities exceed project- and issue-related tasks. They are in charge of motivation, targeting, further training, continual education and the control of results of a collective of employees, i.e., of a team. Executives make use of their professional expertise and social competence in order to accomplish the super-ordinate goals of a department, a business sector or a company, as well as to utilize their potential and to maintain their power. Competition inside a peer group, paired with the expectations of the superior, causes an employee to feel pressure to succeed like a young businessman competing with other companies.

In a family, due to the obligation to provide care, education and support for a child, both parents feel an emotional and material pressure. This reaches its peak between the third and fourteenth year in a child's life. This "double load" by work and family in the emotional respect is nowadays still borne by the woman to the greater extent. The financial load is borne by both parents together or primarily by the man. Both men and women are in the middle of the rush hour of life.

---

6   Luhmann, N., Copierte Existenz und Karriere zur Herstellung von Individualität, Frankfurt, 1994, pp. 199–200.

4 The Conflict of Objectives: Professional Success and Creating a Harmonious Family Life

Upheaval of Values and Living Conditions

Conflicts are part of our human identity.[7] They arise between all people who are in regular interaction with each other, disregarding legal conflicts. There are vocational conflicts with bosses, employees or colleagues and, in particular, people who you actually love and appreciate the most such as a spouse, children and friends. All conflicts have one thing in common: they arise when our expectations cannot be met, regardless of whether we expect something from ourselves or from others. Non-compliance with expectations is called frustration (futile expectations).

To a large extent, expectations and goals determine the way that people act. It is in men's nature that a person is not viable without goals – one gets depressive and prone to suicide. An accomplished goal leads to a feeling of success. Successes make humans active and actional beings. Activity may take place on a purely intellectual level, a quasi activity of thoughts. Therefore, a person always strives for success, i.e. for accomplishment of his/her goals. The stronger the person's identification with his personal goals and the more unrestricted his acceptance of these goals is – seeing them as meaningful and necessary – the greater his likelihood is to achieve these goals. Corell discovered that 82 % of employees in Germany do not really "match" with their professional ambitions but rather, have built up a "cognitive dissonance" between objective target and identification.[8] They pursue their profession without a "primary" motivation but with a "work-to-rule" attitude. These professionals strive to fulfil their tasks, not because they expect to accomplish their goals, but because of secondary benefits, for example, money and occupational advancement.

---

7   Conflict [lat., confligere "beat, smash"], antagonism, quarrel, fight [between persons, countries, or others]; also inner antagonism of motives, desires or intentions.
    Social conflict: clash of interests and disputes of various intensity and violence between persons, groups, organizations, societies, countries or groups of states resulting from that. Conflict contents are controversies on values, goals of life, status, power or distribution fights. About the origination of conflicts, there are different theories: The biologically-oriented behaviour research often assumes human biological basic instincts, which do not vary. This theory postulates a general potential of aggression and sees conflicts as a "natural" social fact. In the view of social psychology and sociology, conflicts are caused by contrariness between a person's mental drives/motivations and standards/requirements of the society order. Alternatively, the reason of conflicts can be contradictions in the structure of obligatory behavioural standards itself (socially structured conflict). Meyer, 1992, Vol. 12, p. 89 f.
8   Corell, W., Psychologie für Beruf und Familie, 18th edition, mvg Verlag, Heidelberg, 2007, p. 13.

The latter seems to be problematic since they have no primary motivation. It should be pointed out that the employer often does not clearly see their primary and secondary motivation, since an increasing number of employed people "learned to camouflage" their lack of primary motivation by hustling and bustling.

We have to realize that, among members of many occupational groups, actual goals of life relocate into non-occupational fields, i.e., leisure, hobbies and travelling. This implies that the majority of people develop expectations in fields that are irrelevant to their careers. Hence, successes are experienced more and more outside of one's job. At the same time, experiences of frustration at their workplaces grow and grow. As such, occupation is increasingly seen as a means to an end.

This negative trend in the development of the attitude of most German employees becomes stronger due to the linkage to other human behavioural patterns. People's expectations in one field grow as much as their expectations in other fields have been met. The wealthier a person, the more he expects. One would think that the more expectations fulfilled, the happier and more expectation-free people would be. However, in reality, this is not the case. Frustration grows to the same extent as the standard of living increases. Moreover, according to Corell[9], not merely the improving standards of living but the entire mental/intellectual development causes us to continuously expect more. For instance, due to progressive emancipation from all kinds of paternalism, we are becoming more self-reliant, mature and responsible. Thus, we boisterously demand for more self-realization by making others take a step back to allow us to take a step forward. The mindset of previous generations – that blows of fate must be endured and taken as an ordeal – is no longer familiar to us. It conforms to today's concept of humankind to live in the notion that we shape our own destiny, i.e., we can "make" our life. While people continue to expect more, clashes between our fellow citizens and us are becoming inevitable, as they are also focused on their individual expansion. The more people live in a tightening space, the bigger the rubbing surface. The means of communication that are available in the modern world allow us to enter close relationships with lots of people. Consequently, the level of frustration we are exposed rises.

Additionally, as we are obviously becoming more this-worldly in our attitude and have swamped out most of our relation to transcendence, the tolerance of frustration decreases incessantly, whereas the risk of frustration increases. As a result, we are getting involved in an increasing number of conflicts that we cannot manage without difficulties because we are no longer willing to accept them.

Society's solution to divide the work between spouses according to traditional gender-specific roles is becoming less and less effective. A growing number of young executives that are available to the "West-oriented" industrial and service society consists of men and women, who take responsibility for both, the financial wealth of the family and looking after the children, either as individuals or dual-career couples.[10]

---

9   Corell, W., p. 14.
10 Ornstein, S., Making Sense of Careers, in: Journal of Management, Los Angeles, 1993, pp. 243–267.

With respect to quality of life (material comfort, opportunities for individual development and disposal of their own time), today's society, in principle, broadly accepts gender equality as equal opportunities for men and women. Finally, however, this cannot be achieved without adequate social structuring of the relations between employment and parenthood. In market-based societies, opportunities in life primarily come from accessing gainful employment. As long as motherhood prevents or, at least, massively hinders women from gaining this access, gender equality cannot be achieved.[11] Hence, another area of conflict opens up between family as a private matter and the collective public interest in the family. However, this conflict will not be the focus of the present research.

Based on economic, social and cultural indicators, the following analysis will discuss why the relationship between gainful employment and family is considered not only as an individual and familial area of conflict but also, as an organizational one. The starting point of this reasoning is based on an unbroken male and a rising female employment orientation, in particular among women with qualified education.[12]

---

11 Auer, M., Vereinbarungskarrieren, Eine karrieretheoretische Analyse des Verhältnisses von Erwerbsarbeit und Elternschaft, Die Deutsche Bibliothek, Hampp, Munich, 2000, p. 44.
12 Bosch, G., Zukunft der Erwerbsarbeit, Frankfurt, New York, 1998, pp. 13–55.

The Area of Tension between Career and Family

Despite a general decrease in employed people's working-motivation, making a career is still a life goal for most people. Especially for ambitious young executives, it is a self-purpose that is not questioned. Successful people (men and women) gain recognition, satisfaction in work, higher-than-average income and power over other people and resources. On the one hand, at work, an executive is expected to constantly produce new ideas and be resilient, unsentimental and tough. On the other hand, in his private life, the same person should be tender, loving and sensitive, and should have enough time for the family. In addition, he is expected to reduce his emotional needs because the emotional care and tenderness of his female partner is mostly focused on the children.

The executives should generate peak performance in the two worlds, despite the fact that, in many fields, these worlds have different rules. For example, the important criteria of one world could have a negative effect in the other one.[13]

The tension between career and family is strengthened by the need for occupational labour mobility. Globalisation, in the sense of Beck's[14] "Enträumlichung" (deterritorialization) of social relationships, and the fact that entrepreneurial activities are no longer tied to a certain location, have led to an increasing need for mobility in occupations. One asks: how much mobility can family life cope with? The investigations of Schneider, Limmer and Ruckdeschel[15] point to people's pursuit of a balance between longevity and change, and between reliability and renewal. On the one hand, a decreed longevity has a paralysing effect. However, if longevity does not exist and if there is no way to establish longevity, disorientation will be the result. Most people want to live in a relationship and not alone. For many people, the partner relationship is the essential supporting pillar of life. Life satisfaction, which is shown in all relevant sociological studies, is primarily determined by satisfaction in a partnership and with family, not by success at work. According to Thadden[16], in today's world, there is a remarkable movement against the availability of executives in the labour market. Even if you believe that the entire coordinate system of the conflict areas changes, it remains clear that it does not reduce the potential for conflicts between profession and family. These conflicts are only deferred. As long as the financial protection of the family is guaranteed by earning money at work and not largely provided by the state, the potential for conflicts persists. Even in the utopian case – if the state will fund the family entirely

---

13 Czwalina, J., Walker, A., Karriere ohne Sinn, Gräfelfing, 1998, p. 18.
14 Beck, U., Was ist Globalisierung?, Frankfurt, 1997, p. 97.
15 Schneider, N., Limmer, R., Ruckdeschel, K., Familie und Beruf in der mobilen Gesellschaft, Frankfurt, 2002, p. 205.
16 Thadden, E., Gesucht: Fachkraft mit Familiensinn, in: Die Zeit, 45, Dossier, 2008.

in the future – the area of maintaining power outside the family remains the driving force for a professional career.

Other issues, like power and social recognition, will be discussed later.

Finally, we can say that mobility, professional career and family development are closely related in terms of interdependence. A high willingness to be professionally mobile promotes one's professional career. However, a high intensity occupational mobility prevents the family-orientation. Family ties reduce the willingness to be professionally mobile and, consequently, the chance to reach a higher level in the professional hierarchy.

The Conflict of Objectives, its Characteristics, Consequences and Possible Escape Routes

The conflict of objectives between the professional advancement of an executive and their family orientation is distinguished by the high requirements of both sides. One side causes pressure to perform and the other side causes emotional pressure. All of the attributes that distinguish a great executive will make private living together more and more complicated. Often, the executive cannot escape from the requirements of both areas, hence they feel unable to cope with the double burden. The non-employed spouse usually knows nothing or too little about the partner's professional burdens. The executive's advancement comes along with the decline in family life. The more success he/she has in his profession, the more he uses his home as a "family hotel" that is managed by his partner.

The concentration on professional success renounces the development of one's personality and causes a fear of abandonment. The executive's fear of abandonment and his/her vulnerability is clearly higher than an employee without leadership responsibility. The further advances the executive makes at work, the more his quality of family life declines. In the family context, this not only means being deprived of love by the partner but also, sexual failure. Ernst Bornemann explains: "All investigations made by my colleagues and me have the same result: people who are primary focused on money, power and authority, fared badly in sexual life. Men, who can really satisfy a woman, have a type of character that totally differs from men who mainly aspire to professional success. In the higher, eventually also in the lower management levels, there are often fights to the finish. Consequently, men do the same even in bed. The switch between the particular professional requirements, like the daily pressure to always be the best during the daytime, and the ability to be capable of loving without any competition in the night-time is not always easy for men. This is a really big problem for people of the higher social class."[17]

Young executives are increasingly trying to get out of the double burden of family life and professional success by making priorities. They either make family life the priority by giving up their next career step or they have a career without any happiness in their family life. To express this in a negative sense: some people accept the disruption of family, the separation and the divorce because they have professional success. Others accept professional stagnation, being sneered at and even unemployment, because they take responsibility for their family.[18] If you access this escape-route over one's whole career, you notice that some forward-looking executives try to escape from the area of conflict by concentrating on their career for one period of life and by tending to more family-orientation in the following period of

---

17 Bornemann, E., Die Zukunft der Liebe, Fischer Taschenbuch, 1997, p. 87.
18 Czwalina, J., Walker, A., Karriere ohne Sinn, Gräfelfing, 1998, p. 20.

life. In our investigated target audience (young executives with children of preschool or primary school age), this route of escape mainly exists as "the light at the end of the tunnel" and not as the current way of escaping. In our target audience, the area of tension increases from day to day (or, as Bornemann says, from day to night). Neither partner tries to bring one world in-line with the other. So, the distance between them grows. The wife, who is not in employment, begins to understand the vocational world of the husband less and less. The husband underestimates the duties of his wife and hardly understands her needs and preferences.

For many people, to focus on one side (job or family) means to fall out of the model of success of the other. As a result, both worlds break down. This breakdown is accelerated by the search for a compensation of losses on both sides. The man tries to compensate for the lack of affection, or becomes a "workaholic". The female partner seeks refuge in other relationships and tries to seek affirmation in hobbies or by concentrating on the household and children. The consequences are foreseeable. Due to the increasing requirements of executives, managers' fears and crises of identity will also increase. As such, the women become isolated and alone, become a single parent and divorce, unless they find their self-fulfilment in the world of work. In the best case, we find some superficial and non-binding relationships between two "social-partners".[19]

Today, we call the consequences of the increasing requirements on executives the "burnout syndrome". In 1996, the University Hospital in Geneva carried out a study with male heart-attack-patients aged between 32 and 45 years. They did not have congenital tendencies to heart attacks but suffered from tensions in their profession and private lives. The study shows that it is not only ambitious careerists in their mid-40s and mid-50s who are especially endangered to "burnout" in their work. None of them were capable of taking leisure and being calm and relaxed – they tried to escape into their professional hyperactivities.

According to Burisch[20], we distinguish three types of "burnout". The first type is a real burnout of the people that self-made their stress – "self-burning people". Such people do not want to say "no" to their own restlessness. The second type is "wear-out-people". These are victims of pressure from the outside and cannot say "no" to others. In the USA, there is also an ironic expression, known as the "rust-out". This is a type of person who wants to be wretched without ever being burned out. Until this situation comes to a head, a process of escalation takes place. A burnout does not suddenly happen at once. There is often a longer chain of frustrating expectations, failed action plans and absent rewards in the executive's profession and family.

Already during his career ascension, the executive realizes that his idyllic vision of a family as a haven of calmness and peace is far from the reality. As well as

---
19 Czwalina, J., Walker, A., p. 22.
20 Burisch, M., Das Burn-out-Syndrom, Heidelberg, 1994, p. 121.

pressure at his workplace, the executive begins to feel under pressure by his family's expectations of understanding and showing them affection, of collaborating and solving problems, which he no longer feels able to do. In a family, the working husband is called more and more into question. The respect that is given to a "hard-worker" decreases.

The partner who does not go to work tries to come to terms with the unsatisfied expectations in different ways, depending on their temper. Mentally independent, self-conscious and well-educated women make the best of this by enjoying prosperity and time for their children, as well as creating their own private relationships. It seems that only the modest and reserved women define themselves only by their men. In better cases, they suffer in silence. In the worst case, they search for the missing satisfaction by: having sexual relationships outside of their partnership, being on medication, abusing alcohol or abstruse searching for their "Higher Self". The partner who is employed but does not want his career to be his whole life is tempted to enter the same escape-routes. Where mutual recognition is missing, the executives and their female partners search for solutions to fill their inner emptiness and to escape from their crises.

The young wives and mothers of our target audience are bred to be more self-confident, regardless of whether they go to work or not. Mostly, they are no longer ready to obey the subordinating role of men. The more that they are alert and educated, the less they accept men's authority.

Analysis of the Conflict

Causes and Motives

We have ascertained that if our expectations of ourselves or of others are not met, both family- and job-related conflicts arise. We have defined such expectations as the kind of goals that largely determine our behaviour. An accomplished goal leads to a feeling of success. Corell refers to this feeling as "fuel for our soul". It makes humans become active beings. Their activities can also be mental ones.[21] Therefore, a person always strives for success, i.e. for accomplishment of their goals. Frustration arises when expectations cannot be fulfilled because we have been expecting something in vain (frustra) or, at least, we expected more than we are able to accomplish within our professional and private environment.

Insight into good and bad in itself is not enough to be able to decide for the good; there must also be reasons for the good that you identify with. This leads to the ethical strength of the will, which expresses our perseverance and determination; if this leads to success, our motivations are strengthened. People's perseverance is a function of motivation and previous experience of success.

Werner Corell
"Psychology for Career and Family", p. 48

In the view of today's value systems, we are becoming more self-reliant due to the progressive emancipation from paternalism and the wish for self-realization. As such, the demands of our respective environments are increasing. Women have increasingly emancipated themselves from paternalism. Spouses are relieved from complete dependency on each other. Children are also relieved from regimentation by teachers and educators. This is because the authority of teachers and educators no longer derives from their official position or their responsibility for children. Employees in a company no longer feel bound to their superiors. An increasing number of employees expect a higher level of participation and co-management and personal acknowledgement in their job. Meanwhile, these employees are becoming more reluctant to act under orders and commands or do the work just to make a living from it.[22] The communication process between young executives and their superiors, and young executives and their subordinate employees, causes an increasing level of frustration among young (mostly middle-level) executives. They cannot refuse to obey the orders that are given by their superiors and demand subordination from their employees at the same time. Consequently, existing hierarchies are starting to dissolve.

Due to a declining positive motivation for suffering in our increasingly secularized society, the human capacity for suffering is decreasing dramatically. As a result, individuals' tolerance of frustration is diminishing to the same extent. Consequently, more and more often, we get into conflicts both at our work and professional

---

21 Corell, W., Das Phänomen Konflikt, in: Psychologie für Beruf und Familie, Heidelberg, 2007, p. 45.
22 Corell, W., p. 46.

life and in the family, as well as in the area of conflicts between these two fields (profession and family). As we do not want to accept these conflicts, we can no longer overcome them without difficulties.

Possible Causes of Conflict

In the conflict scenario presented here, there are several causes of conflict in one conflict situation, which can overlap, reinforce and also replace each other both in the starting point and in the duration. The literature points to numerous attempts at the classification of conflicts, which ultimately have not led to a convincing and final clarification of their relationships. For this reason, the reader should not expect this scientific work to define a system of causes of conflict that will satisfy all requirements.

We limit ourselves to concise definition of those causes of conflict that we consider relevant to the conflict of objectives between family and career orientation, and for the time being in alphabetical order without assessing the significance of the causes of conflict:

Conflicts of values[23] occur when counterparts want to carry out the reconcilable action plans, because they assign a different value to the results and consequences of their action plans.

Distance conflicts[24] indicate different distance requirements of the partners during the development of a relationship.

Development conflicts[25] occur if different development speeds, directions and intensities in a relationship lead to different interests.

Leadership conflicts[26] are defined as conflicts in leadership by formal or informal leadership and insider relationships.

Gender role conflict[27] indicates the conflict between different rights, responsibilities and general behavioural norms of men and women in society.

Group conflicts[28] according to Schwarz, these also include competitive and rival conflicts (in companies and in families), affiliation conflicts, leadership, maturation and replacement conflicts. According to Dessler, these also include line-and-staff conflicts.

Power conflicts[29] – with asymmetric power distribution. Certain decisions can be enforced against the will of the subordinate, even if they are in the right. According to Dahrendorf[30] power conflicts relate to inequality of status, i.e. the unequal

---

23 Rüttinger, B., Konflikt und Konfliktlösen, Psychologie im Betrieb, vol. 5, Goch (Bratt), 1980, p. 69.
24 Schwarz, G., Gedanken zum Konfliktmanagement, Harvard Manager, 1984, br. 1 , p. 60.
25 Schwarz, G., p. 64.
26 Kurtz, H.-J., Konfliktbewältigung im Unternehmen, Cologne, Dt. Inst. Verlag, 1983, p. 88.
27 Zuschlag, B., Thielke, W., Konfliktsituationen im Alltag, Verlag f. Angewandte Psychologie, Göttingen, 1998, p. 105.
28 Dessler, G., Organisation und Management, A Contingency Approach, Englewood Cliffs, Prentice Hall, USA, 1976, p. 187.
29 Schwarz, G., p. 66.
30 Dahrendorf, R., Elemente einer Theorie des sozialen Konfliktes, in: Gesellschaft und Freiheit, Munich, 1969, pp. 197 f.

distribution of legitimate power in social organisations (= companies and families).

Hierarchical conflicts[31] – indicated as conflicts between persons in different hierarchical leadership levels, which can be traced to differences in information, objectives, values, standards and loyalty.

Identity conflicts[32] occur in the function of individuality in a couple or group relationship (family). To what extent does an individual have to give up their identity to preserve the identity of the other party.

Conflicts of interest[33] – arise if irreconcilable interests block targeted action and force painful or improper compromises.

Interpersonal conflicts[34] – conflicts between different ambitions of two or more people.

Intrapersonal conflicts[35] according to Deutsch[36], also known as intrapsychic conflicts – are conflicts between different ambitions within the same person.

Communication conflicts[37]: misunderstandings occur if different bases or acts of communication prevent correct transfer or interpretation of information.

Competitive and rival conflicts[38] occur in competition for status positions, if several people are seeking the same position.

Latent conflicts[39] – unlike open conflicts, these indicate a conflict scenario in which the cause of the conflict is kept secret or is not known to the persons concerned. Conflicts are latent for as long as the persons concerned do not attempt to bring a conflict that is already known into the open.

Couple conflicts: Schwarz[40] understands these to include a group of identity, distance, transaction and role conflicts described here.

Dessler[41] considers conflict situations to be **role conflicts** if an individual or group is integrated into one or several groups that have different and irreconcilable objectives and values.

Substitution conflicts[42] indicate a shift of the actual conflict to another superficial conflict cause. Solving a substitution conflict does increase the awareness of conflict of the persons concerned, but it is not sufficient to solve the underlying conflict.

Territorial conflicts[43] restrictions to expansion or responsibility with regard to sphere of life or influence leads to conflict with the demands of someone else who is focused on their own sphere of life or influence.

---

31 Rüttiger, R., Transaktionsanalyse, Arbeitshefte zur Führungspsychologie, brochure 10, Heidelberg, 1980
32 Schwarz, G., p. 67.
33 Glasl, F, Konfliktmanagement, Handbuch für Führungskräfte und Berater, Bern, Stuttgart, 1980, p. 134.
34 Berkel, K., Konflikttraining, Konflikte verstehen und bewältigen, Berlin, 1995, p. 89.
35 Berkel, K., p. 91.
36 Deutsch, M., Konfliktregelung, Munich, Basel, 1976, p. 139.
37 Kurtz, H.-J., p. 71.
38 Schwarz, G., p. 67.
39 Rüttiger, R., p. 25.
40 Schwarz, G., p. 67.
41 Dessler, G., p. 178.
42 Schwarz, G., p. 70.
43 Schwarz, G., p. 71.

Transaction conflicts, according to Schwarz[44], indicate the asymmetric communication between persons, e.g. where children are treated as adults if they are „misused" as referees in their parents' conflicts. Adults being treated as children also represents a transaction conflict.

Distribution conflicts in our thematic relationship are not conflicts resulting from the distribution of goods and financial resources. According to Rüttinger[45], these indicate conflicts that result when counterparts consider the value of a result or area of responsibility to be equally high, but they cannot achieve this result or take on this area of responsibility at the same time because they cannot allocate themselves to both simultaneously.

Perception conflicts indicate that two people perceive an issue differently. One looks more to the opportunities and advantages of an issue from a positive, optimistic attitude, the other looks more to the risks and disadvantages from a negative, pessimistic attitude.

Conflicts of objectives: conflicts are considered irreconcilable if each objective requires the whole or a least the majority of the available time in order to achieve the objective. The basic conflict in the orientation between career and family is a conflict of objectives in this sense.

The 15,000 interviews with young executives conducted by the author and his partners in the period between 1981 and 2009 confirm the listed conflict types and causes in practice. Apart from the fundamental conflict of objectives, none of the causes of conflict occur in pure culture. These are always a distinct networking of numerous different causes. If you follow-up on the weighting of the causes of conflict over the investigated period of 28 years of social development, you come to the result presented in the following table.

The attempt to separate the causes of conflict into family and career seems to be theoretical at first glance, because the conflict is described here, occurs precisely in the interaction between family and career related behaviour and actions. However, the empirical investigations showed that increasing and/or decreasing „conflict gestation" in the area of family and/or in the career have a direct influence on the area of tension between career and family. On the one hand, this is because the conflict capacity, i.e. the volume of personal conflicts that can be processed, is limited. A releasing of pressure in one of the areas of conflict allows increased conflict in another area. Conversely, increased stress in one conflict area generally causes a reduction in the ability to resolve conflicts in another area of conflict. On the other hand, the weighting of causes of conflict has been significantly displaced. With increased autonomy in time and income of your objectives, and parallel shifting values to greater individual self-determination, regardless of gender, development, identity, distribution and perception conflicts have led to a disproportionate increase in the resulting conflict group of couple conflicts.

---

44 Schwarz, G., p. 74.
45 Rüttinger, B., p. 81.

Causes of conflicts	In the family	At work	Between family and work
Conflicts of valuations	+	–	+ +
Distance conflicts	+	–	o
Development conflicts	+ +	o	+ +
Leadership conflicts	+	+ +	+ +
Gender conflicts	–	–	–
Group conflicts	+	+ +	+
Conflict of authorities	+	+ +	+
Hierarchical conflicts	–	–	o
Identity conflicts	+ +	o	+ +
Conflict of interests	–	–	+
Inter-personal conflicts	+	+	+ +
Intra-Personal conflicts	–	+	o
Communication conflicts	+	–	+
Competition and rivalry conflicts	–	+	–
Couple conflicts	+ + +	o	+
Conflict of roles	–	–	+
Substitution conflicts	–	–	+
Territorial conflicts	+	–	+
Transaction conflicts	–	–	+
Distribution conflicts	+ +	–	+ +
Perception conflicts	+ +	–	+
Conflicts of objectives	–	–	+ +

Table 1: Weighting of causes of conflict during the period from 1981 to 2009
(+ increasing / - decreasing / o none or not conform to the system)

A systematic analysis of these conflicts and how they are dealt with requires looking into people's motivations for actions and action control. We have asserted that humans are beings with motives and aspirations. We are permanently "dissatisfied", as Corell[46] says, and are constantly striving forward. We only manage to satisfy all of our needs either very late or never at all. As soon as you have accomplished a goal, a new goal already starts moving into the foreground and thus, keeps you active. However, constant activity makes people rather easy to lead and amenable. In this case, we should appeal to the particular motive that is of the utmost urgency for the person that we want to lead and persuade.

To further explore people's motivations for the actions behind their conflicts, we will examine the possible sources of their motivations. The motives that apply to all people who are living within a comparable culture and civilization are referred to as basic motives, as they basically exist as a matter of principle. They do not need to be of the same intensity and can vary and alternate. Inside the psychological historical frame, we can determine two fundamental concepts. The first one is the motivational-psychological monism. This assumes that there should be a sole basic motive that all other effective motives derive from. The second one is the motivational-psychological pluralism. This says that there should be multiple motives that drive and control us alternately or at the same time.[47]

The main proponent of classical monism is Sigmund Freud.[48] According to his structural model, action control is affected by the subliminal (by "ID"), conscious free will of decision (by "EGO") or social standards (by "SUPER-EGO"). In numerous case studies, he demonstrated that all of his patients' motivations are still mostly libidinous and sexual nature. Freud and many of his pupils traced people's actions back to their libidinous basic motives, from which their mental efforts can also be derived through sublimation. We have largely overcome the sexual taboos that were once assumed by Freud. In today's society, these are replaced by new taboos preventing us from saying and doing what we want. Such a new taboo is the expansion of an individual's power at the expense of others. Alfred Adler[49] has pointed out that our striving for power and prestige is the basic motive that drives our actions. He allocated a compensatory function to this striving: the more disesteemed one feels, the stronger one's quest for recognition and superiority over others is, even though one may exceed the limits of "political correctness". According to Adler, excessive ambitions and exaggerated striving for professional success can be seen as a compensation for once being defeated and a desire to restore the individual psychological balance.

---

46 Corell, W., p. 25.
47 Corell, W., p. 25.
48 Freud, S., Die Traumdeutung, Frankfurt, 1961, p. 164.
49 Adler, A., Praxis und Theorie der Individualpsychologie, Frankfurt, 2001, p. 109.

According to the doctrine of the psychological pluralism of motivation, humans are not only influenced by motives. We also have several mutually affected tendencies and incentives. Maslow[50] assumes several motives, which only take effect if the basic needs of life are satisfied first. According to today's prevailing opinion of the motivational psychologists, it seems to be more plausible to assume several motivations instead of variations of a sole motive. Contrary to Maslow, Corell[51] ascertains that the motivation of self-preservation obviously does not need to always be satisfied first before other psychological motivations get a chance. In Corell's opinion, the conception of "self-preservation first" is refuted by the fact that humans are capable of committing suicide. If self-preservation were the absolutely highest and most important motive, a human would not be able to kill himself. So, we have to assume that various pluralistic conceptualized motivations equally or simultaneously take effect on us. One day one of these motivations comes to the fore, another day, another of them. Without starting a theoretical discussion about how many motivations actually exist, we will follow the *five "basic motivations"*, which Corell showed in his multi-dimensional motivations-model. This is because these motivations can be clearly defined and validated both in the professional and private environment.

The Five Basic Motivations by Corell

Social recognition

The first of the five basic motivations is the individual's quest for social recognition within one or more groups. This is a quest for prestige and superiority, for status and validity – similar to how Adler designated it with his concept of striving for validity. If someone follows this motivation over everything else, then their behaviour will be particularly ambitious and industrious as they aim to imitate the respective „Alpha person", who is regarded as the leader of the group. A person who seeks social recognition has not yet achieved this to the extent that they planned. They are the upwardly mobile one with an urge to move further up the corporate hierarchy. They are especially common in our target group of younger executives. But a person motivated by recognition directs their efforts towards every group that they belong to – not just in their professional environment, but also their family / private environment. They will be concerned with casting themselves in the best light in any given group, and gaining recognition therein. As for the defeats that they have to deal with as part of their urge for acceptance in a group, they usually try to conceal them vis-à-vis other groups, so as not to lose recognition amongst them. We are familiar of cases of people concealing the loss of their job vis-à-vis their family, or at least their circle of friends, for longer periods of time, or who have concealed the breakup of their marriage vis-à-vis colleagues and superiors. In a society in which State benefits and voluntary ones (in a business setting) are linked to family status (e.g. child support, corporate accommodation etc.) and professional success is marked by status symbols (e.g. company cars, computers, mobile phones), concealment of defeats to the end of social recognition tends to be only short-term. On the other side, it must be noted that people who are predominantly motivated by recognition are expected to perform

---

50 Maslow, A., Motivation and Personality, New York, Harper, 1954, p. 268.
51 Corell, W., p. 27.

and to be bound to their respective group, which will exemplify to them the desired form of behaviour as a means for gaining prestige. People motivated in this way adopt the expected form of behaviour relatively uncritically and quickly. The share of younger executives who are motivated by recognition is significantly higher compared to the total population, and is increasing further.

Certainty and protection

In contrast to extroverted people who are motivated by recognition, the security-motivated person strives for unobtrusiveness, health and economy. They avoid non-transparent risks, unplanned efforts and even blame, and they are opposed to changes – they are mostly even fearful of them. When dealing with such people, one should offer things that are proven, and avoid new things. Both in professional life and in family life, one can motivate this kind of „skeptics" to adopt a specific kind of behaviour only with patience and in small steps, and that's only if it's possible to make it clear to them that there are no incalculable risks associated with it. The increased need for security in Germany's business companies is reflected by increased fear of job loss, illness or loss of one's partner. The skeptics are still a minority in our target group of younger executives, but the need for security will grow in this social group as well in the coming generation, and will ever more frequently clash with the need for social recognition.

Trust

This basic need refers to one's fundamental human striving for other people that they want to rely on, and from whom they can expect trusting affection. Those motivated by these motivations strive neither for social recognition nor for security, but for closeness to other people to whom they can be a trusted caregiver. If one partner in a marriage is motivated primarily by this, it will be easy for the other partner to lead a harmonious marriage, as the former partner totally adjusts to the other, going along with their ideas by making them their own. Such people are referred to as „wake partners" or „slipstream partners" in literature (usually perjoratively) – they clearly want nothing for themselves, instead always preferring to be altruistic for others. If two partners with such a basic motivation get married, there will be the risk of them trying to create a „perfect world", convincing themselves that their other partner is all they need and separating themselves from their social environment (both professional and private). American literature describes this scenario as „cocooning" of pairs, often together with their children. Given that both partners in a relationship often don't develop at the same speed and in the same direction, and one often has more contacts outside of the cocoon than the other, such islands of harmony don't usually last long. Generally speaking, the trust motivation scenario is decreasing in the population of Germany. However, an increase in selfish lifestyles leads to decreasing fidelity of executives to a company and to increasing instability of partner relationships within a family.

Self esteem

A person for whom self-esteem is the most important motivation in their lifestyle, will be exaggeratedly punctual and accurate, but no less uncompromising, perfectionist and opinionated. Normally, they are isolated from their peers, as they lack any generosity in humour. In their professional dealings with superiors and colleagues, they will insist on extreme accuracy and timeliness, and demand a loyal and uncompromising approach in matters of justice. It is difficult to convince them, as they would prefer to suffer personal disadvantages rather than violate their principles. The principles that they consider „right" are not so much for an orderly coexistence with others as for an end in itself. They are completely without feelings of compassionate tolerance toward others, and their actions are defined by cold calculation of respective results and unbending discipline. This kind of behavioural motivation is particularly pronounced in the following life phases: late puberty, midlife crisis and old age; it is marked by bigotry, pessimism and personal bitterness, but also by stubbornness and sanctimoniousness. In both work and personal lives, others can only cope with those intent on such self-respect if they are motivated by trust i.e. if they are capable of devotion and subordination. They must be ready to agree to plan everything until the end, and then to be guided afterwards. There is little to no room for spontaneous decisions here. Those most largely motivated by self-respect are far less commonly encountered in the target group of younger executives surveyed here than in the general population. Along with the type that cares about safety and security, this affects a 74 % share of the population, according to surveys by Corell. Conscientiousness and reliability unite when it comes to socially and economically risky matters, with inflexibility and fear of change.[52]

Independence and responsibility

This basic motivation is people's pursuit of an activity in which they can assume their own responsibility. Those with this type of motivation like to make their own decisions independently, and to form their own lives independent of those above them, and they are ready to accept the consequences that result from it. This basic motivation is the predominant one among executives, whether they are independent contractors or hired managers. They would not have become executives had they not been ready to assume a greater degree of autonomy and responsibility, and they would not have become self-employed entrepreneurs had they not pursued this self-reliance and responsibility despite the risks involved. Such a person is not normally driven to occupy a position right at the top, but it will inevitably happen to them, so to speak, and this is because they are distinguished in particular by their professional attitude, their realism and their willingness to commit themselves for the greater unit of a company or group.[53]

In marriage, this kind of motivation prevents one from being totally open with their partner, and it secures a tolerant and generous form of cohabitation. A woman with this kind of motivation will normally prefer an occupation encompassing an activity related to family and / or domestic matters. If both partners have such motivation, conflicts will develop which cannot be resolved by mutual tolerance alone. They are discussed as the subject of Chapter 7 of this book. This disadvantage of this basic motivation lies not so much in professional environments – after all, those with this kind of motivation will inevitably be successful – as in one's private life, in that they show too little emotional engagement.

The share of people motivated by independence and responsibility in our society is decreasing more and more – according to Corell[54], it applies to only 2 % of Germany's entire working population. This shrinking trend suggests that only a small minority of people develop their own initiatives and responsibility. However, it is this minority that is represented by our target group of younger executives; their „independency motivation" is far higher than that of the general population and is increasing further.

Summarized: The human being who seeks social recognition does all of these things for himself and his prestige, and not for others. Since the human being is focused on certainty and safety, they think of nothing but his/her own safety. Being motivated by trust, the human being does his/her best to help his/her boss at work and his/her partner in family-life, and not for himself/herself. The human is concerned about his/her self-esteem and, as such, is only led by principles and maxims. Basically, only the human being, who is focused on independence and responsibility, is suited to coping with supra-individual tasks in profession and family.

The basic motives that induce human beings to do something do not always appear in the sequence that is shown below. According to Corell, they constantly rotate: one motive is satisfied and shifts to a lower position, giving another motive greater importance. According to this conception, the human being only reaches

---

52 See Table 2.
53 Corell, W., p. 39.
54 Corell, W., p. 39.

complete satisfaction for a short time but never for a long time. This is because a new motive will always induce him, as soon as the old one is satisfied. We have described that there can be tensions and competition between motivations and that the basic motives are differently weighted and prioritized in different periods of life.

> This is elucidated by comparing how the basic motivations developed in the entire German working population and in our target group (young executives) in the years from 1978 to 2014 (see table 2). The data were taken from Corell's research results for the entire working population and from the results empirically collected by the author in many thousands of interviews with young executives in which they were asked about job and family-related basic motivations.

	1978	1984	1990	1996	2002	2008	2014
Social recognition							
Total population	20 %	16 %	15 %	14 %	n/a	n/a	n/a
Young executives	24 %	25 %	25 %	27 %	28 %	29 %	30 %
Certainty and protection							
Total population	30 %	34 %	36 %	38 %	n/a	n/a	n/a
Young executives	22 %	21 %	19 %	17 %	16 %	15 %	15 %
Trust							
Total population	15 %	15 %	12 %	10 %	n/a	n/a	n/a
Young executives	9 %	8 %	9 %	9 %	8 %	7 %	6 %
Self esteem							
Total population	30 %	32 %	35 %	36 %	n/a	n/a	n/a
Young executives	30 %	28 %	25 %	21 %	19 %	19 %	18 %
Independence and responsibility							
Total population	5 %	3 %	2 %	2 %	n/a	n/a	n/a
Young executives	15 %	18 %	22 %	26 %	29 %	30 %	31 %
	100 %	100 %	100 %	100 %	100 %	100 %	100 %

Table 2: The five basic motivations (tendency development of the meaning) (based on Corell, W. and the author's sources)

> At this point, we should explain how we present the research results given in the table 2. We want neither to pretend nor to give an impression that we simply quantified the qualities in the investigation results. The competent reader will interpret the results obtained by the empirical

survey as definite trends and not as mathematical facts. Therefore the motivation model discussed here should be supplemented by a discussion on the „motives behind the motives". Here we emphasise rather the person's attitude to his objectives than on his possibility to change the objective circumstances. Generally, we can distinguish between **a primary and a secondary motivation**, depending on whether one strives for a goal of his own sake (primary or intrinsic motivation) or whether one pursues the goal as a mean for another purpose (secondary or extrinsic motivation). From the imposition of the values which we have described at another point, we clearly see that most Germans are only secondarily motivated in their jobs. They are usually not so fascinated from their activities that they would also exercise them without payment. They work only because they need money to live and financial security for themselves and their families.

The secondary motivation becomes extremely excessive when one loses his job: he feels impelled to do the work which he would never do from his primary motivation and accept such an activity only in order not to fall into "benefits gravy train". If he finds satisfaction and self-affirmation in his new job, his primary motivation will prevail again. Executives who need to overlook wider contexts in their activities and who can make decisions themselves have mostly – and, in case of above-average ambition, almost fully – primary motivation.

To comprehend the meaning of life, you should primarily be motivated in all areas of life, both in your profession and family. Only people who do this can experience the meaning of life directly and carry out their primary motivated tasks. If you are more primarily and less secondary motivated, you can more easily achieve a behaviour that will help you to avoid frustration and aggression. Is there any possibility for people in our society not to become frustrated? To achieve this, we should be independent from the results of our behaviour and congruent with our acting. In Chapter 6, we will search for a solution for this.

The Inner Attitude to Family and Marriage

By describing the causes of conflicts, the impulses for action and the motives, we begin to understand the net of conflicts in which people and especially younger executives are involved in. This understanding is the basis for further explanations. Therefore, we are now dealing with the inner attitude to family and marriage and to professional career in our target audience. We keep track of the norms of family and of professional ethics, but not like a historical review. Instead, we refer to ethical patterns of behaviour and their changes, which are relevant to the social transformation process that the family and professional life are exposed to.

The institutions of family, marriage and state are complex normative structures, controlling human actions. As such, they are overarching forms of life. While social regulations and norms control humans' needs, interests and connotations, institutions control areas of life in which such needs and connotations are put into practice.[55] In thi s case, institutions create guidelines of understanding and help individuals to find a way of ethically and morally sound self-unfolding. The human being needs the help of these institutions since they cannot rely upon their own

---

55 Korff, W., Institutionstheorie, Die sittliche Struktur der gesellschaftlichen Lebensformen, in: Handbuch der christlichen Ethik, Vol. 1, Basle, Vienna, 1993, p. 169.

instincts and his/her actions. The institutions give them security and safety by taking away the burden of their actions. However, it does not mean that the shape and ethos of the family are rigid and do not change. The understanding of the family was always – and still is – subject to continuous change and will also change in the future. What are the family ethics of today?

The change in our society's life conditions is characterized by the fact that self-unfolding values, like emancipation, enjoyment, self-realization and independence, have replaced the previously prevailing values of duty and acceptance such as obedience, readiness for acceptance, discipline and selflessness. Families are also affected by this process of change in the value system. Although living together as a family is still important, the family has become **more fragile** and its manifestations have become **more versatile**.

The increasing instability and fragility of the family is reflected in the rapidly increasing number of divorces and the decreasing number of marriages. The increasing number of unmarried people is a sign of the relativization of marriage as a form of life. Family life has become significantly more fragile due to the decreasing birth rate. Besides the "normal family", i.e., consisting of two parents and two children, there is a variety of other forms of family life in today's Germany: married couples without children, single mothers and fathers with minor children and patchwork-families in married and not married partnerships. Next to pluralization, we see a growing trend to individualization. Decreasing sizes of households and a high number of single households prove this. The individualization process is accompanied by a biographical pluralism of lifestyles.[56] More and more, people experience several of these life forms in their biography. In former times, the biographies of a man and a woman were incorporated into their family. Now, it is just the opposite trend. "Since family relations become replaceable," says Ulrich Beck[57], "independent single male and female biographies peel off inside and outside the family. Each partner goes through several partial families or family-free lifestyles at various life stages. That is why everyone lives more and more his/her own life."

In the last decades, the family as a social group has become – as mentioned – more fragile. It has lost its united appearance and – with regard to the number of children – its productivity. Representative studies have revealed that, today, the institution of marriage, but not the family, is less valuable and less worthy of protection than decades ago. Family as a social way of life is well respected and enjoys high esteem both at the level of attitude and actions.[58]

In the course of society's social differentiation, the family has changed from a work- and economical community to one of emotion and leisure. This means that emotional relationships of married couples or partners become the most important component of family life.

Separation of work- and family life has led to an emotionalization of the

---

56 Beck, U., Risikogesellschaft, Auf dem Weg in eine andere Moderne, Frankfurt, 1986, p. 189.
57 Beck, U., pp. 188 f.
58 Gruber, H. G., Familie und christliche Ethik, Wissenschaftl. Buchgesellschaft, Darmstadt, 1995, p. 9.

spouses' relationship, as well as the parent-children-relationship. This has led to a fundamental change in the attitude to the child. The family has evolved from a reproduction community to a social instance for children. In a socially mobile society, which is first of all built on individual performance and enforced power, now the highest pedagogical imperative is the best possible promotion of children's abilities and fulfilment of their needs. However, in many families, fulfilment of this means waiving many things that lead to a good life and prosperity. Unlike times before, the cost of children's education is now much higher than the economic benefits that parents gain from it. Then, in our days, it is common to have fewer children, but parents try to give them the best possible promotion of their abilities.

With the increasing equalization of men and women's education over the last two to three decades, growing individualization concerns women, not just men, as it was before. While men previously went to work outside their homes, women were expected "to be at home for the others", i.e., for the family.[59] Today, women's employment is far more than a mere intermediate phase. For women, not being employed is an exceptional situation and is more and more limited to the phase of looking after small children.[60] This is a profound change in the institution of marriage and family. The expansion of individualization in the female life context means that today's women are exposed to the same expectations as men, as well as the same requirements of the labour market. The more that men and women have the same options and compulsions of an individual and self-planned life, the more likely that family ties will break. Both incentives and requirements entailed by the individualized labour market refer more to a **single person** than to a partner and the family.[61]

It is unavoidable that the shown individualization efforts of men and women will lead to a change in the social hierarchy of values. If economical and occupational values, such as rationality, objectivity, effectiveness, achievement, individuality and independence, influence the family, then other values, such as solidarity, social exchange and tolerance to others, will likely be lost. Economical values focus on the individual and his/her performance ability. They do not consider any psychological-emotional contexts of family life or their personal and social issues and content. We will continue this discussion to suggest the ways to minimize conflicts between profession and family.

Career and Character

In the interconnected system of marriage and family, there are learning processes in terms of maturity and character building. Here, parents and children learn how to live together. These are learning processes in which people learn: social behaviour,

---

59 Gruber, H. G., 1995, p. 9.
60 Tölke, A., Das Zusammenspiel von Familienentwicklung und Erwerbsverhalten von Frauen, in: Zeitschrift für Familienforschung 2, 1990, p. 14.
61 Gruber, H. G., 1995, p. 54.

taking responsibility, abstinence, thoughtfulness, benevolence, sharing of responsibilities, teamwork, discipline, and the formation of conscience.[62]

Any company that employs younger executives relies on their skill sets, inner attitude and character traits, which the executives have learnt from their families. In this view, the quality of family determines the character qualification of executives in their career. Labour is an expression of the person's creativeness. It is also the basis of his/her professional success or failure, as well as his/her power. Labour is embedded into organized processes that determine whether something is feasible. Family, on the contrary, does not represent the person's creativeness but rather, the energy from which the person was created. So, the family is the basis and precondition for everything that makes the executive manager successful. They are successful, only due to the fact that his/her parents did not decide against family. Czwalina[63] expressed this with some exaggeration: the executive's character attitude towards his family is not all about the relationship between him and his wife but also, about the future of the following generations. As per Christian ethics, family may not be allocated to one's own freedom of decision. A Christian-oriented person shall rather maintain and cultivate the chain of generations. In our society, a growing number of people insists on their autonomy to make decisions and, in extreme cases, to also destroy their families, when striving for power and career become an important priority in their lives and especially in their profession.

Nowadays, making a career is a life goal that is equally strived for by men and women. Successful people (men and women) gain recognition, satisfaction in work and a higher-than-average income. As soon as the first successes have been achieved (like in our target group of young executives who are already progressing in their career), these successes seem to have a "boosting effect", initiating further career ambitions. However, occupation can no longer provide a guarantee for security and life-long employment. Today, people enter their professional lives later but their retirement date is made earlier. Between these two points in time, there are years of insecurity. None of the young executives can say that his career is secured in the long term.

Power as an Internal and External Driving Force

An important criterion for safeguarding professional careers is obtaining power. Generally, power is an energy that encourages a person to live his life. Power moves a person forward but also determines his coexistence with other human beings. Striving for power is part of the basic instincts of a human being, as well as the elementary needs – hunger, thirst and sexual drive. Thus, power defines the possibility and ability to knowingly control one's intentions and goals. Alternatively, as Max Weber says:[64] "Power is the opportunity to get one's way in a social relationship, even despite the

---

62 Czwalina, J., Walker, A., Karriere ohne Sinn, Gräfelfing, 2nd edition, Resch, 1998, p. 44.
63 Czwalina, J., Walker, A., p. 46.
64 Weber, Max, Wirtschaft und Gesellschaft, 1922 (posthum), quoted after Winckelmann, J. (Ed.), Gütersloh, 1978, p. 196.

reluctance of others." Since power always presupposes a desire, will formation and the finding of goals are fundamental elements of it. In other words, power describes the possibility and ability to purposefully fulfil one's goal. In a professional context, "leading power" or leadership means the deliberate achieving of goals, paired with the force to accomplish required measures. According to this definition, leadership always remains intended, giving purposeful control over individuals or groups and their organizational units. There is no leadership without the exertion of power, i.e., without assertiveness and getting the upper hand. Thus, each executive who fulfils his mission always possesses power. With his exercise of power, the executive gains self-affirmation, self-confidence and a self-assertion in conflict situations. If we understand the power as defined above, the power is neither morally good nor bad. Only the way of how power is dealt with and controlled can be good or bad. Striving for power can be creative but it can also degrade and spoil a person. Thus, the matter is how to control one's drive to gain power and, at the same time, to strengthen his willingness to act responsibly at work and in family. The line between professional goals and opportunities to exert influence at work provided by the company, on the one hand, and private goals and benefits, on the other hand, need to be strictly adhered by the power holder. The more trust that is required in the personal integrity of the power holder, the more they should ensure that no advantage over others is misused in their private lives. Since power can be utilized both constructively and destructively, it needs to be controlled by the person's character. Character is an instrument that regulates power, namely the power that can both destroy and create. The destructive power is a desire to be more than what we are made to be and to have more than we deserve due to our performance. If fair competition in profession and family life turns into a fight, one strives for power destroys the human relationship between him and others. Paul Tournier[65] ascertains: "Power is the biggest obstacle in a dialogue. The ability to destroy human relationships is written largely on mankind's face." Everywhere human power unfolds, we see how the once gained power strives for more and the level of destruction increases. In contrast, power in a positive sense, can also be a waiver of exercising power. We can learn how to get along with others only when we have to gain control over our power, and not to be a victim of the latter.

Career as a Personal and Social Challenge

A successful career is a key in striving for power in business and economy. The term "career" is derived from a French word, meaning "successful path" or "the quickest gait of a horse". Herein indicates the elementary meaning of this term – it is a synonym for motivation, power and endurance. Thus, striving for a career as target-oriented and systematic is not only directed to financial independence and securing the means to make a living or provide for old age but also, to men and women's self-affirmation and self-actualization and to taking an active part in society. Over the decades, a career particularly influences the manager's personality and his/her

---

65   Tournier, P., Aus Vereinsamung zur Gemeinschaft, Basel, n. d., p. 37.

family's way of living in a very specific way. It provides financial stability, recognition in society, prestige and social status. Since early childhood, young people are inspired by their father's and mother's profession. This influences social wealth and lifestyle, as well as performance orientation and the pursuit for achieving more. If you know the professional and career ambitions of a person, you can easily allocate him/her to a certain level of social status. People need to be positioned in the social hierarchy in order to classify themselves and others into it and to distinguish themselves from others. If we know one's professional classification and job position, we believe that we know enough of his/her character and personality.

For many female and male managers, profession raises self-esteem and pride, giving them energy to perform highly qualified work. Both work content and the resulting relationship are important to them. Men and women also want to achieve their individual and subjective demands at work – women even more so than men. Female managers tend to bring more emotionality and unfold more of their personality at work than males. People who know how to mobilize extraordinary forces and can make their way up to the top of the career ladder and get opportunities to fulfil the individual challenges of life. A career offers personal learning and the opportunity to gain experience, as well as a chance to do better than others and show them ways to accomplish their professional objectives, i.e. a chance to be an example to others.

Finally, career offers the individual an opportunity to make a contribution to a higher-ranking final result.

In the future, the demand for executives who are ready to deliver an outstanding performance, who take responsibility for themselves and others, and who have the courage to make decisions in complex situations will increase. In this sense, a career is not just a way of living out your own ambitions. It can be an important mission in terms of the common good. Nowadays, to withstand the pressure that the manager is exposed to, they need something more than only specialized knowledge and management techniques. This pressure challenges the whole of his/her personality. In particularly, young managers, who are at the peak of conflicts between their professional and family life, should ask themselves: Am I in the position and willing to endure all of these tensions? How can I get the inner strength and power to conquer these challenges without damaging my soul and losing myself as a human being? How do I achieve a strong character and the integrity to deal fairly with the power that I have acquired?[66]

Character as a System of Value, Measuring and Control

A successful career and the power acquired by it can be used both positively and negatively. The question is how does the manager deal with his responsibility? This leads us to the term of character. We described character as an instrument that controls power. The term "character" will stay value-neutral as long as we do

---

66 Czwalina, J., Walker, A., p. 68.

not connect it to terms like 'good' or 'bad'. Character can also be described as a 'distinguishing feature' or 'the inner shape' of a person. Since the 17th century, this 'feature' has been related to moral norms and values. Therefore, it is not just a rigid combination of features inherited from parents or the social environment but rather, a "way" of being, a development and a dynamic process. Thus, personal competence is not a static, fixed personality characteristic. It is a dynamic and target-oriented approach to situations and tasks and is based on optimistic, realistic, flexible and differentiated objectives and attitudes.[67] Daniel Goeudevert is in agreement with this thesis and ascertains the following: "Someone who wants to lead people should be able to lead himself or herself first, i.e., have an open mind and willingness to develop and broaden his own horizon. In short: learning for and from life."[68] The executive's character development is the amount of decisions that are made by him/her on his/her own personal responsibility. We have to differ between the management abilities and personal attitude behind them, i.e., the value-, measure- and control system followed by the manager. Management abilities, like decision-making skills, value performance, endurance, initiative, intelligence, organizing ability, reliability, interpersonal skills, ability to judge and self-esteem, are only professional requirements. However, they do not make a successful executive. For the executive's long-term success, a valuation of their character is essential:

- An executive needs to be able to cope with tension and pressure without aggression and resignation.
- They solve unpleasant problems related to their professional and private life with moral courage and in a quiet and honest way.
- They sustain both failures and successes with a conscience.
- They support their employees without being afraid of creating competition for them in their own team or company.
- They respect other people's dignity in their professional and private environment.
- They are self-critical and not afraid of putting their own thinking and acting into question.
- They are ready to answer to their own mistakes and do not shift the blame to others.[69]

Herewith, we describe a high character-related demand on the executive. The term is taken from Anglo-Saxon language and is called "leadership". Leadership is the skill to take responsibility and personal risks, and to conduct other people – not due to their own hierarchical leading position but rather, their own performance, personality, integrity and character, all of which are to be proved every day anew.

---

67 Schelp, T., Karriere und persönliche Kompetenz, 1994, p. 25.
68 Goeudevert, D., Die Herausforderungen der Zukunft. Management, Märkte, Motoren, Munich, 1990, p. 274.
69 Czwalina, J., Walker, A., pp. 84 f.

Conclusion: The Conflict can only be resolved by consideration of the other party's motives

The higher the person's identification with his/her goal, the more likely he/she will achieve that goal. However, 82 per cent of all employees in Germany do not identify themselves with their professions. Although they continue to work, they have inwardly quit their professions. Their expectations are oriented towards other goals than their professional ones. For most of them, their profession is the only way that they can earn money. The better they live with regard to finances, the more they expect to fulfil their goals. Their frustration grows equally to their standard of living. Since many of them pushed aside their relation to transcendence, their frustration tolerance decreases more and more. Young executives should behave in another way. We see an increasing **job orientation** of male and especially female executives with a professional education background. They have to deliver top performances in two worlds. In many ways, these performances are contrary to each other. All of the attributes that distinguish a great executive will make private living together more and more complicated. There seem to be many ways to escape from this situation but none of these ways solve the conflict – they just make it even worse.

A systematic classification and evolution of conflicts have to reveal the actors' motives. Social acceptance, the feeling of safety, trust, self-esteem, independence, and responsibility are the main motives behind many secondary motives. In the early 21st century society, such **self-experience values** like emancipation, enjoyment, self-actualization and independence have almost replaced the former **predominating values** like allegiance, willingness to accept, discipline and unselfishness. As a result, families have become much more versatile, however, more fragile, too. Concerning occupation, the executive's character, which is connected to moral norms and values, comes under career pressure. Power was – and still is – the main drive of our professional success, which makes having a career a personal and social challenge.

Conflict Resolution based on Salutogenic Model by Antonovsky

The conflict between the goals of professional orientation and family focus has become a more and more significant issue in the social policy of all high-developed industrial countries. It is now generally recognized that this goal conflict suffuses all social classes and negatively influences the people's living together. In Germany, some consequences of this conflict are already recognized: Measurably increasing health problems,[70] continuous decline of number of families[71] and therefore decline of number of children. In spite of increasing life expectation, the reproduction rate decreases further.

All socially relevant groups (especially political parties) have been busy with this issue and, in the meantime, promised some legal changes (allowance, child support, part-time jobs, tax-deductible childcare costs, day-care supported by the government, etc.). It is conspicuous that most of the plans focus on the family, and not the professional orientation, or the conflict between them. All aid programs of direct or indirect family support have one thing in common: they only offer **formal solutions** (e. g. increasing financing of family costs by the state, income-loss refunds by the state, day-care in governmental institutions) and **not so much content**. The government and the business world try to diminish the consequences of the conflict, but do not try to mitigate its causes within the family.

> *In his famous metaphor, Antonovsky compared health and life to a river. With this metaphor, he was able to present the perspective change of the salutogenesis in a fascinating way. It presents an image of people swimming in a river full of dangers, bends and rapids.*
>
> *The doctor, according to Antonovsky, could use his pathogenetically orientated medicine to try to pull the driving people out of the current. But salutogenesis is about more than that: It's about making people into good swimmers. So what helps them to master dangerous spots and rapids without medical help?*
>
> Aaron Antonovsky
> Preface to „Salutogenesis"
> Demystifying Health

On the contrary (or, better to say, in addition) to the formal concepts of resolving the conflict between the family and career, we offer an approach based on the

---

70 Federal Statistical Office of Germany (Statistisches Bundesamt), „Haushalt, Familien und Gesundheit, Ergebnisse des Mikrozensus 2005", pp. 55 f.
71 Federal Statistical Office of Germany (Statistisches Bundesamt), „Mikrozensus 2005", pp. 41 f.

salutogenic model of A. Antonovsky.[72] We will look into the question how a single person (not a society) dealing with stress factors can manage to activate his/her individual capabilities and to efficiently and adequately control the conflict situation.

---

72 Antonovsky, A., Salutogenese, Zur Entmystifizierung der Gesundheit, translated into German by Alexa Franke, Deutsche Gesellschaft für Verhaltenstherapie, DGVT Verlag, Tübingen, 1997.

The Salutogenic Model

In recent years, the subject of salutogenesis has attracted a lot of attention in social sciences and in medicine, especially in such areas as illness prevention and health promotion. The concept was brought into the health science and health policy discussion by the Israeli-American sociologist Aaron Antonovsky (1923–1994). He criticized approaches based on pure pathogenic cures and compared them with a salutogenic approach. The most important question is why people remain healthy and not what are the causes and risks of an illness. Accordingly, the salutogenic approach primarily explores conditions for remaining healthy and health-protecting factors. In some way, it is a paradigm shift from an illness-centred pathogenic model to the health-centred, resource-oriented and preventive approach of salutogenesis. Using the salutogenic model Antonovsky tries to answer the question which is central for him: Why people remain healthy despite many potentially health-endangering influences? Some people who endured many hard physical and emotional stresses stay healthy – against all medical doctrines. What is special about the people who do not fall ill despite all the stresses? Some people develop amazing resistance against illnesses in daily life, too, and their well-being does not always owe to a healthy lifestyle. Quite the contrary: they live sometimes "unhealthy" and are still healthy. What keeps such people from illness?

These notices take centre stage in Aaron Antonovsky's studies. His aim was not to find out the ways of avoiding the risk of illness. Instead of that, he looked for explanations of health beyond the risk-avoidance patterns. Consequently he developed a new viewpoint of coherence between health and illness.

"Generally speaking, both the health-oriented viewpoint and the illness-oriented viewpoint of curative medicine are based on the assumption of a fundamental dichotomy between healthy and ill people. Who takes the first position aims his attention and resources on keeping the people well and prevent them from illness. Who takes the second view is focused on illness healing trying to prevent death and chronic diseases and – as far as possible – to restore health. The first ones argue that it would be much more efficient to invest energies in maintaining health. The second ones reply – if any dialog takes place – that no human society can ignore the suffering of those who are ill now."[73]

However, both pathologically oriented approaches do not answer the question why the person remains healthy. Health was defined and is partly still defined up to now as "not being ill". Health itself seems not to be an independent and self-contained quality.[74]

Antonovsky considers the human organism as a system permanently exposed

---

73 Antonovsky, A., pp. 23 f.
74 Bengel, J., Strittmatter, R., Einführender Vortrag vor der Bundeszentrale für gesundheitliche Aufklärung (BzgA), Cologne, 2001, A. Antonovskys Modell der Salutogenese, p. 138.

to natural influences and processes causing disturbances in its order, i.e. health. Health is not a stable balanced condition. The organism needs to continuously re-establish its health when dealing with sickening influences. Illness is not an exception, peculiarity, or health disturbance. Bengel[75] asserts that an average person feels ill even more frequently than healthy in the light of chronic diseases, civilisation sicknesses and psychosomatic illnesses. He points out that between 30 and 50 per cent of people in the higher-developed industrial countries are ill or have illness symptoms – if not only physical symptoms are included. If sickness is considered as the normal condition, it is certainly worth thinking whether health is something more than simply not-being-ill.

Based on the above mentioned notices Antonovsky worked out his salutogenic model. The model is based on the statement that health and illness do not exclude each other. They are extreme poles on a continuum and can be imagined as a continuous movement on a line between two extremes – health and illness. He calls it **health/disease continuum**[76] and says: "We are all non-eternal. We all are also healthy to a certain extent as long life still smoulders in us. The salutogenic approach intends that we investigate the position of each person on this continuum at any point of time. Epidemiologic research is to be concentrated on distribution of groups on the continuum. Clinical medicine would support the individuals under its care in their change toward the health pole."

In Antonovsky's opinion the organism strives to multiply its healthy shares or, at least, to establish a balance between its healthy and ill shares. The aim of the salutogenesis-oriented therapy is not only to heal illness symptoms but also to strengthen the organism's healthy shares and to enable the person to use his resources. This is the point where the paths of the pathogenetic approach and the salutogenic one go separate ways. The pathogenetic therapy is focused on healing of conspicuous symptoms – independent from the patient. The aim of the resources-oriented salutogenic therapy is to generally call up the healthy shares of the patient, e.g. to find out and to support the personal resources of the person.[77]

Since Antonovsky's theory structure does not offer any definition as to what "health" does mean, we will try to fill this gap and to offer a definition hitting the core of salutogenesis: "Health is a subjectively experienced and estimated as well as externally perceived and estimating genuine quality of life processes in the development of the body and its living environment. A healthy person integrally and differentially perceives himself in bodily connection with his life context (context and continuum). According to his vitality or vulnerability, potential coping, competences and resources situation the person is in the position to deal with critical personal experiences and problems, to control and to preserve himself when facing interchanging protective and risk factors, i.e. supportive and exonerative lifestyle. Based on that he is able to co-creatively and constructively flower out his physical, spiritual, social and ecological capacities and to develop a feeling of

---

75 Bengel, J., Strittmatter, R., p. 141.
76 Antonovsky, A., pp. 23 f.
77 Bengel, J., Strittmatter, R., p. 142.

coherence, meaningfulness and well-being. Usually a good immunological and physical condition is also provided, although it does not need always be so."[78]

Health as depicted above is thereby a dynamic balance controlled by given chances of using both protective and restoring factors that the person possesses himself and that are provided to him by his environment. Instead of asking the question what caused the illness and which stressors influence the person, Antonovsky places the main emphasis on the person's coping resources.

---

[78] Petzold, H. G., Steffan, A., Gesundheit, Krankheit, Diagnose- und Therapieverständnis in der „Integrativen Therapie", Jubiläumsausgabe 2001, pp. 75 f.

The Sense of Coherence

Antonovsky determined in his explorations that healthy people possess a certain spiritual global orientation that he called "Sense Of Coherence (SOC)". We will use this term (the sense of coherence)[79], since it exactly expresses our sensory perception in conjunction with our thinking and feeling and especially individual issues of life orientation, as well.[80]

This Sense Of Coherence which healthy people possess to a markedly great extent takes centre stage in salutogenesis. To say simply, the people with strong sense of coherence can manage their lives better. They are "good swimmers" (if we use Antonovsky's river metaphor). They feel themselves fit for challenges and solving problems, find their ways in their world and searching for the meaning of their lives.

In in-depth interviews and, later, by standardized questionnaires Antonovsky searched for typical characteristics of good coping in life histories of the respondents. His main question was what really matters for fates and destinies. His research suggests that in the given conditions some individuals and groups felt better than the others. That was the mystery which he searched for. The focal point of his research was not the question what are the problems to be solved, but how to do it. He determined three factors of behaviour patterns and lifestyles and summarized them to a term called Sense of Coherence:

„The **SOC (Sense Of Coherence)** is a global orientation that expresses the extent to which one has a pervasive, enduring though dynamic feeling of confidence that

1. the stimuli deriving from one's internal and external environments in the course of living are structured, predictable and explicable;
2. the resources are available to one to meet the demands posed by these stimuli;
3. these demands are challenges, worthy of investment and engagement."[81]

The SOC can be measured and recorded by means of questionnaires developed by Antonovsky that withstood scientific examinations. When evaluating the protocols of the investigated groups Antonovsky came across three recurring issues considered by him as three focal components of the SOC.[82] Thereby the sense of coherence shall not only be understood as a mere feeling, but as a perception and estimation pattern. The SOC includes:

Comprehensibility
People possessing a strong sense of coherence experience the world as orderly, predictable and explicable. The same applies to their internal experience. Healthy

---

79 Coherence = interrelation; coherence principle = basic principle of interrelation of all existing things.
80 Lorenz, R., Salutogenese, Ernst Reinhard Verlag, Munich, 2004, p. 36.
81 Antonovsky, A., pp. 36 f.
82 Antonovsky, A., pp. 34 f.

people with a strong sense of coherence also have a feeling that other people understand them, too. Antonovsky assigns this comprehensibility to the cognitive part of the person's experience.

Manageability
Manageability is a belief that you generally have the resources necessary to solve problems and take challenges and that all difficulties are manageable either by yourself or with the help of others (spouse, colleagues, God, the Nature, or a physician – anybody whom you trust in). Manageability is allocated to the cognitive part of the person's experience, too.

Meaningfulness
People with a high sense of coherence believe that their lives, life histories and deeds are really worthwhile. This third dimension of the sense of coherence shows how strong your confidence and feeling is that your life has an emotional meaning and your challenges are worth to invest energy in them – no matter how the things will turn out. People with a high sense of coherence see their lives as interesting, worthwhile and wonderful. Antonovsky sees this meaningfulness as an affective motivating component in the salutogenic model. According to Antonovsky, this element is the most important of all.

Antonovsky does not consider The Sense Of Coherence as a criterion for the person's typology. This term only describes a dispositional and outlasting orientation, i.e. a stable pattern of the person's perception of himself and of his environment. The Sense Of Coherence has nothing to do with moral. People acting beyond the rules of ethics can have a high sense of coherence, too. Moreover, The Sense Of Coherence does not relate to the whole world. As determined by Antonovsky, we all draw border lines. We are not so much concerned about what happens beyond them – it is not so important for us whether we can understand or manage it or discover its meaning. One with a high SOC can also be a philistine or a couch potato. However, drawing such border lines does not mean that we are not influenced by external factors. An absolutely apolitical person can also get a military draft and be sent to the war where he will be killed.[83]

According to Antonovsky there are some areas of life which are absolutely essential for a high SOC and can never be excluded from that. They are:

- the person's own feelings;
- direct interpersonal relations;
- the person's most important own occupation;
- existential vital issues (death, unpreventable failures, his personal mistakes, conflicts and isolation).

---

83 Antonovsky, A., pp. 39 f.

"Too much of our energies and a large part of our Self is so inevitably connected with these areas of life that we cannot ignore their significance. If you ignore it you have a low degree of meaning – as per definition. If you realize how they are important in your life it is still a question whether they shall be perceived as a challenge" [...] „It can be so that you do not really enjoy your work, e.g. housekeeping, going to school or to serve in the army. But if you are confident that your work has meaning (supporting your own family, looking after the children, preparing to your career, or defending your own country) you can still have a high SOC."[84]

The limits of importance attached by the person to a problem are not constant. Making them sometimes narrower or wider depending on the situation can even be an expression of a high SOC. In the first case you avoid getting stuck into your excessive demands and in the second case you broaden your horizon to gain new experiences.

Antonovsky also points to the limits of the coherence principle. "I have the feeling that in some way it would be wrong to assume a strong SOC in the person who asserts that there is always a solution for any problem, that he understands almost everything and shows no tolerance for doubts."[85] He also points out that there can be an extremely high SOC which is, however, not authentic on closer inspection; such SOC acts as a program that the persons learned or got prescribed by a higher instance, but not experienced by himself. For example, it can be religiosity transmuting into fanatic optimism because of not being sufficiently grounded in life experience (a highly topical reference at the beginning of the 21st century).[86] According to Antonovsky, a healthy sense of coherence cannot be of a hundred per cent; SOC is always situated in an area that also tolerates doubts, unanswered questions and human insufficiencies. His practice of research eliminated values to a certain extent.

As per Antonovsky, a healthy person possesses an arsenal of resistibility with which he comes up against problems, stresses and difficulties. Antonovsky calls this arsenal of resisting power **Generalized Resistance Ressources, GRR**:

"At the most general, preliminary level, I defined a GRR as any characteristic of the person, the group or the environment that can facilitate effective tension management."[87]

Those resisting power is a significant health protective factor. Although these resources do not directly influence health Antonovsky underlines their decisive importance for health. Stressors and tensions resulted from them can cause illness if they anyway coincide with already existing pathogens or physical weakness. However, the resources facilitate coping with tensions which are bad for health. Generalized Resistance Resources (generalized because they are effective in situations of any kind) are not by far the body's defences only. This term of Antonovsky describes

---

84 Antonovsky, A., pp. 39 f.
85 Antonovsky, A., Health, Stress and Coping, New Perspectives on Mental and Physical Well-Being, Jossey-Bass Publishers, issue 1985, pp. 158–159.
86 Antonovsky, A., pp. 158–159.
87 Antonovsky, A., Breakdown: A Needed Fourth Step in the Conceptual Armamentarium of Modern Medicine, Social Science and Medicine, 1972, p. 541.

cultural and social skills and abilities to solve problems and to manage difficulties. The GRR also includes financial safety, ego strength, intelligence, practical managing strategies, as well as genetically dominated und organic factors. Development of these resources especially takes place in childhood and adolescence. Deficits arise if early experiences are inconsistent, i. e. the children's or adolescents' environment overstrains or under-challenges him/her, or if they cannot participate in decisions.

Stressors are another component of the salutogenic concept. Antonovsky incorporated still applicable stress models of his generation into his concept. Factors potentially capable of trigger stresses are primarily neutral stimuli. They do not become stressors before they cause stress reactions. It can be so that one person does not perceive a certain stimulus as a stressor at all whereas the same stimulus cases severe stress reactions in another person. What underwhelms one person can set another one off. As per Antonovsky, the "stress reaction" term is also neutral. Stress reaction initially means simply a situation in which an individual does not know how he should react. He is "unbearably helpless"[88]. This reaction induces a physiological stress condition. Then the challenge of the organism is to treat the stressor and to ease the tension. If the stressor is processed positively the reaction on the alarm will be adequate and the organism will come to its balance again without suffering any damage. It depends on the individual scoring model and on the personal resisting power resources whether a stressor induces a tension reaction and whether this reaction is really damaging. According to Antonovsky, it is only reasonable to speak of stressors in conjunction with the person in whom the stress reaction is induced. Therefore, stressors are not objective factors. They directly depend on the individual factors. The higher the person's SOC the better he will cope with the stressor alarming him or he will not be alarmed by that stimulus at all.

The salutogenic model components – sense of coherence, generalized resistance resources and stressors – shall not be regarded in isolation from each other. They are linked together in dynamic interdependence and can positively or negatively influence each other. Who experiences the world as explicable, manageable and meaningful due to his high resistance resources develops a good sense of coherence. In other words: a good Sense of Coherence mobilises the Generalized Resisting Resources. However, Antonovsky emphasizes that the SOC development does not only depend on the individual's resources availability. He holds the society and its supportive conditions responsible for it. If the society provides good development conditions for children and adolescents they will be in the position to form a good sense of coherence. Insofar, all environmental, social and political measures of the government for a child-friendly family policy support the SOC development.

In conclusion, the SOC degree can directly influence the organism in its changing towards health. At the same time, SOC acts as a stressor perception filter and can

---

88 Bengel, J., Strittmatter, R., A. Antonovskys Modell der Salutogenese, in: Was erhält Menschen gesund?, BzgA, 2002, pp. 144 f.

mobilize available resources. In short, it makes a person to a good swimmer in a sometimes dangerous river of life.

The Antonovsky's coherence theory is a reasonable research approach and an improved viewpoint due to reproducible research results. However, it does not deliver any action concept. Antonovsky doubted that the SOC can be influenced by any supporting measures at all, but he did not exclude such a possibility. He assumed that the SOC is a character trait brought to the person in his childhood. The Sense Of Coherence as a perceptual pattern develops "from the cradle". According to Antonovsky, in early adulthood it only matures and being consolidated, but it cannot be considerably changed.

This sobering statement brings us to a fatalistic resignation: you either have this high sense of coherence or not! Since Antonovsky assumes a high self-responsibility of each individual which can also be learned we will search for approaches for further-development of SOC in an individual person, as well as of SOC in couples (partner SOC) and in groups (group SOC), e. g. in families and working teams. In the following, we will refer to the newest researches which indicate that the SOC can also be considerably changed in adulthood.

How The Sense Of Coherence changes in Course of Life and how it can be applied to our Target Group

Antonovsky's main thesis says that a strong sense of coherence is a decisive factor for successful management of omnipresent demands and stressors and, therefore, for health maintenance. He considers the sense of coherence as a stable property formed by historical and cultural conditions and not by individual ones. In his opinion, the SOC development is completed in adulthood and can be only slightly or shorty changed in course of dramatic events. However, he still gives no answer to the question how the SOC changes in course of life. He does not tell much on possibilities how to change and to develop the SOC by targeted and planned measures and interventions. He only points out that such insignificant and short changes can be very meaningful in many situations and it may be important to accompany the person in such critical situations to prevent him from a short-time SOC value descent.

Structural and social measures enabling an individual to influence and to participate in socially recognized decision-making (participation) are considered by Antonovsky as a promising opportunity to positively influence the SOC. From that we can deduce that it is important to create such a world for children and adolescents where it would be possible to gather consistent experiences, to compensate stresses and to participate in decision-making processes. (We will return to this point again when we come to the discussion about Coping Concepts for families.)

Antonovsky is obviously convinced that health promoting and preventive measures should be aimed on changing a wide spectrum of individual, social and cultural factors – so that such a participation in relevant decision-making processes would provide a social approval to the person. According to Lorenz[89], this assumption refers to personal attributes, e. g. gender, age and educational background. Larsson and Kallenberg[90] could point out that women have a lower coherence experience at average. This finding is confirmed by clinical studies of other authors. (We will try to interpret this finding in Chapter 7.) There are only few researches dealing with SOC changing in course of life. Due to basic considerations we shall handle the survey of Schumacher, Gunzelmann and Braehler conducted in 1998 in more detail.[91] The authors report on age- and gender specific standard values (percentile ranks) for Antonovsky's Sense of Coherence Scale. The standard values were based on a population-representative survey conducted in Germany in 1998 (N = 1944; age of 18–92). In line with Antonovsky's approach, this study considers the SOC as a dispositional managing resource making people more resistant against stressors and

---

[89] Lorenz, R., Salutogenese, Grundwissen für Psychologen, Mediziner, Gesundheits- und Pflegewissenschaftler, Ernst Reinhardt Verlag, Munich, 2004, pp. 96 f.
[90] Larsson, G., Kallenberg, K. O., Sense of coherence, socio-economic conditions and health, in: European Journal of Public Health No. 6, pp. 175–180.
[91] Schumacher, J., Gunzelmann, T, Brähler, E., Deutsche Normierung der Sense of Coherence Scale von Antonovsky, published in: Diagnostica, 46, 2000, pp. 208–213.

thereby contributing to health maintenance and promotion. In 1987 Antonovsky developed a so-called Sense of Coherence Scale for empirical study of his hypotheses. The scale contained 29 (SOC-29) or 13 items (SOC-13) in its short version. Both scales were theoretically examined in a number of studies throughout showing good consistency coefficients. Antonovsky's sub-scales derived by him from his theoretic pre-considerations (comprehensibility, manageability, meaningfulness) could not be factor-analytically reproduced to a satisfactory extent up to now. Therefore, the "standardization" is exclusively referred to the current total value (sum of all items) of SOC-29 or SOC-13. Before that study, no standard values were available in Germany for any of these SOC scales. This gap is filled by Schumacher's research.

As a result, we can assert following: as long we only consider total values of all items and cannot break them down according to SOC subscales we will get the pattern predicted by Antonovsky. The SOC-29 scale's average value is the highest at the age of 18–40 (151.31 for men and 145.03 for women). With advancing age it descends continuously but slowly. The same applies to the average values of scale SOC-13. The scale's average value for 18–40 years-old women is still considerably lower than for 41–60-years-old men, but it descends synchronously with men's average values. In all age segments it remains considerably lower than the men's one. It may be due to the fact that women still less participate in decision-making processes than men.

In the sum of all SOC components, the degree of SOC thereby turns out to be **dependent** both on the **age** (age-correlated SOC descent) and on the **gender** (women's lower SOC). Concerning our target group (young managers aged 30-40) we can note that this age group can develop the best sense of coherence. In other words: our target group possesses the largest Generalized Resisting Resources of three parameters (comprehensibility, manageability and meaningfulness). Our target group has a high consistency concerning understanding coherences between family and occupation. This group is in the best position to manage life challenges and to create a balance between over- and under-stress. And since this group actively participates in decisions and solving conflict between family and occupation it is meaningful for social interaction.

Age and gender are not the only factors correlating with the sense of coherence. There are also other correlations important for our target group, for example, **educational background** and **socioeconomic condition**. Larsson and Kallenberg[92] proved in their study that social groups with higher earnings have a higher SOC whereas manual workers and low-income groups have a lower SOC. According to Lindberg[93], high sense of coherence is primarily typical for occupational groups in leadership positions.

---

92 Larsson, G., Kallenberg, K. O., Sense of coherence, socio-economic conditions and health, in: European Journal of Public Health No. 6.
93 Lindberg, O., Childhood conditions, SOC, social class and adult ill health, exploring their theoretical and empirical relations, in: Social Science and Medicine 44, pp. 821–831.

As explored before, the target group (young managers) investigated by us has the best chances to develop a high sense of coherence compared with target groups of other ages. Therefore, this group is in the best position to manage the goal conflict between business success and harmonic family life.

Influencing the Sense of Coherence by psychotherapeutic Measures

Psychotherapy is the generic term for various methods of trying to influence and – as far as possible – to eliminate disturbances on behaviour, psychical disorders and other sufferings (psychogenic diseases, pains, disorders) by communicative means (often verbal ones). The usual aim is to diminish the symptoms disturbing the patient. In most of the cases it should occur by modification of the personality structure. The therapist and the patient should establish a stable relation to each other. Psychotherapy is primarily carried out ambulant in therapists' practices (they are mostly clinical psychologists) or stationary in psychiatric or psychosomatic clinics.[94] There is a number of various psychotherapeutic schools. Behaviour therapy, psychoanalysis and talking therapy are the most common ones. There are also other schools: gestalt therapy, systemic therapy and "psychodrama". Psychotherapy is generally based on a theory of psychical disturbances and a theory of therapeutic behaviour modification.

In psychosomatic and psychotherapeutic specialists literature you can hardly find the term of salutogenesis. The theoretic discussion was continued e. g. by Schüffel and Brucks showing a diagnostic model of Epicritic Case Study (ECS).[95] In the following, we will more refer to the practical use of the research written by Sack und Lamprecht which delivered comprehensible results important for the further discussion.[96]

As already mentioned above, large changes in the sense of coherence occur very seldom. Even if they ever occur it never happens due to a single modified confrontation or a single decision. Such a change is a result from concrete changes of living conditions and incitation of a new live management pattern. In Antonovsky's opinion, the SOC can gradually change if this new pattern is kept up for many years.

Antonovsky doubts the possibility of psychotherapeutic influence on the SOC. However, he relativizes this skepticism himself and says that it would be quite possible to slightly modify the SOC measured by his questionnaire within the range of approx. +/-5 points by therapeutic intervention.[97]

That was the starting point of Sack & Lamprecht's study[98] aiming on an empiric examination of Antonovsky's hypothesis of the SOC's independence of age and impossibility to be influenced. Using SOC Questionnaire 1993/94 all patients of the Psychosomatic Polyclinic (N = 1061) and all in-treatment patients at the psychosomatic station of Prof. Lamprecht at the Medical University of Hanover (N = 35 or N = 30 –

---

[94] Bengel, J., Strittmatter, R., Willmann, H., Was erhält den Menschen gesund? Antonovskys Modell der Salutogenese, Diskussionsstand und Stellenwert, BzgA, Cologne, 2001, pp. 73 f.
[95] Schüffel, W. (Publisher), Handbuch der Salutogenese, Konzept und Praxis, Beitrag 3, Brucks, M., Wahl, W.- D., Schüffel, W., Ullstein Medical, 1998, pp. 37 f.
[96] Sack, M., Lamprecht, F, Lässt sich der SOC durch Psychotherapie beeinflussen?, in: Salutogenese, ein neues Konzept in der Psychosomatik, VAS 1997, pp. 186 f.
[97] Antonovsky, A., p. 124.
[98] Sack, M., Lamprecht, F., p. 186.

shortly before their admittance and shortly before their discharge) were examined on their SOC. The SOC values turned out to be very dependent on the age. It is remarkable that evaluation of sub-scales showed considerable age dependence in the Comprehensibility and Manageability sub-scale only. The Meaningfulness sub-scale turned out to be relatively age-independent.[99] Comparison of provided test results of 30 patients who filled the SOC questionnaire at the beginning and an the end of stationary therapy[100] (usually 8 weeks) showed considerable increase of the SOC total value in course of therapy (8 points at average). The largest increase was in the Comprehensibility sub-scale.

	Tr. beginning	Tr. end	T-test
Comprehensibility	36,9 +/-7,7	41,3 +/-8,3	(p≤.012)
Manageability	37,2 +/- 8,1	38,0 +/-7,3	(n. s.)
Meaningfulness	33,1 +/-7,9	35,9 +/-7,5	(n. s.)
Total SOC	107,2 +/-20,1	115,2 +/-20,5	(p≤.041)

Table 3: Comparison: beginning of the therapy and end of the therapy[101]   Inpatient treatment (N = 30)

On the premise that the SOC questionnaire delivers reliable results we see that Sack & Lamprecht's results contradict the Antonovsky's hypothesis of the SOC's age- and treatment independence – even in a smaller group of patients. The significant increase of the total SOC value within the period between the patients' admittance and discharge from their stationary psychotherapeutic treatment (8 points at average) allows a suggestion that psychotherapeutic treatment may support a person's health-protecting resources.

Furthermore, Sack/Lamprecht detected considerable age dependence of Comprehensibility and Manageability sub-values. With advancing age the people seem to see the world as more explicable and clear and assess coming challenges as easier manageable. It was surprising that Meaningfulness remained neither age-dependent nor changeable in course of a stationary psychotherapy, in whole.

However, exactly the Meaningfulness is considered by Antonovsky as "the decisively motivating share of the sense of coherence".[102] Therefore Sack & Lamprecht conclude: "If, as per Antonovsky, meaningfulness is really the most decisive SOC factor it shall be put more emphasis on it in therapeutic treatment, e.g. attach more significance to life orientation, meaningfulness and faith in course of therapy.[103]

In the psychoanalysts' majority opinion, meaningful life orientation develops in the person's "inner world", i. e. in his subjective cosmos that mediates between

---

99 Sack, M., Lamprecht, F, p. 189.
100 A covariant type of treatment, i.e. polyclinic vs. station, did not achieve any significance in the research.
101 Sack, M., Lamprecht, F., p. 189, Table 4.
102 Antonovsky, A., Unraveling the mystery of health, Jossey-Bass, San Francisco, 1987, p. 22.
103 Sack, M., Lamprecht, F., p. 192.

external strain, decompensation and symptom development. Therefore, for a stable health, the entire regulating system shall be able to withstand and to compensate conflict tensions between the current life demands and the inside representing world.[104]

---

[104] Lamparter, U., Deneke, F. W., Stuhr, U., Die „Hamburger Gesundheitsstudie", in: Lamprecht, Johnen, Salutogenese, Ein neues Konzept in der Psychosomatik?, Kongressband.

Conclusion: The salutogenic model is a promising method to solve the conflict

All socially relevant groups dealt with the issue of the conflict between family and career. All aid programs and approaches have one thing in common: they mostly offer formal solutions, e. g. more income-loss refunds by the state and the enterprises, more day-care by governmental institutions, etc. There are no offered contents and approaches how to change own behaviour in order to live in a harmonic partnership. **All formal approaches try to diminish the consequences of the conflict, but do not try to mitigate or to eliminate its causes within the family.**

We will investigate the question how an individual person (not a society) can adequately and effectively solve this conflict situation by changing his behaviour. Here we apply Antonovsky's salutogenic model. We show how to make the conflict endurable, tolerable and compensable by learning making it comprehensible and manageable and by feeling the meaningfulness of solving it. **Solving the conflict between the occupation and family by changing own behaviour is the concern of the present book.**

6 Looking for Individual Resources

Despite all the critics towards Antonovsky's salutogenic model in recent years (see Bengel, Strittmatter und Willmann)[105] and under appreciation of related concepts of stress research, we see the salutogenic model as very well applicable for our issue. Since it considers many determining factors and variables on the social, psychological, emotional and cognitive level, it has a high integration value for our subject. It is a complex meta-theoretic and heuristic process model[106] and can be used as orientation frame to order and illustrate complex interrelations. Up to now it was discussed in three application ranges (prevention, psychotherapy and rehabilitation) which are particularly important for a co-evolution of occupation and family. Change of perspective from risk factors to protective factors and resources goes along with a modern interactional definition of health where psychical and social issue are as important as somatic ones. Strengthening the sense of coherence becomes the main concern of health promotion. The **positive person's self-portrait of actionability** formulated by Antonovsky is seen as an important element of health. "The older the more independently from others, the person alone can and must find and arrange his true calling himself as spiritual and physical being – on the one hand, by self-critical reflection of his and others' experiences in the past, and on the other hand, by trying over and over again to design new enhanced and extended possibilities of thinking and acting in the future".[107]

In the following, we will try to determine resources and competences of our target group (young managers) – at first, theoretically and, at second, practically and empirically, independent from risk factor, using positive forms of communication and interaction. It is the question how to avoid turning tension into stress and which resources can be mobilized for that.

Our attention is centred around the question of successful coping, i.e. management strategy providing necessary tools to a person to find some „SOC improving experiences" within his area of life, as it is called by Antonovsky.[108] This Antonovsky's term embraces all therapeutic measures making easy a sustainable consistent change in the person's real experience. In his opinion, one of the most important measures is **social assistance** (i.e. his meaning in the social co-operation).

---

105 Bengel, J., Strittmatter, R., Willmann, H., pp. 88 f.
106 Jerusalem, M., Gesundheitspsychologie, Zur Mehrdimensionalität der Salutogenese, in Seelbach, H., Kugler, J., Neumann, W. (Publisher), Von der Krankheit zur Gesundheit, Huber, Bern, pp. 389 f.
107 Schmidt, H.-L., Leben als Wagnis, Hilfe zur Bewährung und Bewährungshilfe, Festvortrag anlässlich des 25-jährigen Bestehens des Vereins Förderung der Bewährungshilfe in Schwaben e. V, diritto Publikationen, Eichstätt, 2003, p. 10.
108 Antonovsky, A., pp. 119 f.

Antonovsky points out that it directly influences the illness resistance and is not solely a buffering effect. However, he makes a reservation that social assistance is only one of many factors which he calls Generalized Resistance Resources (GRR) and Resistance Deficits (GRD).[109] Moreover, there are also other factors of the same importance as social assistance – **consistency experience** (i. e. understanding coherences) and **manageability of life demands** (creating a balance between over- and under-stress). "At the same time the person is only slackly bound by moral laws and not strictly coerced. He stands between necessity and freedom. This space is the most fateful range for his actual mission and challenges. It is insecuritas space for his free self-determination, for his choice and decision, for his large risk to find his dimension and to live between any alternatives.[110]

But what resistance resources can be mobilized by the person to make his life demands and challenges manageable? We can come closer to the answer if we follow up the emotional control, development of a positive self-esteem, meaning finding and identity forming, as per Antonovsky.[111]

---

109 Antonovsky, A., pp. 123 f.
110 Schmidt, H.-L., p. 17.
111 Antonovsky, A., p. 138.

Control of Emotions

For psychical health it is decisive to create a positive self-esteem. The person strives to effect something in his environment and to be perceived and honoured by others for deeds and activities in relation to other people. In this interaction with others he revises his personal constructs through real experiences. An important task of his ego is to form his identity arising from his stabilized images of himself. A positive self-esteem can only develop and survive as long the person is perceived in the current context, feels to be needed and finds tasks in which he feels to be supported and experience his life as meaningful.

In the viewpoint of psychoanalysis, the "self-esteem" term is reflected in Freud's narcissism theory,[112] as well as in further-going Mentzos's narcissism theories[113] and others. In their view, the narcissistic homeostasis (self-esteem control) very much depends on the narcissistic supply, i.e. from objects. A psychologically healthy adult needs reflections by self-objects, too. If the reflection is positive, runs indifferently and follows the pleasure/reluctance principle, it is primary narcissism. Psychoanalysis also defines secondary narcissism: the individual tends to create object relations aimed on increasing his self-esteem. Mentzos[114] describes four possibilities of compensation of shaken self-esteem:

- ***Regression into the primary condition:*** phantasies of merging with something indefinitely great and rise in value and power;
- ***Denying bitter reality by means of delusion of greatness:*** a child feels confirmed in his belief that he is „handsome, smart and grown"; harmless reveries of adults, from delusion of greatness up to megalomania;
- ***Compensation by idealizing:*** the child identifies itself with omnipotent and omniscient objects to save or to idealise his self-esteem; according to his experiences of reality, he corrects and relativizes his strongly idealized image of his parents only slowly, bit by bit;
- ***The Ideal Self*** makes a person rather independent of praise and reprimand. It allows for inner surety, self-awareness and a quiet self-assurance. Faulty or missing idealized objects can lead to weak points which may cause disorders in the case of stress.

Control of emotions affecting self-esteem is important for inner balance restoring. Lorenz[115] sees self-esteem Janus-faced. Strong feelings of self-respect, inner satisfaction, surety, sense of scale and contentedness can be alternated with insufficiency,

---

112 Freud, S., students' edition, volumes I to X and a supplementary volume, Fischer, Frankfurt on the Main, 1969 f.
113 Mentzos, S., Neurotische Konfliktverarbeitung, Einführung in die psychoanalytische Neurosenlehre unter Berücksichtigung neuer Perspektiven, Fischer, Frankfurt on the Main, 1997, p. 53.
114 Mentzos, S., p. 56.
115 Lorenz, R., Salutogenese, Grundwissen für Psychologen und Mediziner, Gesundheits- und Pflegewissenschaftler, Ernst Reinhardt Verlag, Munich, 2004, p. 54.

self-doubt, inferiority and being hurt up to self-contempt. In 1956 Selye[116] already described a characteristic sequence of stressor reaction phases called **general adaptation syndrome**. The first reaction on an alarm is followed by a phase of resistance. In this phase such symptoms as headache and tiredness disappear until an exhaustion phase comes which leads to inability of the organism to adapt to stress permanence. Simonton et al.[117] point out that the degree of emotional overloads evoked by external occurrences depends on the person's subjective interpretation of the current occurrence and how he manages it.

Motivation researches also contain notes and thoughts what kind of dynamics can be affected by tensions, energies or even forces and how they can be processed. Heckhausen[118] deals with the "person-environment interaction model" of Lewin[119] and describes changing tensioned conditions in different personal areas within this model. Tensions activated in the person model are depicted in the environment model as forces. Dealing with these conditions is ruled by homeostatic dynamics resulting in forces balancing and not in reduction of tensions. Antonovsky explains these dynamics so[120]: *"The fundamental philosophical view of salutogenic concept is that the human organism prototypically stays in a dynamic condition of a heterostatic imbalance. Tension is the brain's acknowledgement that some demand is not fulfilled and the person must meet this demand, i.e. must do something if he wants to reach his goal."*

When investigating correlation between the SOC and a successful control of emotions, Antonovsky presumes that the human organism cannot tolerate abidance in a strong emotional tension without deleterious consequences – even if the emotion is pleasant. He comes to the conclusion that persons with high SOC have other emotions as the ones with low SOC – emotions which easier get under control.[121] He describes focussed emotions where feeling is bound to a relatively univocal goal (unlike unfocussed ones). "You are angry about something you did or something what happened. Dimensions of angriness are confined in the same way as its perceived consequences. Rage is quite another thing: it aims on the world, life and people in general. You boil in rage, the steam dissolves and you simmer in wrath endlessly. There are similar differences between fear and anxiety, between grief and feeling to be abandoned."[122] **Thus the focussed emotions are more controllable than unfocussed**. Furthermore, Antonovsky distinguishes emotions by degree of the person's **awareness of them**. A person with strong SOC is more aware of his emotions, he can easier describe them and he feels not so endan-

---

116 Selye, H., Stress mein Leben, Erinnerungen eines Forschers, Kindler Verlag, Munich, 1979.
117 Simonton, O. C., Simonton, M. S., Creighton, J. (Publisher), Wieder gesund werden, Eine Anleitung zur Aktivierung der Selbstheilungskräfte für Krebspatienten und ihre Angehörigen, Rowohlt, Reinbek bei Hamburg, 1995, p. 73.
118 Heckhausen, H., Motivation und Handeln, Lehrbuch der Motivationspsychologie, Springer Verlag, Berlin, 1980, p. 176 f.
119 Lewin, K., Die Lösung sozialer Konflikte, Christian, Bad Nauheim, 1953.
120 Antonovsky, A., pp. 130 f.
121 Antonovsky, A., pp. 139 f.
122 Antonovsky, A., pp. 139 f.

gered by them. He can easier manage these emotions adequately to the situation. The third distinguishing characteristic of emotions is connected with **stressors and assignments of guilt**. Persons with low SOC tend to blame other people or circumstance because they are afraid to take responsibility. Persons with strong SOC can blame others, too, but only if the others are really guilty. According to Antonovsky, guilt is easier to manage when it stems from what you do, and not what you are.[123]

Creating a positive feeling of self-esteem is decisive for psychical health. In interaction with other people the person examines his acts and opinions comparing them with real experiences. So he is confirmed in his perception, thoughts and feelings. An important task of his ego is to form his identity arising from his stabilized images of himself. A positive self-esteem can only develop and survive as long the person is perceived in the current context, feels to be needed and finds tasks in which he feels to be supported and experience his life as meaningful. Lorenz[124] concludes that relations distinguished by respectful and appreciating attention of the counterpart (spouse, boss or colleague) have an enduring quality and provide important resources for a good experience of self-esteem in the current period of life. But as noted by Mentzos[125], it needs sustainable regulation of self-esteem to create an inner balance since strong feelings of self-respect, inner satisfaction, surety or sense of scale and can be alternated with insufficiency, self-doubt, inferiority and being hurt up to self-contempt. According to Mentzos, the person has to be permanently busy with maintaining his inner balance all his life. Besides the problem-solving or instrumental aspect, Antonovsky speaks of "emotional regulation"[126] as a reaction on an occurrence or non-occurrence. In his view, regulation of managing impulses, feeling expression and cognitive estimation of the occurrence are important levels of emotional control.

Lazarus and Launier[127] point out that emotion is cognitively estimated by how a stimulus influences the condition. They investigated people's coping with endangering and stress triggering situations and came to a conclusion that there are two estimation phases *(the primary and the secondary)*, which are important for interacting with environment.

In the **primary estimation phase** the individual checks whether the situation is related to his goals. As soon as he has realized that his personally important goals can get solutions or even be achieved a positive emotion comes into effect. If the personal goals seem for him to be unachievable or to be difficult to reach he will feel negative emotions.[128] As already mentioned, our emotions are enmeshed with our self-perception and identity. Lazarus and Launier present this relation in six values

---

123 Antonovsky, A., pp. 140 f.
124 Lorenz, R., p. 52.
125 Mentzos, S., p. 56.
126 Antonovsky, A., pp. 188 f.
127 Lazarus, R. S., Launier, R., Streßbezogene Transaktionen zwischen Person und Umwelt, in Nitsch, J., (Publisher), Streß, Huber, Bern, 1981, pp. 213–259.
128 Lorenz, R., p. 58.

that show which personal values could be concerned by the primary estimation phase:[129]

- Self-respect and Reputation (how I see myself and how others see me?)
- Moral values (what is important for me, what are my convictions?)
- Self-ideals (how I would like to see me?)
- Life meaning (how I can organize my life meaningfully?)
- Other persons and their well-being (how my goals affect other important persons in my environment?)
- Individual aims in life

And yet feelings are the most important thing of life, since they first generate that force and tenderness, sheen and cloudiness which makes the humans feel something actually important for them.

Hermann Schmitz
quoted after Lorenz, R., Salutogenesesis, p. 52

Dealing with this concept, Antonovsky presumes that a person with strong SOC sees life demands rather as challenges than as stressors and knows how to use his resources adequately to the situation and goal-oriented. Usually they utilize ability to recognize their own strengths which should be used. In this connection, Hüther speaks of "individual estimation of the stressor's controlability"[130]:

"As soon as the stress has turned out to be controllable everything suddenly goes into reverse: threat becomes a challenge, fear becomes confidence and courage, helplessness evolves into will and finally when we managed it, we feel how our confidence has grown in all what we know and can."

The **secondary estimation** goes beyond the individual's associating the current situation with his goals. In the secondary estimation, the person checks the **accountability** attachable to the situation. As soon as he has reasoned that it is only his own fear and nobody but he himself can be called to account it he will deal with his coping resources. Coping potential that can be activated by a person in a concrete situation is always estimated due to negatively rated occurrences and coupled with feelings associated with these occurrences. Therefore Lazarus and Launier distinguish between coping with situation and coping with emotions connected with it. How the person finally estimates the situation and emotion depends on the time frame within the estimation takes place, especially on his future expectations. **Future expectations** are a further aspect of the secondary estimation since the person also checks the occurrence on long-term consequences of his decision. In long decision-making processes so called "reappraisals"[131], i. e. one or several new estimations can appear. Reappraisals are significant for emotion control since they can initiate a modified and situation-adequate coping. Later we will return to this point in discussing coping concepts within a family.

---

129 Lazarus, R. S., Launier, R., pp. 213-259.
130 Hüther, G., Biologie der Angst, Wie aus Stress Gefühle werden, Vandenhoeck & Ruprecht, Göttingen, 2002, pp. 39 f.
131 Lazarus, R. S., Launier, R., pp. 213 f.

Antonovsky distinguished between **primary estimation I and II**. **Primary estimation I"**[132] is the step when the people with strong sense of coherence do not ever perceive the occurrence as a stress and can activate their resources to meet the life demands (situation-adequate tension does not endanger their well-being). He adds a further step – **primary estimation II**: a person who really perceives a stimulus as a stressor and checks whether this stressor is endangering, auspicious or irrelevant for his well-being. As soon as he has found it favourable or irrelevant, the tension will be defused and no stress will arise. Future expectations are very important for emotional regulation: positive thinking and presumption of a successful solution for the problem leads to diminishing of felt tensions and, at the same time, confirms positive self-esteem, taking individual abilities and skills into consideration.[133]

Alongside with emotional regulation, an individual's **instrumental estimation** takes place. Strong sense of coherence helps the person to see the problem more clearly, in more detail and, first of all, as a challenge for active dealing with it. Then he chooses the suitable resources for facing the stressor. On the contrary, a person with low sense of coherence loses his hope and resigns. This process of emotional control connected with instrumental aspect is called by Antonovsky **"primary estimation III"** [134].

Furthermore, Antonovsky describes a further step of the coping process – **"tertiary estimation"**[135]. The secondary estimation phase includes the choice of resources suitable for coping with the stressor. As soon as the found resources are implemented the person receives a feedback from his environment. If he has a strong SOC he incorporates the received **feedback** in his further thoughts, evaluates it and looks for **alternative acting** to avoid mistakes. In contrast, a person with a low SOC remains in his intent because he did not perceived any feedback and cannot thereby consider alternative acts. People with strong SOC are usually familiar with casting about for such a feedback and even provoking it in order to make an evaluation and reorient their acting. On the contrary, a person with low SOC ignores signals from their environment and finds no motivation to quit the way leading into a dead-end and to look for alternatives.

Since stressors permanently exist in our lives we are permanently called on to cope with them. People with strong SOC make mistakes in thinking and acting, too, but the probability of taking wrong coping actions is lower among the people with strong SOC.[136] Regardless which potential possibilities are available in the reality there is a big chance to bring them into being. If there is really no solution for a problem a person with strong SOC will be able to adequately deal with this problem and to bear a life with less pain and sorrow.

---

132 Antonovsky, A., pp. 126 f.
133 Lorenz, R., p. 62.
134 Antonovsky, A., pp. 129 f.
135 Antonovsky, A., pp. 137 f.
136 Antonovsky, A.,pp. 136 f.

Searching for Meaningfulness

Antonovsky does not provide any references to semantic difference between meaningfulness and importance. As per Lorenz, "meaning" refers to multifaceted terms:[137]

- "Meaning" as spiritual attention to the world (cognitively). In relation to the outside world, we speak of our senses, for example: sense of touch or sense of sensuality. In relation to the inner world, we speak of attitude or way of thinking.
- "Meaning" as interpretation of relation between the person and its environment.

The latter corresponds with Antonovsky's term of ***"meaningfulness"***. When evaluating his interview protocols Antonovsky discovered that test persons possessing high SOC always spoke of areas of life which are important and dear to them and which have "meaning" from their point of view; they also spoke of it emotionally and not only cognitively.[138] In order to "find a meaning" a person should have a certain commitment, i.e. he shall be committed to a thing which is worth it.[139] That results in vouching for own goals and ascribing meaning and importance to them. This high degree of meaning does not mean that the person is still happy with blows of fate, e.g. serious disease or loss of job. But if such a person is befallen with negative experiences he accepts the challenge more willingly. He will be able to ascribe a meaning to it and to mobilize all his resources to overcome it with honour.

A person is usually perceives the situation as meaningful if he has possibilities to participate in decision-making processes, i.e. to actively influence the processes, both in business world and in the family.

In the context of social approval, i.e. participation on decision-making processes in the society, "meaningfulness" just begins to be formed. According to Antonovsky, for instance, a person can have a role providing him enough consistence and a good balance between over- and under-stress, however, his decision-making ability is ignored and he cannot participate in decisive processes. That is applicable to a classic role of a stay-at-home housewife. Antonovsky concludes that such a role would lead to high values of comprehensibility and manageability as SOC components, but the meaningfulness remains low.[140]

Becker und Minsel[141] point out the role allocation leading to different chances for genders. They cited a research in which housewives have problems with their identities and fell into a self-esteem crisis because of low self-confidence. On the

---

137 Lorenz, R., p. 68.
138 Antonovsky, A., pp. 35 f.
139 Lorenz, R., p. 69.
140 Antonovsky, A., pp. 37 f.
141 Becker, P., Minsel, B., Psychologie der seelischen Gesundheit, vol. 2, Persönlichkeitspsychologische Grundlagen, Bedingungsanalysen und Fördermöglichkeiten, Hofgrebe, Göttingen, 1986, p. 162.

contrary, working mothers seemed to be much better balanced and were especially psychically well-adapted even though they complained about lack of time and were worried about insufficiently available time for their kids because of their "double" work. Therefore, workplace factors affecting a person for a long time decisively give him life experience forming a high or low sense of coherence. Those factors are corporate citizenship (an enterprise's prestige in the society) and enjoying occupational tasks at the enterprise. Both can be promoted if the person can use his skills and knowledge gaining recognition.

People who can make their experiences with meaningfulness, find meaning in fulfilling their tasks and feel themselves challenged possess much more active stress respond strategies than people who tend to escape problems. The reaction of the latter is resignation and refraining from activities along with self-incrimination, self-pity and, consequently, social isolation.[142] In chronic existence-endangering critical situations an experience of meaningfulness becomes a decisive factor for a possible coping-strategy. Comprehensibility and manageability take back seats. In survival issues, to ascribe meaning to the situation is often the only way to find orientation, to draw hope and to look for new solutions.[143]

Antonovsky considers the meaningfulness as a motivating force decisively affecting health. He says, if a person ever experienced affordance something by his own activities and decisions he will not feel himself as a mere object fulfilling rules given by others; by his own acting with another conscience he experiences a feeling of being meaningful strengthened by self-responsible acting together with others.[144]

---

142 Schmitz, E., Hanke, G., Sinnerfahrung, innere Langeweile und die Modi der Stressverarbeitung, in: Integrative Therapie, vol. 1, pp. 42 f.
143 Lorenz, R., p. 71.
144 Antonovsky, A., pp. 39 f.

Self-respect, Identity, Self-protection

How self-concepts relate to identity and sense of coherence? Petri[145] speaks of "self-coherence" as a core of self-respect, identity and self-protection. In the following, we will investigate this question and cite Ruediger Lorenz[146]. He describes how a person's identity gets formed and develops in course of life and how self-esteem and sense of coherence relate to each other.

People's experiences and behaviour are influenced by their self-perception. Self-feelings affect one's attitude to oneself (how useful do I feel myself in general) and self-evaluation. The latter is the evaluating component which forms the self-esteem. There are following questions in the focus of these self-judgements: How I think about myself? What images of myself do I have? How am I evaluated by others? The person herewith strives after favourable experiences reflected in his wants, evaluated and forming his self-estimation. Emotional expression is reflected in self-value and self-acceptance, but also in self-humiliation and self-hate. Our "self" is the dimension of our identity. By creating identity projects it strives after positive experiences constructing positive feelings.

Identity development directly depends on the self-feeling. A person develops very different feelings to himself in course of his life. The Self dimension is Janus-faced and is shaped by self-images and other's feedbacks from the current context and within life dynamics. It is elastic and shapeable in course of life and undergoes continuous changes. The **identity** term can be traced back up to William James[147] moving the social dimension into the focus of his thoughts, while Erikson (1959, 1973) deals with this term focusing on individual. In the inner perspective the identity experience is, on the one hand, an act of self-perception, self-estimation and self-judgement. On the other hand, an individual's understanding his own identity is guided from outside in course of social co-operation that influences him. Both dimensions shape the identity whereas the individual is imbedded into social cooperation from the beginning of his life.

In the following, we present diverse identity problems in a heuristic model. Petzold[148] distinguishes **five pillars of human identity**:

- *Bodiliness* as a cornerstone of identity against the background of personality and theoretical development of the self – as a basis for forming of the ego and its identity. Among other things bodiliness embraces physical integrity, health, performance ability and satisfied sexuality.

---

145 Petri, H., Geschwister – Liebe und Rivalität, Die längste Beziehung unseres Lebens, Kreuz Verlag, Zurich, 1994, p. 158.
146 Lorenz, R., pp. 72–75.
147 James, W., The Principles of Psychology, Holt, Rinehart, Winston, New York, 1890, 2 vols.
148 Petzold, H. G., Integrative Therapie; Modelle, Theorien und Methoden für eine schulenübergreifende Psychotherapie, volumes 1-3, Jungfermann, Paderborn, 1993, pp. 68 f.

- *Social network* – incorporation in social contexts; originally – the family, later – friends and colleagues.
- *Work, performance, leisure* as dimension of self-realisation both by our job performance evaluated by others and by recreational activities in social interaction. This area is very important in countries and cultures where a person is particularly identified by his occupational status and job performance.
- *Material securities* generally ensuring financing and holdings, e.g. food, home and ecological connectedness. Material goods play a leading role in our society, and that is why people often associate their own value with them. Financial resources also offer some leeways to stabilize our identity.
- *Values and valuable priorities* which the person responsibly admits to and can be identified with, both by himself and by others. Beyond doubt, one of such identity-providing sources can be membership in organizations connected with such values, e.g. communities of faith, political associations, or humanitarian and ecologically oriented groups.

In terms of recognizing life-determining structures, this model of "five pillars of identity", as described by Petzold[149] offers an approach to learn entire understanding oneself. Besides survival issues and material basis securing, his job is a decisive component for his self-realization and, thereby, for promoting his identity. Our job roots in our bodily basis. We do our job bodily, our body decides on our life both in healthy and ill days. Moreover, we organize our job on a higher-level, i.e. in cooperation with others. We are identified by our job by others and can achieve a self-identification ourselves, as soon as both aspects are in line with it.

Risk and daring to do something have their special meaning in times of societal uncertainness and a variety of choices. We live in a period of societal upheavals characterized by inconsistences. Things once been familiar and trusted in are now called into question. What once was certain and sure begins to totter. In times where flexibility and mobility is so highly required, there is a danger to lose the balance and to suffer losses of identity. Risks make necessary to act in the presence in the light of future consequences. Despite all required flexibility, the individual is expected to take risky actions in light of future effects with restrain and nevertheless develop a feeling of his own identity. Thus we have to remain functioning and healthy in an inconsistent and fragmented society and to develop a stable identity at the same time. Therefore we need "life experiences in which individuals can conceive themselves as governing their lives, as self-producers their biographies and designers their identities" since it is "obviously important conditions for maintaining health", as pronounced by Keupp[150].

Connection between identity and salutogenesis allows for following the aspect how far a stable and sustainably developed identity is directly correlated with sense of coherence. As we know, the sense of coherence as a focal salutogenic component provides motivation to organize life self-responsibly and independently. That

---
149 Petzold, H. G, p. 73.
150 Keupp, H., Ermutigung zum aufrechten Gang, dgvt Verlag, 1997, p. 57.

generates confidence that the individual can use permanently available resources adequately to his situation.

For further comments, it has to be critically scrutinized whether the sense of coherence is really a stable personal characteristic since the person's working on his identity is process running all his life.

In his scripts Antonovsky refers to an already mentioned identity of Erikson[151]. However just Erikson refers to a normative step model as a phase model. He is geared to the psychoanalytic tradition saying that a person runs different development steps approximately up to the end of his adolescence until he formed a stable core for a successful life management. This concept came under criticism merely for that. Today it is premised that development processes run all life. The person constitutes himself all his life within the scope of dynamic identity development and change.

These thoughts result in the conclusion that the identity development and change of coherence experience is embedded in a process of continuous change, i.e. a process of his evolution. Doing this the person is continuously busy with his beliefs about himself that also continuously change and about his own abilities and skills in terms of managing daily life.

Our self-esteem, identity and sense of coherence get new orientation under condition of continuity and discontinuity in our society. Working on our own identity runs in daily balancing between inner demands and demands from outside, thus in permanent communication with our environment. Identity is a permanent contact and a dialog with yourself and others. In this connection, self-esteem is a quality and kind of the person's relation to himself. The same applies to sense of coherence that based on estimation processes within the scope of daily life management. Therefore, the sense of coherence is also defined by Antonovsky as an orientation frame depicting the person's relation to the world.

The issue of sense of coherence broached by Antonovsky is based on above-mentioned evaluation of life order maintaining the self-value dynamics. Goals set by the person himself or by others find expression in assessments of experiences and creations and form feelings of Comprehensibility, Manageability and Meaningfulness:

- Problems and strains in implementing projects and goals strived for can be understood and interpreted as a person's way influenced by the environment but still governed by his own acts, to the large extent.
- Projects and goals strived for can be basically undertaken as identity projects if estimated realistically; the person has available resources that he is in the position to use at a right moment.
- It is worth to campaign for own identity projects as for the ones which are meaningful for one's life. For this purpose the person invests his energies in order to reasonably use them at a right time.

---

151 Erikson, E. H., Growth and crisis of the healthy personality, in: Psychological Issues 1, 1959 und Identität und Lebenszyklus, Suhrkamp, Frankfurt, 1973, pp. 50 f.

The sense of coherence and self-esteem feeling result from identity processes. In this respect, the person has to permanently keep his own goals and wants in balance with demands given from outside. A successful working on his own identity would strengthen his self-feeling and sense of coherence. **The sense of coherence is thereby a decisive factor for successful identity processes.** The permanently acting identity dynamics can also stagnate if our identity in danger, especially if tensions cannot be eased anymore because of too long lasting stress. The sense of coherence is then correspondingly stabilised or decreases.

The said working on identity takes place in future-oriented projects for further-development of the own personality and in projects with others for joined organising our living environment. The identity itself changes over and over again since our living environment continuously changes, too. These complex processes, on one hand, demand from the person a high flexibility of roles and ambiguity tolerance up to risky manoeuvres with all thinkable dangers for coherence experiences, and, on the other hand, offer chances for successful life management and health.[152] But if the person's identity changes in course of all his life the Antonovsky's concept is too narrow as long he sees the sense of coherence as a stable personal characteristic remaining the same from adolescence till into old age. Since Antonovsky designed his theory based on psychology of an individual there is a lack of theory which could show how the sense of coherence is formed and acts in different social conditions.

Bandura's[153] **concept of self-eficacy** is also a psychological construct that, in our opinion, overestimates a person's potency of self-steering and disregards social and cultural determinants of his acting and experiences.

Besides Lorenz's comments described above, the **concept of bonus crises in occupation** by Siegrist[154] also offers an approach providing socio-scientific substantiation. The keynote of his concept is to interlink three systems of organism, of the acting person and of his social environment giving or blocking his chances via the construct of "socio-emotional motivations". Salutogenic or pathogenic effects are postulated in a stress theory paradigm from consonances or dissonances between these three systems.[155] There are three experience modes of self-regulation in the focus of the concept:

- Experience of self-efficacy by successful acting on daily life;
- Experience of self-value via feedbacks from other important persons;
- Experience of self-incorporation via own integration of an individual into large (social, intellectual, or spiritual) communities.

All three forms of self-regulation have in common that they are only possible in one transaction process between the person and social environment and that they need

---

152 Lorenz, R., p. 77.
153 Bandura, A., Social foundations of thought and action, Prentice Hall, Englewood Cliffs, 1986.
154 Siegrist, J., Selbstregulation, Emotion und Gesundheit – Versuch einer sozialwissenschaftlichen Grundlegung, in: Lamprecht, F., Johnen, R., Salutogenese, Kongressband VAS, Frankfurt, 1997, pp. 102 f.
155 Siegrist, J., Soziale Krisen und Gesundheit, Hogrefe, Göttingen, 1994, p. 139.

a field demanding active influence and, at the same time, providing participation on rewards. Readiness to act oriented to creation and maintenance of this transaction between the person and his social environment with the goal of successful self-regulation is called **socio-emotional motivation**, as per Siegrist.[156] Such socio-emotional motivation of a person faces a social structure of chances given in the society around him (in a stricter sense – at his workplace and in his family). This structure of chances can either allow or impede implementation of this motivation. Therefore, positive self-regulation is integrated into the societal system of acting and reward. From these general principles of socio-psychosomatic analysis Siegrist derives his model of bonus crises in occupation. In this model the correlation of influence and recognition in occupational distribution of roles at the age of mature adulthood is a focal point. Concerning exercising of influence the person experiences effects at this workplace depending on his expenditures in his career. The model distinguishes between two sources of high expenditures – an extrinsic and intrinsic source. While extrinsic expenditures mostly depend on quantity and quality characteristics of the job specification, intrinsic expenditures derive from personal achievement motivation. Concerning rewards Siegrist distinguishes three levels of bonus experiences[157]:

- **Salary payments** as equivalent to fulfilled job performance;
- **Recognition**, appraisal and prestige;
- **Occupational status control**, i.e. possibility of occupational promotion or, at least, promising a safe working place as long-term gratification options.

Chronic stress results from workplace conditions characterized by continuing or increasing expenditures and, at the same time, poor salary, lack of promotion possibilities and recognition and even danger of losing the workplace.

The model of bonus crises in occupation was originally referred to lower classes of the society. In a newer study it could be proved that the model is applicable to managers belonging to upper classes. In this social group, too, occupational bonus crises increase risk of coronary diseases in mature adulthood and affect somatic risk factors. Unlike the both salutogenic concepts restricted to personality of an individual (of Antonovsky and Bandura) the model of occupational bonus crises refers to structural level of mechanisms of work organisation and employment policy.

---

156 Siegrist, J., p 103.
157 Siegrist, J., p. 104.

Conclusion: The Sense of Coherence is Decisive

If a person obtains social support and understands coherences of live conditions he will be in the position to create a balance between over- and under-stress. That results in behaviour to vouch for goals and to ascribe meaning and importance to them. Forming own identity begins with self-respect and self-protection. The sense of coherence developable by an individual is the decisive factor for successful identity processes. To leverage these processes without losing balance the person needs permanent self-control by social/emotional motivations. They are mainly act/reward systems effecting exercise of influence and appreciation.

Co-evolution of Family and Career by Changing the Sense of Coherence of Interacting Individuals

The reader shall not get an impression that the subject of this chapter quasi forestalls the result of the process to be surveyed. Rather, it will be depicted that the co-evolution of family and career means very complex and interdependent development systems. Constantly balanced management of different relationship systems is only possible in an ideal case, without disturbances, inhibition and erratic behaviour of one or another interacting person.

Urie Bronfenbrenner[158] portrayed a systematic networking of these relationship systems: **Microsystems** are relationship systems in which the person holds direct relationships, takes roles on and carries tasks out. Correlations of different microsystems are called **meso-systems**. For instance, a meso-system is a correlation between a family, school and neighbourhood or between a working team and a sports group of the company. **Exo-systems** are systems which other microsystem members take part in and thus influence the person directly. For instance, the father's working team is an exo-system for his child. If the father is abased or hard done by his employer, it can influence his parenting behaviour. Occurrences in the exo-system can also affect the immediate surrounding of the person concerned even if he himself is not a part of this system. A **macro-system** means the whole complex of multiple interdependent systems of a definite culture or sub-culture. A macro-system can be a community, a country or a language area. For instance, it can be a problem for children of foreign employees since the microsystem of their family is not a part of the macro-system which they live in. They may come into conflict with their identities because of feeling themselves belonging to two different macro-systems that are not easily compatible with each other. Each person develops his own history that becomes visible by its implication on the person's environment. It leaves traces and marks in which it recognizes itself and is recognized by the environment.

The conflict between professional success and a harmonic family life is a conflict in a meso-system between two micro-systems being an exo-system for another one. In our case, the macro-system is mostly a German speaking area with its economy and culture.

In the following, we will clarify how to develop the both microsystems (family

---

158 Bronfenbrenner, U., Die Ökologie der menschlichen Entwicklung, Klett-Cotta, Stuttgart, 1981.

and work) and, at the same time, to diminish the conflict between them. We are aware of the fact that we shall tackle it in three steps. At first, we will describe co-evolution concepts and processes in the Family Microsystem and, at second, we will describe how to bring the gained knowledge into the practice of the Working World Microsystem. Then, in Chapter 8, we will search for approaches for a holistic co-evolution process in the superior meso-system (which connects the both micro-systems) and ask about family-ethical consequences of the described processes.

The report is based on a viewpoint that is focused on the family. In our opinion, developing a conflict-free family as much as possible is a cornerstone for the further success of the economies of our macro-system. **We need family-friendly workplaces. Not work-oriented families.**

Now it is time to exactly define what does the **"co-evolution"** term means and how it shall be used here. The term was introduced to the psychotherapeutic literature by Jürg Willi[159] who has written the book "Co-evolution – the art of common growth" in 1985. He describes co-evolution as mutual influence of partners living together on each other's personal development. They can further or cumber each other, and they can support forming certain personal qualities, or limit certain behavioural patterns in each other. The point is how the people develop themselves in living together and in going certain ways which cannot be understood without the partner. Co-evolution is a mutual interaction between the partners who are in a specific relation to each other, or live or work together for a long period of time.[160]

The dialectical tension between want for freedom and the want for binding creates wealth, dynamics and fullness in the partner's life, but, to a significant extent, it also creates tension in the marital conflict.

Jürg Willi
"Dyad", p. 10

The more harmonious the relationship, the more the interests of the individual draw back and are overlain by the interests that develop from the partnership, without one being completely absorbed in the other. The product of direct interaction between the partners is the inner and the outer world jointly created by the partners which provides dwelling for their relationship and stability to their personalities. The inner world built by the both partners is a spiritual micro-cosmos for their spiritual dwelling – that means, their ideas and issues which they are busy with, their commonly accumulated experience, their memories, values, norms and meanings that structure and bond their spiritual world. The partners aspire to a private and intimate world which is completely governed by their beliefs and try to create such a world together. This world should provide them a familiar framework and a possibility to feel in the societal reality as at home. This

---

159 Willi, J., Koevolution, Die Kunst des gemeinsamen Wachsens, Rowohlt Verlag, Reinbek bei Hamburg, 1985.
160 Willi, J., Was hält Paare zusammen?, Rowohlt Verlag, Reinbek bei Hamburg, 1993, pp. 220 f.

dyadically built world[161] ("dyadic" means "by two parties") depicts societal relations, on the one hand, and tries to separate itself as privacy from the outer world, on the other hand.

Georg Kelly[162] and Ernst von Glasersfeld[163] dealt with this matter within the scope of constructivism discussion. In their opinion, the person is not able to see the world objectively or to know what is true. Rather, the person builds his experience due to occurrences in which he sees repetitions and abstracts them to patterns, templates and regularities, i.e. to so-called "constructs". These constructs enable him to distinguish usual and special things in the repeating occurrences, to assign ranks to the occurrences in their value and meaning and to determine reasonable correlations in them. Occurrences which are recognized as repetitions become habitual and bring order and structure to the world. However, such constructs governing our perception are only valid as long as they fit with our daily experience. If it is not so any more, the constructs should be modified and aligned with our perception again.

By watching each other in their family and their colleagues at work, the spouses validate their personal constructs, convictions, as well as their political, philosophical and religious attitudes – down to the details of their daily lifestyle. Often they are even not aware of their own personal constructs until being advised of that by the spouse or a colleague.

In the view of them[164] married people are emotionally more stable. Their emotional expression is under a stronger control. They hold "more matured views" since they dwell in a better secured world which is compatible with expectations of the society. Contingently, they are even more self-confident since they feel more vindicated in their definition of themselves. The dyadic world construed by the spouses is a tangible and consistent world for them. Such a world is not only more tangible at the moment, but accumulates more memories, too.

However, the person does not live in a dyadic word only. You also live in other worlds, e.g. at work. These worlds build the person's reality according to their own values and oblige the person to their own construct system of economically reasonable division of labour – mostly bindingly and not co-operatively. Constructs of the job world contain relatively rigid schedules as well as a system of values based on subordination – up to now, even if disguised as a "team philosophy". As we already mentioned in Chapter 3, these two worlds often conflict with each other. Each one of these worlds is a holistic building with more or less definite ideas of the right lifestyle and personality development. Therefore, a person as a member of different construct systems has also to absorb their opposites and contradictions. However, that also means that he can identify with each of these worlds only partly because they often exclude each other.

---

161 Willi, J., p. 268.
162 Kelly, G., die Psychologie der persönlichen Konstrukte, Jungfermann, Paderborn, 1986.
163 Glasersfeld, E. v., Einführung in den radikalen Konstruktivismus, in: Watzlawick (Publisher), Die erfundene Wirklichkeit, Piper, Munich, 1984.
164 Berger, P L., Kellner, H., Die Ehe und die Konstruktion der Wirklichkeit, in: Soziale Welt 15, 1965, pp. 220–235.

With Antonovsky's salutogenic model we get a solution how to significantly diminish the conflicts between the both micro-systems (family and work) and construct systems behind them. The focus of our considerations is the sense of coherence (SOC) defined by Antonovsky[165] as a point of reference. The SOC indicates the person's gaining the pervading, enduring and dynamic belief that his own inner and outer world is predictable and that the things will go so as reasonably expected – with a high probability. We concentrate our attention on coping resources and coping processes which show how the conflict between professional orientation and family becomes ***comprehensible, manageable and meaningful***.

Before doing that, it is reasonable to describe the platform which societal processes of our macro-system run on. ***We portray the social-demographic situation at the outset and depict the ethical and social transformation process running in families nowadays.*** This is quasi a slowly moving coulisse on the stage which we want to let the persons act on.

---

165 Antonovsky, A., pp. 16 f.

Basics of Family Ethics

The term of "**ethics**" should not be mixed up with **ethos**. Whereas ethics as a teaching of human action reflects the latter by distinguishing good and evil, ethos is a concrete moral constitution of a person, group, or society (in our case, a family) as it shows itself in its moral experiences, attitudes, opinions, norms and institutions.

Such institutions as matrimony and family are comprehensive forms of lifestyle and its organisation which both control and unburden the human behaviour. Their aim is to give a point of reference to an individual in his/her concrete dos and don'ts and to help to act ethically right in his/her complex immanent world[166]. Such forms of life and organisation as well as individual moral norms should reflect current societal and economic conditions. Any change in living conditions of the society leads to a transformation of institution of marriage and family. Gruber[167] explains that people's imagination of human happiness and success depends on how they understand the meaning and aims of their existence. Such anthropological pre-understanding is the basis of all human experiences and precedes them all. Norms and values derived from it get their special character by interpretation in the light of certain understanding of the people and world, for example, the Christian, Islamic, Jewish, or secular/laicistic one. In modern European and North-American secularized societies there is no homogeneous understanding of world and human being anymore and, thus, there is no unified system of values. Modern societies are characterized by a **pluralism of values**. What we now begin to see in such countries and regions is mostly a mere **societal consensus** on certain values and meanings ensuring living together.

Does it mean that the Christian understanding of a family is forever lost? We have good reasons to answer "no" on this question. For instance, Weimer[168] asserts that the largely secularized Western culture is simply no longer aware of its underlying religious structure and demands that the own culture should be mobilised first before a dialog between the cultures takes place. For instance, if parents send their children to an international school where traditional German cultural goods are taught only marginally they pay tribute to the competitive constraints of globalization, but the own cultural tradition will be destroyed by hyper-pluralism.[169] More and more parents call such education method into question. They realized that their moral and ethical action cannot be solely and exclusively measured by own sense of conscience because moral does not speak with one voice. Finally, it needs "Archimedean points" of ethical codification. Such points can only be set by

---

166 Gruber, H.-G., Familie und christliche Ethik, Wissenschaftliche Buchgesellschaft, Darmstadt, 1995, p. 59.
167 Gruber, H.-G., p. 60.
168 Weimer, W., Credo – Warum die Rückkehr der Religion gut ist, Deutsche Verlagsanstalt, Munich, pp. 33 f.
169 Weimer, W., p. 55.

religions and that characterizes a culture.[170] Societies which no longer recognize their immanent meaning and do not know other goal than to protect own rights and possession develop less force, activate less aptitude reserves and, finally, get fewer children. According to Erich Fromm[171], the difference between "having" and "willing" cultures is indicated by the birth-rate. Renaissance of cultural and religious awareness raises the readiness to grow again, to have and to want the future in form of descendants.

It is obvious that the Christian understanding of a family is so further developed that it fits with social and economic conditions of the today's society – neither by granting normative quality to the existing facts nor even by sacrificing the ethical groundwork to the spirit of the age. The both pillars – the value of life and the power of love – still characterize the form and ethos of a Christian family.

In the **ethical respect**, the modern family is to be defined as intergenerational community of persons[172]. This term contains **three functions**: the function of **parents**, the function of **community** and the function of **personality**. The first function implies that a family includes at least two generations in a more or less close community. The second one is the function of living together. Unlike a former family that was primarily a working and economic community, a today's family is, first of all, a community of people living together. Parents live together with their children in the same house about a quarter of a century ("Hotel Mum"). The third function (personality) is decisive for a modern family in the ethical respect. The family is not only a community governed by economic aspects, but a personal long-term community. Closeness and intimacy is more decisive for the quality of family relations than objectiveness and practicality. Family life is not characterized by competition and mutual "usefulness", but by fiduciary duty and solidarity. In the Christian tradition, the decisive meaning of a family is to allow a fulfilled personal life.

From the **Christian viewpoint**, the family should be seen as a repository of **social, personal and religious contents**. The division in social, personal and religious contents turns out to be a mere theoretical one. In reality these three family dimensions are simply different sides of the same issue. Gruber[173] expresses it so: Specific contents of the family can be qualified as personal, social or religious ones solely in terms of the viewpoint which the family is regarded from – whether by an individual, by the society or by the Christian belief." The Pastoral Constitution of the Second Vatican Council ("Gaudium et spes") pointed out the **interdependence of culture, education and family**: "The real order of reality are especially easily learned by children surrounded by love in the family, quasi from their mother and herdswoman of upbringing; the proved form of human culture imprint souls of adolescents quasi on its own."[174]

We can illustrate it on following example: parents experience bearing and up-

---

170 Weimer, W., p. 78.
171 Fromm, E., Haben oder Sein, Deutsche Verlags-Anstalt, Munich, 1976.
172 Gruber, H.-G., 1995, pp. 65 f.
173 Gruber, H.-G., 1995, pp. 66 f.
174 Zweites Vatikanisches Konzil, Gaudium et spes, p. 61.

bringing children as highly meaningful. This family content is a part of realization of their personalities. However, the society sees bearing and upbringing children as an eminent social matter insofar it is relevant for its survival. In the view of Christian religion, transfer of human existence finally means fulfilling the mission of the Creation. "Life guidance, education and coping with daily practice are processes decisively furthered by the family. One who wants to withstand challenges of the society getting more and more complex needs a strong personality structure and a firm groundwork of values to stand on. However, what is the place where these properties can develop? It can only be the place where the children grow up, that means, in families", says Reinhard Marx[175] and explains: "Family policy is a forward-looking social policy, like educational policy. That is why to strengthen families is also economically vital for our commonwealth."

In the theological respect, parenthood means relinquishment of "You and Me" for the sake of the comer, i.e. overcoming of stagnation and death. According to Ratzinger, it is "readiness to become a past and to abdicate in order to give way to the comer. If the partners only want to see themselves, it means that they arbitrarily make their time to the last time, and, factually, abandon future to death when trying to eternize the presence and escape the mystery of death."[176] In our time of exaggerating egocentrism and individualization of the society, that is something more than a mere hint.

In the opinion of Christianity, a family is based on marriage. That means, marriage and family is an inseparable entity. Growing numbers of extra-marital cohabitations and extra-marital families put this principle more and more into question. A family without marriage is posited as an equal alternative to a marital one. Such an opinion made the family independent of the marriage and established so strong that it seems no longer tenable to grant to the marriage more rights and tax privileges than to other forms of co-habitation. It is required from the government that instead of marriages it only privileges concrete upbringing performance, regardless the co-habitation form which is done in.[177]

This assessment only refers to the "family period" of a marriage and not the

> *On the one hand, it would not be honest to claim that once there was an ideal form of family and we could hold to such a chimera, even while the other relationships in the society were changing. On the other hand, it would also be wrong to assume that an intact social system could exist without the emotional support and concern which, apparently, only the parents can give a growing child.*
>
> *No matter how many shapes a family may have assumed in history – a constant of a family remains unchanged: a family includes adults of both sexes who have taken the responsibility for their mutual well-being and for their descendants.*
>
> Mihaly Csikszentmihalyi
> "Living Well", p. 116

---

175 Marx, R., Das Kapital, Ein Plädoyer für den Menschen, Pattloch Verlag, Munich, 2008, p. 215.
176 Ratzinger, J., Zur Theologie der Ehe, in: G. Krems, R. Mumm (Ed.), Theologie der Ehe, Regensburg, Göttingen, 1969, p. 109.
177 Schenk, H., Freie Liebe – wilde Ehe, Über die allmähliche Auflösung der Ehe durch die Liebe, Munich, 1988, pp. 234–236.

whole life period of the spouses' living together. Today's couples usually live together alone many years before the first child is born and, in addition, a quarter of a century (in average) after the children become grown and leave the home. The today's family period is only a relatively short period of the entire period of living together. It is even less than a half of a whole marriage period. Today, the starting, middle and final point of the marriage and family life makes the conjugal community an essential and extensive partnership between a man and a woman. Therefore, the modern Christianity considers the marriage as a personal encountering of two people of different genders; the basic and instantaneous meaning of this encountering is common coping with life. The first and the most important function of today's marriage is its protective function, i.e. mutual personal stabilization on various stages of a long period of living together – almost a half of a century.[178]

The power triggering and motivates the people's will to cope with their lives together again and again is **love**. Love is the core of what is profanely called "ethos of the family". One who tries to define love more exactly is faced with a problem: there is no unified definition of this term in marriage and family discussions – neither concerning its contents nor concerning its functions. Therefore, both the Christian marriage model and the secular model of co-habitation can be a form of love. Especially partnerships motivated by much individuality are aimed on self-understanding of the man and woman based on their equal rights. That means not only political and legal rights, but also equal chances of both genders to realize their own lives, skills and life plans. As far such partnerships are guided by intimacy, the main focus is set on psychical and emotive level. The aspired goal is psychical and personal self-realization of the both partners. Such understanding of the partner's love is dictated by individualistic goals of self-realization. The ruling criterion of such love is primarily well-being and happiness of the own life and not of the other partner's life. Finally, love to the other partner is only a way to achieve this goal. In this context, love has primarily a psychological and not an ethical function. Thus, love as a feeling (i.e. subjective and emotional love) is the partnership's base, goal and measurement of its quality. That is what the relationship is valued by. The partnership is kept up as long as it is useful for this goal. As soon as the partnership becomes an obstacle for this goal it is no longer maintained and the partners break up.[179] Such an individualistically reduced idea of partnership conflicts with the desire of today's people to find meaning, support, concealment and protection in their personal relationships. If the mutual attachment is only measured by its usefulness to an individual, the marriage becomes something governed by the "cost vs. benefit" principle – calculability, rationality and economic viability – so as it is common in the world of work. Concealment and support originally arise from awareness and experience of ability of the one to rely upon the other in the case of conflict or a crisis, too, since he/she is loved as a person and not only due to his/her properties and achievements. Emotional warmth and mutual trust cannot develop in insecurity and apprehension. In

---

178 Gruber, H.-G., pp. 75 f. and Gen. 2.18.
179 Gruber, H.-G., 1995, p. 85.

such an atmosphere, it is not finally possible for an individual to grow and mature as a person.

These expectations from a family relationship can be much better realized by the Christian family and marriage model based on love which is more decided, devoting and hoping than in the simple "partners" model. According to Gruber[180] the idea self-discovery and personal development by means of relationships with others (in our case, with a spouse or children) originates from the basic Christian principle. Unlike partners of the individualistic love relationship described above a Christian expects gaining personal stability, self-discovery and maturity not by means of the other partner's behaviour but exactly the reverse – by his own behaviour and devotion to the other. According to his conviction, a Christ finds God and, thereby, himself in his serving the neighbour. The mystery of such devotion is to surrender with the hope to completely retrieve oneself back in a changed form. **However, a real devotion requires personal autonomy and loving oneself. Ability to be devoted without to lose your own self-sufficiency is a part of our approach.**

"Person" as a Term establishing Family Ethics

Family ethics – as it is described in already made explanations that will be specified in following – is based on the Christian definition of a "person". In this definition, the person is considered as "**being**" and "**co-being**" with others, i.e. as an individual and as a social being.

We quasi let go anchor and position the family ethics in the ethical identity, as it is seen by the Christian beliefs in the modern world. For this description, it is necessary to distinguish **between the quest-based ethics of choosing aims and the duty-based ethics of demarcation of moral subjects' interests**. In the quest-based ethics, the human existence is seen as persons acting in the aspect of a good life always taking certain forms.

The human as a person is an individual subject on the one hand and a co-being with other people on the other hand.

Human personality is only possible as mediation of individuality and sociality.

Arno Anzenbacher,
"Christian Social Ethics", p. 181

The form taken by life consists of various actions, deeds, or clusters of actions by which objectives are pursued and adversities are repelled, and all of these actions should be integrated into a consistent course of life. Setting aims and proceeding actions are inseparably connected with evaluative attitudes of the "good" that are realized, concretized and proved in them. In these actions, the acting person actualizes himself as a historical person who lives together with others in a collective and institutional context, i.e. lives and also suffers his life. The quest-based ethical rationality means a transparent and consistent choice and pursuing of aims when observing and compensating own desires that sometimes conflict. Such quest-based

---

180 Gruber, H.-G., 1995, p. 115.

ethics of lifestyle differ from so-called duty-based ethics that emanate from a conflict between interests and goals of individuals and groups and consider compensation between them as legitimate rights, e. g. moral duties.

The ethical identity consists of developing a self-concept which integrates both quest-based life-competence and duty-based ethics (fulfilling moral obligations) into the open biographical coherence of a certain lifestyle which, in turn, concrete deeds are realized in. The ethical identity is depicted in the person's convictions, i.e. their attitudes and values which they experienced as important in their lives. They include his basic concepts of the good and were proved during living together with others, in moral conflict situations, too. The person can identify himself by these convictions only. Against this background of convictions, the person can see himself as empowered to act and challenged to do a concrete "good" with regard to others.[181] In the Christian view, a personal identity is thereby a certain moral concept of a culture forming an ethical identity. It is reflected in historically transformable options of lifestyle which will be parts of the scenario for diminishing conflicts between family and career.

Sociodemographic Situation

Looking at the situation of the family in the modern society, we see that the family is though in crisis now, be not in a situation of collapse and that this crisis is rather a change of the family importance than of the life form itself.[182] The last decades of the 20th century have been distinguished by a profound change in the living conditions and human values conceptions. In this period of time, our way of dealing with time and space, communication and transport has been fundamentally changed. Today modern technology determines not only our life at work (information technologies), but also our life at home (communication, home and household technology) and in our leisure (transport and communication technology) to an extent never seen before. At the same time, there was a great change of moral and ethical values. Such self-experience values like emancipation, enjoyment, self-actualization and independence have almost replaced the former predominating values like obedience, willingness to accept, discipline and unselfishness. As the sociodemographic trends show, families are also affected by this process of change in the value system. Although living together as a family is still important, the family has become more fragile and its manifestations have become more versatile.

In the social debate at the beginning of the 21st century, the family is a focal point. According to the article 6,

> *The traditional family is still, by far, the most common form of family. However, unmarried cohabitation is the most frequent today's form of all families defined in the microcensus who bring up minor children.*
>
> *Federal Statistical Office*
> *Mikrozensus 2005*

---

181 Mandry, Ch., Handbuch der Ethik, Düwell, M., Hübenthal, Ch., Werner, M. H. (Publisher), Verlag Metzler, Stuttgart, Weimar, 2002, pp. 506–507.
182 Gruber, H.-G., pp. 5 f.

par. 1 of the German Basic Law, marriage and family are under the special protection of the state. However, the German Basic Law contains no definition of the term "family". "Family is where children are", as defined by Horst Koehler, the Federal President of Germany at the annual reception of the Protestant Academy in Tutzing on the 18th of January 2006. Even without a clear definition, the Germans agree that living together with children requires a special protection. This definition of "family" is allowed for by the microcensus. Since the reporting year 2005, the microcensus has been the standard for publication of family-related results from the data collection. According to this standard, all child-parent communities are statistically recorded as families. In detail, child-parent communities are married or not married cohabitations of people of two sexes or of the same sex, as well as single mothers and fathers with unmarried children living at their homes. Regarding the "family", the microsensus makes no difference how old the children are and whether they are birth children, stepchildren, foster children, or adopted ones. In the microcensus, a family always includes two generations.

In 2005 there were 12.6 million families in Germany. More than 10 million of them (80 %) lived in West Germany and 2.5 million (20 %) in the former DDR. Since 1996, the number of families in West Germany and especially in East Germany has been steadily decreasing (with the exception of the year 2005). In April 1996 there were still 13.2 million families in Germany. About 10.2 million of them (77 %) lived in West Germany and 3.0 million (23 %) in the former DDR. So the number of West German families has decreased by 1 % and of East German ones even by 16 % since 1996.[183]

The decreasing number of families in West and East Germany was caused by different development trends in individual family models. While the number of traditional families (married couples with children) decreased, the number of alternative families (single parents and co-habitations with children) increased. In the Eastern Federal States (the former GDR) the number of alternative families grew by 14 % to 0.95 million in 2005 compared to 1996. At the same time, the number of married couples with children fell by 27 % to 1.6 million. In West Germany the number of alternative families grew by 25 % to 2.4 million in 2005, the number of traditional families decreased by 7 % to 7.7 million in 2005. So the number of alternative family forms in West Germany grew almost twice quicker than the one in East Germany (25 % compared to 14 %). At the same time, the number of traditional families in the former GDR decreased almost four times more than in West Germany (27 % compared to 7 %).

The growing importance of alternative family forms led to a shift in family structures where married couples with children still clearly predominate. **The traditional family is still by far the most common form of family.** In 2005 more than three quarters (76 %) of the families living in West Germany were married couples with children (in April 1996 it was 81 %). About three fifths (62 %) of the East German families were married couples with children in 2005 (in April 1996 it was 72 %).

Between the different forms of families there are also significant differences in how often they have minor children. The relevant living conditions of alternative family forms between East and West Germany have levelled out. At the same time, the living conditions in traditional families have been developed completely different. In April 1996, still almost three quarters of East and West German non-childless couples (74 % in each) brought up minor children. In 2005 it still applied to 74 % of the West German

---

183 Federal Statistical Office of Germany (Statistisches Bundesamt), Leben in Deutschland, Haushalte, Familien und Gesundheit – Ergebnisse des Mikrozensus 2005.

non-childless couples, but only to 62 % of such couples in East Germany. Thence the traditional family has definitely lost its importance for upbringing of minor children in the now called federal states of the former GDR.[184] **Not married partnerships are the most frequent today's form of all families defined in the microcensus who bring up minor children.**

Regarding the family size, it becomes more and more common in West Germany to have only one child in a family. In 2005 49 % of over 10 million West German families and 62 % of over 2.5 million East German were one-child-families (in April 1996 it was 49 % resp. 55 %.) Only 38 % of West German families and 31 % of East German families had two children living in them (in April 1996 37 % in each). Three or more children were in 13 % of the families in West Germany and in 7 % of families in East Germany (April 1996: 14 % resp. 8 %.) Thus since 1996 there are less and less families with minor children in East Germany; at the same, the number of children in them also decreases. In all over Germany, families with children under the age of 18 brought up 1.61 children on average in this age group (April 1996: 1.65 children).

If we investigate fathers and mothers with regard to family form and main earning a living, we see that in 2005 6.7 million husbands with minor children in all over Germany earned their living by occupation and economic activities. Among non-marital male partners, 80 % earn their living mostly from occupation and economic activities. And only 49 % of 6.7 million marries women with children younger than 18 earned their living from occupation and economic activities. Among non-marital female partners, 62 % earn their living mostly from occupation and economic activities. **In 45 % of all German traditional married couples and 55 % of all heterosexual partnerships, both partners earn their living from their work.**

Without intention to discriminate against one or another kind of partnership, only these two types of families can be considered as relevant for the present research. Homosexual partnerships or single mothers and fathers are not taken into consideration. The reason is that, in many cases, single mothers and fathers do not remain such ones for a long time. Such kind of living is only a transitional stage toward the first two types of families. Co-evolution in terms of our topic needs an emotional community of values, as it can especially be created by heterosexual partnerships (with or without marriage certificate).

If we now correlate the presented socio-demographic data with the family net income, we reach our target group of young executives with minor children. From 6.7 million German traditional families with at least one minor child, 37 % families have net financial income between 2,600 and 4,500 Euro monthly and 11 % of them have net income of 4,500 Euro monthly or more. From 600,000 heterosexual partnerships, 29 % have net income between 2,600 and 4,500 Euro monthly and 6 % have an income of 4,500 Euro and more. If we only consider the highest income class, we can count a target group of more than 1.5 million people in Germany. If we add the upper part of the recipients of net financial income of between 2,600 and 4,500 Euro to our core target group, we get a total of **over 2 million young executives who have children in heterosexual partnerships**.

---

184 Federal Statistical Office of Germany (Statistisches Bundesamt), Ergebnisse des Mikrozensus 2005, p. 44.

Ethical and Sociological Metamorphoses of the Family

The analysis of family lifestyles shows different trends – **pluralisation**, "patchwork family", etc. and also a very typical trend of **individualisation**. The demographic data show today's variety of co-habitation getting more and more individualized. It is especially visible in the fact that families and households become smaller. The share of single-person households is 35 % on the average in all regions of Germany. In agglomerations of German large cities it even exceeds 50 %. While the number of families with more than two children gets less and less in Germany, the trend to live as a single grows further. The process of individualization can be even more exactly recognized in biographical pluralism of lifestyles. Many people practice more than one social lifestyle in their life – from life in as a step-child and extra-marital co-habitation up to being a single parent or a single at all. In former times, the individual biography of a man or a woman was integrated into their families. Today we have just the opposite priority, as stated by Ulrich Beck[185]: "The more exchangeable family relationships become the more autonomous are individual biographies of a man and a woman in the family and outside it. Each person experiences several kinds of lifestyle in a family and without family on his certain life stages and, therefore, his life becomes more and more exclusively his own one." The family as a social group became more and more fragile in the last decades. It has lost its overcoming and unified appearance and its productivity, too, if we concern decreasing numbers of children. However, the family as a social lifestyle still enjoys high appreciation, namely both on the attitude and action level[186]. For instance, the representative questionnaires on the attitude to marriage and family[187] done by the Institute of Public Opinion Research in Allensbach came up to the result that marriage is not so valuable and protectable today as it was in the middle of the 20th century, but the same does not apply to the family. Up to now, the rewards for a family as a lifestyle (defined as a couple with children and a common household) seems to be much higher than limitations and stresses suffered in connection with it.

In the last two decades, it was visible that more and more unmarried couples decided for marriage when they expected a child. **It confirms the impression that people legalize their decisions to stay with their partners mostly in connection with children.**[188] Sociologists call it "child-oriented family". Seeing the growing number of divorces that now hits the mark of 37 % per cent of all marriages whereas 60 % of them are initiated by women, we have to conclude that not the family has got into crisis but the marriage. Not the family lost its power of commitment and attraction, but the marriage. In the social and historical context, such a "crisis" turns out to be not really a crisis, but a change. The change is the result of a structured social differentiation process in the society. During this process, marriage and family

---

185 Beck, U., Risikogesellschaft, Auf dem Weg in eine andere Moderne, Frankfurt am Main, 1986, pp. 188 f.
186 Gruber, H.-G., p. 9.
187 Vgl. Einstellungen zu Ehe und Familie im Wandel der Zeit, Eine Repräsentativuntersuchung im Auftrag des Ministeriums für Arbeit, Gesundheit, Familie und Sozialordnung Baden-Württemberg, Stuttgart, 1985, pp. 134 f.
188 Lüscher, K., Familie und Familienpolitik im Übergang zur Postmoderne (Ed.), Konstanz, 1990, p. 22.

lost some of their functions and tasks. However, they got other important ones. In the last two centuries the society has more and more divided itself in different social organisation complexes.

Tasks and functions belonging to the same system (e.g. a family) in the former traditional society are now distributed on function-specialized and relatively autonomous social systems that, however, very dependent on each other.[189] The modern family type originates from separation production and household in the 19th century, establishing of a public school system and a central medical care and old age benefit system by the state that took over the family tasks of taking care of each other. The family lost some of its functions and was disburdened at the same time. The both important functions special for a modern family are mutual emotional stabilization of partners and bearing and upbringing children. **Emotional relations of the partners become a more and more important component of family life.**

Industrialization and urbanization lessened traditional bindings between relatives and neighbours and made directly close persons important for the person's awareness, self-consciousness and his inner place in the world and his physical and psychical well-being.[190] Historically, this is the beginning point of the today's type of marriage with its special functions of binding, protection, psychical stabilizing, and balancing recreation.[191] The separation of family and work made marriage and family more intimate and so marriage was entered by love – even if in a compromise form. Love became more and more the motive for beginning and maintaining a marriage. The above-mentioned separation of family and work also led to an intimatization of the relation between the parent and children and therefore to decisive changing the attitude to childhood. Like all other activities of a married couple in the pre-industrial society, children and their upbringing were aimed at ensuring survival. A child or an adolescent did not have "childhood" and "youth" in that way we provide them nowadays. Children were seen and treated as little adults.

After the enormous drop in the birth rate in the second half of the 20th century children seem no longer be the most important objective of marriage and family and the majority of people seems to foreground the relation between partners. In some way, it is right: nowadays, children become the object of life-planning calculation more than ever. More and more people see other alternative life objectives more attractive than to have children. It becomes apparent that children now occupy quite another place in the spouses' life as before. It can be also recognised in changes of upbringing and education methods. New ethically-based guidelines of upbringing said that the parents should recognize positive tendencies of their children and optimally further them by assistance, guidance and care. **The primary goal of upbringing consisted in socialization of the child to a sensible and internally controlled**

---

189 Tyrell, H., Probleme einer Theorie der gesellschaftlichen Ausdifferenzierung der privatisierten modernen Kernfamilie, in: Zeitschrift für Soziologie, 5, 1976, pp. 393 f.
190 Beck-Gernsheim, E., Von der Liebe zur Beziehung?, Veränderungen im Verhältnis von Mann und Frau in der individualisierten Gesellschaft, in: Berger, J. (Ed.), Die Moderne – Kontinuitäten und Zäsuren, Göttingen 1986, pp. 209 f.
191 Gruber, H.-G., p. 18.

person.[192] Moreover, development of motivation, flexibility and assertiveness were of particular importance. They were qualities enabling an adolescent to improve his economic situation and social status by being successful in his future work life. The optimal promotion of the child's skills is the pedagogic priority in such a mobile society primarily based on individual achievement and assertiveness.

Due to technically perfected contraception the question of reproduction is no longer in focus of family life. The more important subject is the optimal upbringing of children and living conditions which the parents can offer them. Apparently, the main reason of drop in birth rate is the change in upbringing methods, a tremendous demand on emotional attention and pedagogic promotion, as well as equal rights of the both partners on self-realization and financial well-being. Separation of sexuality and procreation offered the possibility to enjoy sexuality outside the procreation. Such sexuality became an object of delight and to a special mean to express intimate and personal relation and love between partners. At the same time, the sexuality is exposed to the danger to be practiced in a self-centred and egoistic manner and to miss its personality-related objectives.

To exactly position a today's family in ethical and sociologic change we should view the pluralization and individualization of today's social worlds once more. These processes are especially visible in **separation of work and family**. One of the consequences of this separation was **dichotomizing of life into a private and a public domain**, and that is the most typical attribute of the today's society.[193] Individualisation of life was promoted not only by pluralizing of social worlds but also mechanization of the economics. Superior systems of care allow a **small family to emancipate itself** and to **withdraw from kinship bonds**. However, the newest researches prove that a network of relatives of different generations is still preserved if they live not so far away from each other. In the past, family networks were fixed in one place, and now they are distributed over many regions and states. Former strong religious bonds in families lost their influence because of growing secularizing. Today, a single person no longer recognizes himself as part of a large superior whole but increasingly as an individual. He no longer lives in a consistent world but moves between different worlds such as between the highly specialized work world, public life and family. He has always to accustom to new roles and behaviour types. Many people see a danger in such a situation. Privacy of their families gets a quite new meaning and function. It serves as a kind of balancing mechanism that provides meaning contents and meaningful activities as compensation of dissatisfaction caused by structures of the today's society.[194] People who see the marriage and family as a kind of shelter for finding meaning of their lives, self-realization and self-determination often overstrain their partners. At the time when traditional guidelines and societal concepts become fewer and fewer and, on the contrary, exogenous stressors increase, idealized imaginations of marriage cause

---

192 Gruber, H.-G., pp. 29 f.
193 Gruber, H.-G., pp. 44 f.
194 Berger, B., Berger, P. L., Kellner, H., Das Unbehagen in der Modernität, Frankfurt, New York, 1987, p. 160.

too high demands on the relationship quality and lead to unfulfilled needs and thus to conflicts and tensions in the family.[195]

To complete the description of changes in family, we should specially mention the individualisation process in women's lives. The formal stability typical for a former family was primarily based on division of labour between the genders. According to the today's societally recognized concept, such division of labour contradicts the basic principle of the modern society where chances and circumstances shall be fairly distributed, namely, only according to individual merits and without respect to any estates given by birth. However, individualizing of women's lives has a double meaning: on one hand, a female individual is no longer the one who needs to be controlled and fended for and on the other hand, she can fend for herself on the labour market. Accordingly, all consequences of this individualization are "double". Individualization in the meaning described above extends freedom of action for an individual and so allows for an individualized biography. At the same time, the individual is faced with diverse uncertainties, insecurities and a necessity to fend for oneself in circumstances of market economy.[196]

Educational expansion in the 60s of the 20th century was decisive for equalling the chances of man and woman. Large differences in chances between the genders have been overcome in only two decades: the share of boys and girls in schools and even in universities was nearly the same. Such equalling the education chances had a multiple influence on women's lives and co-habitation of the genders. At first, women got more knowledge and thus more power: the man lost his guaranteed privileges since his education was not better than the woman's one. Women got a larger economic independence since they were no longer dependent from marriage as fending institution. For our subject it is especially important equalling education chances gave women a higher sense of coherence which was much lower than the men's one before since the women's participation in decision-making processes grew. Women with good education understood that they generally possess all necessary resources to solve problems and take challenges. **Finally, women got the same feeling of manageability as men – one of three perception and evaluation patters which the sense of coherence (SOC) consists of.**

That has a deep meaning for marriage and family institutions. After the individualization process also involved the female world, women also got exposed to the lures of professional career. That points up a conflict between demands of family and demands of world of work. As long the individualization was limited to men, and women were complementarily obliged to "live for others"[197], the family could well stay together. However, from the moment of getting the same chances and underlying the same necessities of self-designed life plan the relationship between man and woman may collapse. Not only incentives but also requirements of an individualized existence in the world of work are more related to the **own personality** and not to the partner or family.

---

195 Matthias, H., Scheidungsursachen im Wandel, in: Frauenforschung 8, Bielefeld, 1990, pp. 27 f.
196 Beck, U., Beck-Gernsheim, E., Das ganz normale Chaos der Liebe, Frankfurt, 1990, pp. 12 f.
197 Gruber, H.-G., pp. 53 f.

Such egocentrism of man and woman heightens the potential for conflicts in marriages, partnerships and families. As already mentioned above, all formal, institutional and financial solutions for creating balance between family and work offered by government grow further but will never replace the necessity of private solutions between the partners. **The partners have rather to look for individual solutions and negotiate with each other – not only one time, but again and again – how to agree all necessities and ambitions concerning supporting the family, career and profession with their family wishes and beliefs.**

Coping Strategies for the Family

According to Lazarus[198], the "coping" term includes all efforts of an individual to manage stress-related situations. His model considers stress situations as complex reciprocation processes between the demands arising from the situation and the demands of the acting person.

Coping Strategies and Social Groups

In contrast with earlier stress theories, Lazarus assumed that it is not the nature of stimuli or stress response situations that are important, but rather the individual cognitive processing of those affected. As Antonovsky also pointed out in his remarks on salutogenesis, people's response to a particular stressor can be highly varied. What means stress to one affected person (for they have a relatively low SOC) can mean no stress to someone else (for they have a relatively high SOC). Each person assesses situations and their burden differently, as well as, for this reason, their level of threat. Lazarus applied three different levels here:

- **Primary appraisal**
  In the primary appraisal phase, environmental stimuli are seen and assessed as to whether or not they pose a threat. Situations may be assessed as positive, irrelevant or potentially dangerous.

- **Secondary appraisal**
  In the secondary appraisal, one examines whether or not the situation can be overcome with the resources that are available. A stress situation is triggered only if there are insufficient resources. One will proceed to develop a coping strategy – one which will in no way be dependent on the situation or on the personality and cognitive structures of the individual. This threat handling is called coping. Possible behaviours include:

  - Confrontational coping
  - Cognitive distancing
  - Self-control
  - Search for social support
  - Taking responsibility
  - Escape prevention

Over time, a person learns how to apply coping strategies selectively, on the basis of success and failure outcomes.

---

198 Lazarus, R. S., Emotion and Adaption, Oxford University Press, London, 1991, pp. 213 f.

- **Re-appraisal**
  After a person has responded to a threat, internal and external conditions will change; there shall be a comparison with the original situation in retrospect. If the initial situation prior to the threat could not be recalled, a change in expected values shall take place.

Lazarus[199] differentiates between two types of stress coping:

- **Problem-oriented coping**
  Under this, he understands that the individual attempts to overcome problem situations, or to adjust to circumstances, by looking for information, direct actions or omitting acts. This coping strategy depends on the level of the situation.

- **Emotion-regulating coping**
  Emotion-regulating coping is also known as "intrapsychic coping", where an attempt is made to reduce the emotional impact caused by a situation without having to deal with the cause.

The coping strategies as described above, which people apply for themselves, usually fuse with a highly individualised coping style which does not clearly distinguish between problem-oriented and emotion-regulating stress management. However, recent studies have indicated that men prefer problem-oriented coping strategies while women prefer emotion-regulating ones. Nicholls & Polman ascertain: "Problem-focused coping mechanism may allow an individual greater perceived control over their problem, while emotion-focused coping may more often lead to a reduction of perceived control. Certain individuals therefore feel that problem-focused mechanisms represent a more effective mean of coping."[200]

We refer to the theoretical statements on how individuals cope which are included in Chapter 6 under the heading "Controlling the emotions" and now ask about coping strategies **between** *individuals – specifically, coping concepts within families.*

While stress has so far been defined mainly in the context of the individual and – according to the transactional stress approach of Lazarus which is today a leading one – has been understood as interplay between the requirements made of a person and their perceived resources for dealing with them, since the 90s the concept has extended to social concepts.[201] **With this, in the modern day, next to individual stress, terms like dyadic, familial or social stress have also been introduced and conceptualised.** Although the approach of Lazarus and Folkman[202] is based on a correlation between the person and their environment, social exchange and reciprocal processes were neglected. There follows a discussion of social coping forms (in the context of interaction of individuals), whereby stress and coping in partnerships – our topic – receives special attention.

---

199 Lazarus, R. S., p. 214.
200 Nicholls, A. R., Polman, R. C. J., Holt, N. L., The effects of individualized imagery interventions on golf performance and flow states, in: Athletic Insight: the Online Journal of Sport Psychology, 7(1), January 6th 2006, www.athleticinsight.com/Vol.7Iss1/ImageryGolfFlow.htm.
201 Bodenmann, G., Stress und Coping bei Paaren, Göttingen, Hogrefe, 2000, quoted in Grau, J. und Bierhoff, H. W., Sozialpsychologie in der Partnerschaft, Springer 2003, pp. 483 f.
202 Lazarus, R. S., Folkman, S., Stress, appraisal and coping, Springer, New York, 1984.

According to Bodenmann[203], stress can be defined to the effect that multiple persons are affected by the same stress event, and will attempt to cope with it with the application of joint, coordinated coping efforts. One special form of social stress fosters stress in partnerships and families – alongside a high level of common concern, there is also a high level of intimacy and closeness between social interaction partners / the family members.

So-called dyadic stress is understood as stress between persons in a partnership resulting from an experience which affects both partners, directly or indirectly, an experience which unbalances the relationship in a couple wherever the individual and dyadic resources of both partners are not sufficient for reasonable coping of the internal and external requirements with each individual / the couple. In the conflict between family and professional orientation that we have outlined, professional orientation can be the cause of burden inside or outside the dyad, affecting both partners; whether at the same time, on a staggered basis or sequentially. In this way, the stress of one partner can become the stress of the other if the first one is not able to reasonably cope with the burden themselves. In addition, the stress coping of the first partner can trigger stress in the other if strategies are employed, which involve a conflict of interest or come at the expense of the other.

If, in addition to the couple, other members of the family (children in particular) – as in our target group – are affected by a conflict event, one can speak of family stress. Family stress is defined by Perrez[204] as circumferential stressors which are experienced not by one sole family member alone, but by several, or all at once, at the same time. As such, it's about the relative amount of overlapping stress experienced by the individual within a family if more than one person in the family – or, at the maximum, all family members – are involved in the coping process in response to a stressor. In their concept of family competence, Bodenmann-Kehl[205] designate family stress and family coping as fully familiar phenomena which are based on common assessments and which combine the complementary coping activities of multiple or all family members. According to the **stress coping cascade model** of Bodenmann[206] it should be assumed that, in cases of persistent, prolonged, severe stress, children will believe the existence of first individual stress, and then, should it not be successfully coped with, dyadic stress, then family stress. Finally, when people who are close to the couple (friends, relatives and work colleagues) are included, social stress can develop, which could be countered only by the coping concepts of all involved.

In the individual stages of this cascade model, we distinguish between several determinants of coping with stress. Thus, in the coping phase, there is a close correlation between the dimensions of closeness, intimacy and familiarity and that of consternation. With dyadic and family coping, high intimacy and confidentiality of the participants fuse with a level of being affected by the stress event which is high. This is a process of *mutual "contamination"* of the interacting individuals which will be all the more inevitable the closer the persons are to each other and the more they are affected by the stress event.

---

203 Bodenmann, G., Stress und Coping bei Paaren, p. 484.
204 Perrez, M., Familienstress und Gesundheit. Familienleitbilder und Familienrealitäten, Leske & Budrich, 1997.
205 Bodenmann-Kehl, C., An integrative model of family competence, in: European Review of Applied Psychology, 47(2)1997, pp. 143–147.
206 Bodenmann, G., Stress und Coping bei Paaren, p. 486.

What coping concepts are to be recognised with dyadic coping?

Partnership coping was formerly defined either as individual coping within the partnership or as dyadic coping in the real sense.

While the individual coping concepts of some authors assume that each partner manages independently of other sources of stress[207], other authors do assume that all involved will manage independently; however, it is claimed that the coping efforts of the two partners (which take place separately) are related and are either **congruent**, i.e. the two partners cope with the situation in a similar manner or **discrepant**, i.e. both partners choose different coping strategies.[208] The findings of the cited researchers indicate that, with emotion-related coping strategies, congruent coping behaviour of both partners is more appropriate; in the event of problem-related coping strategies it is different i.e. discrepant coping efforts of the two partners that are more appropriate.

Amongst the examined target group of younger executives (with 5-10 years of professional experience and growing children at pre-school and primary school age), dyadic coping is employed for coping with the dual pressures of family and professional life at a family level (mostly flanking with individual coping efforts) – it is invoked if individual coping resources are insufficient. In addition to the stress-reducing effect, it has mostly positive effects on partnership quality and stability, in which the feeling-togetherness of the couple is strengthened, partner confidence increases and intimacy and emotional attachment increase.

Self-realization and Variety of Roles

The term of "self-realization" as a delimiting one defined in the last decades stands in the way of all coping concepts that seemed to be thinkable and manageable already in the beginning of the 21st century and outrun the individual. People tried to gain self-knowledge and awareness by concentration on themselves. The person strived to learn to stand up to other people and to repel heteronomy. People were afraid to surrender and to get under the partner's influence whereas they did not really recognize that they would be aware of themselves just in their distinction to the partner.

Here we will not describe the history of this special term of self-realization aimed on the demarcating one and how this term was developed by Descartes and Hobbes and later by Kant, C. G. Jung up to Maslow, Rogers and Perls. We only underline that in spite of the boom of self-realization concepts in the 60s and 70s of the 20th century the self-realization is still not a new thing of the present time but a further step of the European culture more and more tending to emphasize the distinctiveness of the individual.

If this term of self-realization stands no longer in way of the discussion of coping

---

[207] Pearlin, L. J., Schooler, C., The structure of coping, Journal of Health and Social Behavior, 19, 1978, pp. 2–21.
[208] Revenson, T. A., Social support and marital coping with chronical illness, Annals of Behavioral Medicine, 16, 1994, pp. 122 f.
Pakenham, K. J., Couple coping and adjustment… in: Family Relations, 47, pp. 269–277.

strategies, we will try to develop this term further. We will follow Jürg Willi who described two additional aspects of self-realization: "One thing is the **self-realization in the people's meeting together, especially in a love relationship**. Being engaged into a dialog the person call forth many things which he was not aware of before. By meeting the partner many such things are drawn into life. Another form of **self-realization is realization of deeds** in which the person becomes fruitful."[209] The first aspect concerns self-reflection of the individuals, the second one concerns the partner's relationship and, in the broader sense, the family, and the third one primarily the **professional domain of the person where he performs his activities and success**.

All three forms of self-realization – by self-recognizing, by meeting others and by performance done – will be a basis of coping processes portrayed in the following. We represent the idea of a person which is not only centred on self-recognition and consciousness of self as a method of independence and self-determination but also includes active implementation by creating one's own world in the family, partnership and work.[210] The human personality needs a so-called **"self-transparency"** (as it is called by Frankl), that means **being responded by its own environment,** to remain vivid and to grow personally. "The person is asked questions by life itself. He has nothing to ask. Rather, he is the one who is asked and has to give answers to life."[211]

We live only a small part of our opportunities – that means, only the ones which become apparent by means of interaction with our specific environment.

Jürg Willi
„Turning Point in the Biography", p. 61

Consequently, the person is considered as a part of processes which he cannot always and completely control and which, at the same time, convey him an outlook on life oriented at fellow humans. In the period between the years 1981 and 2009 (28 years), we have found out in many thousands of interviews with executive managers that at least this target group of people presses for realization. Executive managers want to make their outcomes visible for themselves and for others and to be recognized in them. **But what is visibly realized by a person is always only a part of his personal possibilities. What comes into being, takes certain forms and becomes visible is not in the exclusive power of the person but is dictated by his circumstances in the family and work and by other persons acting in this field.** This conception corresponds with the idea of human in the today's psychotherapy. The person is seen as the main player on the stage of life. He cannot play his history without his team-mates who grant him his role. What can be realized by him in this play and what not? To answer this question the person's approach has to include other persons whom he interacts with. The goal is to make a good history from life. Such values of personal development as autonomy and self-

---

209 Willi, J., Wendepunkte im Lebenslauf, Klett-Cotta, Stuttgart, 2007, pp. 116 f.
210 Willi, J., p. 117.
211 Frankl, V. E., Grundriss der Existenzanalyse und Logotherapie, Urban & Schwarzenberg, Munich, 1972, quoted in: Riemeyer, J., Logotherapie Viktor Frankls, Eine Einführung in die sinnorientierte Psychotherapie, Quell, Gütersloh, 2002.

discovery are important. However, their real trial in the practice is to organize the course of life and to actively bring into being concrete things.[212]

Allocation of one or several roles to the person makes it easier for him to find his own location in his configurable environment. Jürg Willi calls it **"his personal niche"**[213]. The role gives the person tasks which come along with expectations on his behaviour. Up to now such expectations are governed by societal norms adapted to the roles and related expectations of co-acting persons. Well-known roles are the ones of a partner of a spouse, of a father, mother or of a boss at job. The role expects certain behaviour and limits it, too. Up to now, roles allocated to the person by the society offer not only a certain freedom of role practicing, but also some protection from taking the role or its parts by other persons and even by the government.

The enduring and strongly increasing individualization of our society and, thus, shift in values have drastically changed traditional allocation of roles or, at least, put them into question. Such changes are recognizable and understandable. For example, a working wife will put her traditional role of mother into question and dispute her husband's former control of family income because now she can earn herself. She will also review her sexual role. If one of the partners is going to change his/her workplace, the final decision can only be made by both of them because the career of the other partner is also concerned. **Conflicts on allocation and distribution of roles break out in many marriages and partnerships in our target group,** especially if the partners seek a high degree of self-determination. However, in more and more cases, people do not come up to the roles given them by the society, or do not want to do it. When these people finally win through to some roles which were not originally allocated to them they feel overburdened by this **"roles accumulation".** In an extreme case they begin to disrespect the roles accepted by the society or the ones "captured" by them. Such behaviour affects both close persons in the family, especially children, and colleagues and others at work. In all described cases people lose the freedom of role exercising ensured them before, as well as protection that was formerly provided to them by their undisputed roles.

If **the government** believes to recognize that the caring persons come no longer up with their former roles within their families or they cannot do it because they both have to go to work, **it increasingly offers its "help" and takes over a part of "parent" role in diverse forms, up to day-care for small children**.

Changes in allocation of roles also change our personal opportunities that we can or cannot realize in the course of our lives. We can realize only some of our opportunities, namely the ones which are brought into appearance by the interaction with our specific environment.[214] **If we assign a further part of our remaining opportunities to the government, it will have an effect of de-individualization of our society.**

---

212 Willi, J., pp. 52 f.
213 Willi, J., pp. 79 f.
214 Willi, J., p. 115.

We came to the conclusion that the majority of male and female roles are at a turning point. Unlike women's movement into "men's area" that took place long ago, men's movement into "women's area" goes much more slowly. Women acquire more and more **variety of roles**, and men can only painfully surrender their limitation of roles. As already mentioned above, the variety of roles causes both stress (or sometimes even overstress) and relief, flexibility and implication of social support. Hibbard and Poe[215] came to the conclusion in their researches that professional occupation of women often diminishes stress caused by the role of mother, wife and carer of relatives. **Being a wife and mother has no positive effect on health of not working women. On the contrary, working women experience such roles as a health-promoting buffer, however under a precondition that their marriage is based on equal rights of the both partners and women can be decision-makers.** In the men's world it is not the case. Men usually do not possess the same variety of roles as women. Stress in job is not mitigated by their roles as fathers or husbands because they exercise those roles not with the same intensity as women.

American and German researchers[216] point out that men still did not learn to tell about their fears and apprehensions to other men and to get an emotional support from them in such a way as women do that. Men often have too few persons whom they exchange emotions with. Their social network is mostly oriented at job and competition. When men get older they do not have the same social resources as women because they had neglected their private relationships during their working life. It is reasonable to require that men no longer assign maintaining social relationships to women. They have to begin to allow and sense feelings in order not to emotionally take more than they give. First of all they have to free themselves from fear to be devoured and taken by women and to lose their independence.[217]

Men keep their bodies for a possession, which they proliferate indefinitely. They use their bodies as performance machine and are amazed when the body no longer function. Men do not see their bodies as a component of their personalities, and it is a contradiction to the ideal of the classic male stereotype (mens sana in corpore sano). Finally, careless and hurtful treating own body leads to a lower life expectancy and a higher death rate for men. A man is well-advised if he behaves more carefully with his health, does not exploit his body ruthlessly, but looks after it and maintains in a good condition already at younger ages.

Although medical diagnostic findings assert that the difference in male and female life[218], expectancy has genetic reasons, we can assume that existing vulnerabilities of men can be influenced and modified by the environment and socialization

---

215 Hibbard, J. H., Poe, C. R., The quality of social roles as predictors of morbidity and morality, in: Social Science and Medicine 36, 1993, pp. 217 f.
216 Brod, 1987, Connel, 1987, Farell, 1995, Williamson, 1995, Griffiths, 1996, Pilgrim, 1986, 1989, Hollstein, 1990, 1991, 1992a, b, 1993, Willems und Winter, 1990, Winter und Willems, 1992, Brzoska, 1992, Winter, 1993, Sielert, 1993a, b, Böhnisch und Winter, 1994, Engelfried, 1997, Gottschlach, 1997, Möller, 1997, Zimmermann, 1998.
217 Hollstein, W., Die Männer, Vorwärts oder zurück? Deutsche Verlags-Anstalt, Stuttgart, 1990.
218 Bründel, H., Hurrelmann, K., Konkurrenz, Karriere, Kollaps, Kohlhammer, Stuttgart, 1999, p. 175.

(even if the environment cannot abolish them). Thus the importance of health awareness and active protection of health remain beyond dispute.

Traditional family models in which the man is the master of the family and the only decision-maker are slipping out of their existence in all modern European societies. Urban agglomeration regions where new structures are tested govern the speed of the changes.

Women have captured the terrene of gainful occupation and win more and more power in leading positions due to their appropriate education. Thus they have won a larger right to say in a matter. Men are mostly no longer the only money-earner of the family. So the family needs a new distribution of roles. Men have to surrender a part of their power and to win a new relation to the power. **A democratic society requires balanced power relations between the genders and equal rights for men and women in its smallest cell, too (i.e. a family).** That also includes overcoming a gender-specific division of labour at work, as well as fair division of work in family life and housekeeping.

Balance of power between genders formulates new concepts of masculinity and femininity concepts, releases from gender-specific restraints und can lead to an extended view of sexuality. Both genders will get a larger variety of roles and agree a reasonable division of roles between each other.

Today's power relations between man and woman sometimes cause helplessness and thus dealing with own fears and scares, namely for both genders. According to Bründel[219], a sign of weakness is not expression of feeling but denying them and blocking out. Strength and weakness are not boundary relations between the genders, but within the genders. People are not strong or weak in themselves, there are strong and weak men and women. Dealing with himself, a man can discover his inner core and develops inner strength and power basing on the own strength and not on oppressing femininity. The key to a new form of masculinity seems to be a discovery of own sensitiveness connected with empathy that should be more developed in men.[220]

Instead of hegemonic masculinity, a new term of masculinity is developed which also includes admission of the powerlessness. The unilateral right for power traditionally belonging to the male role should be changed and extended in favour of self-efficacy and coherence in terms of Antonovsky's models[221]. The decisive thing is not the power and striving to control everything, but a realistic and always recoverable feeling to cope with requirements of inner and outer world and to experience them as comprehensible, manageable and meaningful when applying a suitable coping strategy. A coping strategy does not mean to manage all problems alone, but to allow help and support and to see emotionality as a fortitude and not as a weakness. Not claiming for almightiness, but flexible coping comes to the fore. The latter is supported by positive attitude to own abilities and being sure that a broad

---

219 Bründel, H., Hurrelmann, K., p. 177.
220 Lenz, H.-J., Männerbildung, Ansätze und Perspektiven, in: Möller, K. (Ed.), Nur Macher und Macho? Geschlechtsreflektierende Jungen- und Männerarbeit, Juventa, Weinheim, 1997, pp. 165–184.
221 Antonovsky, A., Salutogenese, pp. 34 f.

social network is able to help.[222]

Old ideals of masculinity and femininity have almost lost their importance. They were replaced by new ones that extend the spectrum of behaviour, experience and feelings of men and women. Mutual attraction of genders, i.e. erotic link between them should remain anyway, and love between man and woman should not be lost because of this new orientation. **Increasing flexibility of gender roles and images of man and woman does not diminish attraction between them. On the contrary, it is sparked anew.** It acquires a new quality since there is a larger freedom for shaping own behaviour by agreement with the partner. Even if ready stereotypes no longer exist, emotional attachment and love and sexual relations between man and woman remain exist due to mutual imaginations and expectations. However, they are individual and personal (as far as possible, agreed with consensus) and no longer pre-programmed by societal beliefs considered as reasonable before. Individualization always includes abandoning some accustomed and firmly bound patterns. It causes some scare in the beginning, but can lead to new forms of relationship. Such scaring for a moment can start a creative process: social, cultural and individual development of genetic material has much more potential than supposed before. We are at a turning point when everyone is responsible for developing one's own personality, for choosing one's own action plan and, thereby, for imagination of masculinity and femininity.

It remains to be seen whether this self-responsibility of everyone will stay free from new societal expectations, influences and even necessities positing a new idea of human.

Open Discussion of the Dilemma and sensitive Dealing with the Conflict by Family Members

In our culture, such individual-related values as success, self-realization, self-reliance and independence rank at the top of the scale of values. As stated by Gruber[223], they highly influence family life since the family has quite other rules and values. Profit maximization, mobility and assertiveness are not important in the family. More important things are to understand and to be understood, to accept and to be accepted. Family members need social values, e.g. solidarity, faithfulness, considerateness and ability to devote and to surrender to live together in peace. The spouses have to synchronize these legalities between the economically organized and individual-oriented work of world and consumption and the alliance-oriented and personal family world. In apprehension of exposing family togetherness to egoism and lopsided individualized aims, Gruber[224] requires *reduction of individualization dynamics* by societal propagation of family-friendly concepts and ideals, as well as socio-political

---

222 Hurrelmann, K., Alte und neue Bilder vom Mann und der Männlichkeit, Vortragstext, Fakultät der Gesundheitswissenschaften der Universität Bielefeld, 1997.
223 Gruber, H.-G., 1995, p. 158.
224 Gruber, H.-G., 1995, p. 159.

influence by the legislation in order to make family life as attractive as occupation. He agrees to the socio-political advocates speaking louder and louder in unison that the dilemma between family and professional orientation can be solved by refund of family costs by means of regulating laws. Like Ulrich Beck[225], he recommends laws which could forbid mobility coercion and would legally recognize immobility due to family reasons.

We do not follow the approaches of these authors because they do not consider changing of education structure in our target group, i.e. young executives. As we said before, the education and cultivation are the same among men and women in this group. **Female young executives are not lower educated than their male colleagues (soon they will be even better).** In families of young executives both partners have the same level of education and interaction culture allowing them to work out solutions in their small social group (the family) without waiting for ready solutions from the state. **Solutions can be found in an open dialog and co-operation between two people with equal intellectual skills; such people are able to sensitively deal with each other and to negotiate "agreed careers", as well as to arrange emotional correlation of love and care of children in their new understood roles.** The focus of our view is new understanding of roles allowing the partners to agree of work and parenthood.

,I' becomes ,You'.
All real life is encounter.

Martin Buber
"The principle of dialogue", p. 15

My wife is the heaven of my soul,
But also often my pain and hell.
…
My wife is often amenable and good;
…
She is my freedom and my choice
And often my prison and cause of nostalgia…
She is also often angry and furious.
She is my bliss and my heavy load.
She is my wound and my bandage.
She is my heart's delight
And she makes me old and grey.

Hans Sachs (1494–1576)
"Bitter-sweet Married Life"

Mutual Evolution of Couples – Personal Resources

As already described in Chapter 3, our understanding of career includes not only occupation but the whole biography of an individual. In this way, family life, parenthood, and partners' career come to the fore together. The focal term is an **"agreed career"**[226] – such a career stage at which occupation and parenthood (especially if the children are not grown yet) converge and should be organized in such a way that

- the conflicts happening are made structured, predictable and comprehensible;
- resources are found and made available to face with these conflicts;
- coping with the conflicts (or, at least, their diminishing) is seen as a challenge which is worth efforts and commitment.

---

225 Beck, U., p. 202.
226 Auer, M., pp. 27 f.

A possible solution can be strengthening of Generalized Resistance Resources (GRR) in terms of Antonovsky's salutogenic model of stress prevention.
"The belief that conflicts have their meaning and are comprehensible and manageable provides motivation and a cognitive basis for a behaviour which allows for an easier coping with problems caused by stressors than a behaviour based on a belief that the world is chaotic and overwhelming."[227]

Antonovsky's salutogenic model is individual-based. He says that a person with a strong SOC is more in the position to identify the nature and dimensions of the instrumental problem. Rather, the person tends to see the problem as a challenge and so it is a higher probability that the person chooses from his resource repertoire the adequate ones and uses them reasonably. But what will happen if more than one individual is involved into the conflict or even gets stuck in it? Antonovsky does not deal with reciprocity between the individual and the dyadic stress assessment. Therefore, to describe the couple's common development in the conflict between career and family we choose a systematic extension that stress and coping are seen in their social influences and responses from the social environment. We assume a complex reciprocally between different actors (in our case, the both partners and their children). In this situation, both the response processes (mutual escalation of stress situations) and helpful dealing with the situation by a dyadic coping can occur. How the stress will be felt and how the coping process will run mainly depends on the anxiety of the stress and possibilities to control it by the co-acting persons and sometimes even external persons. Such situation attributes depend on the motivation factors (e.g. satisfaction with the partner) and competences of the both partners. ***Consequently, dyadic stress and dyadic coping are a function of extended partner- and dyadic-oriented estimation processes and aims.***[228] If a person or a dyad comes to a conclusion in the primary estimation that her/his own well-being or well-being of the partner or of the dyad is endangered, it will be examined in the secondary estimation which individual, dyadic and extra-dyadic response capacities are available to cope with the situation. Own resources, resources of the partner and common dyadic resources and resources of external persons are examined within the scope of the dyadic coping.[229]

Dealing with common development of the partners we should discuss existing process models exactly described by their originators which concern our target group. The phase model of Schneewind[230] for couples with small children goes further: a child is born, the woman becomes a mother and the man becomes a father and often the only wage-earner. In this phase both partners have to grow into changed roles. Structures of power, affect and communication of the young

---

227 Antonovsky, A., Salutogenese, p. 137.
228 Bodenmann, G., p. 49.
229 Bodenmann, G., p. 50.
230 Schneewind, K. A., Graf, J., Gerhard, A.-K., Paarbeziehungen, Entwicklung und Intervention, in: Rosenstiel, L. v. Hockel, C. M., Molt, W. (Publisher), Handbuch der angewandten Psychologie (pp. V-6.1, 1–20) ecomed, Landsberg/Lech, 1999.

family are changed and a new phase of the **"family career"**[231] begins. Similarly to individuals, development tasks can be also defined for couples and families in terms of the normative expectations. Development tasks for couples with small children are following:

- adaptation of the couple system to the care of own children,
- distinguishing between parental role and role of the partner,
- exercising a parents' alliance that works.

The matter of this life period is to develop agreed careers, i.e. to negotiate roles in the family and the couple.

The partners can easily find what is important to change in their behaviour if they know which development tasks they have to cope with in a certain life period and what competences are required for that. However, according to Schneewind and Wunderer[232], we have to consider that in the research publications there is no unity on the questions how many development tasks should be and what events lead to new phases in the family cycle. To say strictly, neither family development theory nor even unified process theory is available. Facing increasing pluralization of lifestyles the idea of development tasks in terms of more or less universally valid normative expectations should be assessed critically, anyway.

However, there are different **process models of partnership development** important for coping strategies in the family in terms of co-evolution of partners. The first one is the **attachment theory** of Shaver.[233] The theory explains continuity of attachment patterns over all life, from attachment between a small child and his caregivers up to emotional attachment in love relationships of adults with reference to cognitive models that continue to exist all the time. So-called internal models are already developed in the very early childhood. They are the person's internal representations of himself and his social environment created due to concrete experiences with important close people. In the course of growth the working models of the child get firmer and become a part of his personality. The resulting representations are more generalized and abstract. Researches show that attachment experiences got in the childhood and behaviour patterns resulted from them influence and form later relations in adulthood. Children and adults have the same functions of attachment behaviour: looking for closeness, protest in case of separation, a secured basis and a safe harbour.[234] How does it influence the relationship between the parents and the child? In all probability, one who experienced responsive parents and a coherent and balanced attachment to them will offer his own children similar positive attachment experiences.

---

231 Aldons, J., Family careers, Rethinking the developmental perspective, Sage, Thousands Oaks, CA, 1996.
232 Schneewind, K. A., Wunderer, E., Prozessmodelle der Partnerschaftsentwicklung, in: Sozialpsychologie der Partnerschaft, Grau, J., Bierhoff H.-W. (Publisher), Springer Verlag, Berlin, 2003, pp. 226 f.
233 Shaver, P. R., Collins, N., Clark, C. L., Attachment styles and internal working models of self and relationship partners, in: Fletcher, G. J. O., Fitness, J. (Publisher), Knowledge Structures in Close Relationships, A Social Psychological Approach, Mahwah, NJ, 1996, pp. 25–61.
234 Feeney, J., Noller, P., Adult attachment, Sage, Thousand Oaks, CA, p. 90.

Internal representations also influence relations between partners. Hazan and Shaver[235] have classified different **attachment styles of adults** rooting in attachment styles in childhood:

- For adults with **secured** attachment style it is easy to be close to others; they can have trust in others and have no anxiety to be alone and not be accepted.
- People with **anxious** attachment style have difficulties to get involved on others and to have trust in them completely because of fear to be hurt.
- A person with **dismissive (avoidant)** attachment style says "I am comfortable without close emotional relationships" and desires a high level of independence.
- An adult with **possessive** attachment style does not like to live without close relationship. However, it seems to him that the partner does not want to come close to him. In such cases, the partner usually responds with **avoidant** attachment style to diminish psychical pressure exercised by the possessive person, purposely or unconsciously takes up a subordinate role to the possessive partner in a **dependent** style.

Since early 90s some theoretical and empirical dissertations on adults' attachments (Bartholomeus, 1990; Main, 1995; Shaver & Hazan, 1987) and attachments in partnerships (Grau, 1994; Kobak & Hazan, 1991; Levy & Davis, 1988; Lussier, Sabourin & Turgeon, 1997; Shaver & Brenman, 1992) are available. We cannot discuss all these dissertations in detail here. It is enough to conclude that results obtained from researches up to now point out that a secure attachment goes along with a good and satisfactory partnership. There are more self-openness, mutual trust, positive emotions and tenderness in relationships of **partners with secure attachment**; they have also a higher capacity to solve problems and conflicts. Moreover, partners with a secure attachment more often have a marital relationship (about 80 per cent of married couples show secure attachment style) and have a joint household. **Anxious-avoidant** and **anxious-ambivalent couples of unsecure attachment** seem to have no such sustainable partnership. They have not so much emotional self-openness. The relationship is not clearly defined, there is no strong mutual orientation at each other, and the stability of the relation is lower than of the ones with secure attachment. An interesting finding of these researches is that persons with secure attachment more often find a partner with the same style (the secure one), and anxious-avoidant persons more often choose partners with anxious or ambivalent attachment.

Researches on individual coping have confirmed that different attachment types cause different coping behaviour. Secure-attachment couples more often practice issue-related coping. Anxious-attachment ones tend to emotion-relat-

---

235 Hazan, C., Shaver, P., Romantic Love conceptualized as an attachment process, in: Journal of Personality and Social Psychology, 52, 1987, pp. 511–524.

ed coping and avoidant partners – to avoidant coping. Exact allocation is not always possible, but the tendencies can be recognized. At least, there is a moderator influence of individual coping between attachment style and partnership quality. Correlation between dyadic coping and attachment styles mentioned above is described in Cina's research[236]. Based on knowledge acquired up to now, we can draft hypotheses on correlations between different dyadic coping forms and attachment styles. It is expected that dyadic coping as important indicator of a functioning and satisfactory partnership positively correlates with the secure attachment style. On the other hand, the anxious attachment style of one partner points to avoidance of dyadic coping by another partner, while the woman's dependent attachment style predicts the dyadic coping of the man.

Women with possessive attachment style demonstrate the strongest correlations. They show consistently negative correlations with the positive dyadic coping and positive correlations with the own hostile and ambivalent coping, as well as avoidance of dyadic coping.[237] The more possessive a woman designates herself in Bartholomew's scale the less she communicates her stress to the partner and less she is involved in a joint dyadic coping. Anxious attachment style of men shows less stress communication and less dyadic coping, as well as a higher avoiding of dyadic coping by the woman. The woman's dismissive attachment style goes along with less stress communication, less joint dyadic coping and more avoiding of dyadic coping by the man.

Attachment styles are only one side of a coin in the further-development of couples. The other side is gender roles orientation. Only two sides together can provide a complete overview of relationship representations that we will explain in this book in more detail. Gender roles orientation usually means a pattern of behaviours, attitudes, feelings and attributes expected from the male or female gender.[238]

A number of international researches on gender role stereotypes show that the typical man is relatively consistently seen as active, dominant, independent, rational, logical, brave, aggressive, goal-oriented, self-confident and strong. A typical woman is seen as expressive, hearty, friendly, tactful, emotional, but also fragile, fearful etc. However, the researches show that differences due to biologic sex are less representative than differences due to gender roles orientation.

According to Bem's 2D-model[239], developed in the 70s, femininity and masculinity are considered as two independent dimensions. A person can have both masculine and feminine qualities at the same time. This 2D concept separates understanding of biologic sex and social gender. The latter term includes not only a pure sex type but also a mixture of feminine and masculine qualities.

---

236 Cina, A., Dyadisches Coping bei verschiedenen Bindungstypen, Unveröffentlichte Lizentiatsarbeit, Fribourg, Institut für Familienforschung und -beratung der Universität Fribourg, 1997.
237 Bartholomew, K., Avoidance of intimacy, An attachment perspective, in: Journal of Social and Personal Relationship, 7, 1990, pp. 147–178.
238 Eagly, A. H., Sex differences in social behavior, A social role interpretation, Hillsdale, NJ, 1987.
239 Bem, S. L., Sex-role adaptability, One consequence of psychological androgyny, in: Journal of Personal and Social Psychology, 31, 1975, pp. 634–643.

The gender roles orientation becomes more and more important for a partnership. Empirical researches on this subject show that the gender orientation (femininity vs. masculinity) causes more important differences in communication behaviour between the partners than biological sex. Both men and women with strong feminine qualities turned out to be considerably more negative in their communication than masculine or androgyne persons. Antill's[240] research also points out an important correlation between gender roles orientation and the partner's satisfaction. He concludes that there is a correlation between femininity or masculinity of the person and the partners' satisfaction with relationship. Both men and women said that a feminine partner is better for a relationship. Femininity of the woman is more important in the beginning of a relationship, but as soon children are born femininity of the man visibly gains importance. Data collected by Antill show that femininity in terms of gender roles orientation is the best predictor of a high degree of satisfaction with the partner. Androgyny shows no advantages for the majority of respondents. It seems to be good for the partners' satisfaction that their role orientations are similar.

We can analyse you, see through you and despise you. It brings us no benefit – we lose you, and also lose our femininity.

Eva-Maria Zurhorst

In connection with gender roles orientation and coping, Nezu & Nezu[241] have found out that partners with high masculinity tend to practice issue-related dyadic coping and persons with high femininity practice emotion-related dyadic coping.

Bem's Sex-Role Inventory dated 1974[242] revised by Schneider-Düker and Kohler in 1988 provides sophisticated results. According to them, only the feminine scale correlates with dyadic coping, not the masculine one. However, the supposed higher correlation between femininity and emotion-related dyadic coping is clearly proved only in men. Women's high femininity does not lead to a higher tendency to emotion-related stress communication. On the contrary, feminine men demonstrate the highest correlations to the emotion-related dyadic coping categories and emotion-related stress communication. It is to summarize that feminine persons (both men and women) tend to practice positive dyadic coping. The influence of gender role behaviour on coping has to be seen as relevant. In following chapters, suggestions to be made for therapeutic interventions for solution of conflicts between career and family **are provided not only for biologic sex but also for social gender**.

---

240 Antill, J. K., Sex role complementarity versus similarity in married couples, in: Journal of Personal and Social Psychology, 45, 1983, pp. 145–155.
241 Nezu, A. M., Nezu, C. M., Psychological distress, problem solving and coping reactions, Sex role differences, in: Sex roles, 16, 1987, pp. 205–214.
242 Schneider-Düker, M., Kohler, A., Die Erfassung von Geschlechtsrollen – Ergebnisse zur deutschen Neukonstruktion des Bem Sex-Role Inventory, in: Diagnostica, 34, 1988, pp. 256–270.

The partner's map: to know, to recognize, to understand

To investigate stress and coping of a couple we use self-reporting data (questionnaires, interviews, behaviour protocols shortly after event), behaviour monitoring (third-party assessment data) and physiologic measurements (objective body parameters). Since we do not develop any own empirical researches in the present book and are not going to send our target group to the family therapist we have chosen a pragmatic approach of self-help. Due to several hundreds of interviews that we conduct for filling executive positions every year we know that one or both partners of our target group do not really exactly know delights, preferences, antipathies, fears, or efforts of their partners. Couples possessing emotional intelligence are mostly very familiar with the world of the other. They often have a very detailed "partner's map"[243] containing all important information on the partner's life. Such couples have worked out a **cognitive space** for their partnership. They remember important events of the other's past and renew this information over and over again. Facts and feelings of their partnership change in the same way. Couples possessing exact maps of the partner's world are better prepared for coping with difficulties and conflicts. They have resources to diminish stresses and to develop dyadic coping strategies. Researches by Bodenmann and Cina[244] confirmed that the majority of couples see themselves highly stressed in their daily life and that stress at work, with children, financing and health are the most often areas of stress – regardless of the partnership quality. Differences between stabile-satisfied and stabile-unsatisfied couples only concerned such fields as **adversities in daily life** and **stress at leisure time**. Thence, it can be assumed that couples of the risk group have lack of competence to mitigate additional stress if they did not work out any cognitive space for understanding their partners. Couples which have partner maps in more detail protect their marriage during dramatic times of changes, especially when they get children. Radical changes do not get them off course since they were already used to be attentive and to unconsciously care what the partner feels and thinks. The higher the understanding and knowing each other between the partners the easier it is for them to maintain the contact to each other when they are faced with conflicts.

In terms of strengthening of generalized resistant resources defined by Antonovsky[245], the development of a partner's map is a further step to stress prevention and making the conflict between the partners comprehensible and manageable. The starting point is an analysis of the relationship focused on the partner's estimation and his understanding derived from it. For this purpose, Gottman and Silver[246] have developed a **questionnaire** which we give here.

---

243 Gottmann, J. M., Silver, N., Die 7 Geheimnisse der glücklichen Ehe, Marion von Schröder Verlag, Munich, 1999, p. 66.
244 Bodenmann, G., Cina, A., Stress und Coping als Prädiktoren für Scheidung, Eine prospektive Fünf-Jahres-Langzeitstudie, in: Zeitschrift für Familienforschung, 12, pp. 5–20.
245 Antonovsky, A., Salutogenese, p. 137.
246 Gottmann, J. M., Silver, N., Die 7 Geheimnisse der glücklichen Ehe, p. 69.

First, each partner has to answer following questions to himself:

1. I know the best friends of my partner.
2. I can say what problems my partner now faced with.
3. I know names of some people whom my partner had difficulties recently.
4. I know some lifelong dreams of my partners.
5. I am familiar with religious ideas and convictions of my partner.
6. I know basics of my partner's life philosophy.
7. I know which of his/her relatives my partner does not like so much.
8. I know my partner's favourite music.
9. I can name three of my partner's favourite movies.
10. My partner knows problems which I now faced with.
11. I know the most important life phases of my partner.
12. I know the most fatal event in my partner's childhood.
13. I know the most important hopes and wishes of my partner which he/she is desirous of.
14. I know the strongest anxieties which my partner is now haunted by.
15. My partner knows my friends.
16. I know what my partner would do if he/she suddenly won the lottery.
17. I can exactly describe my first impression of my partner.
18. I regularly ask my partner about his/her ideas and experiences.
19. I think my partner knows me well enough.
20. My partner is familiar with my wishes and hopes.

This list of questions is wilfully compiled "without any system": qualities and quantities, as well as relation to the ego and to the other are mixed in order to avoid possible derivation effects in answering. According to Gottman & Silver[247], one has a secure partnership if he answered more than 10 questions positively; he/she has a quite exact map of the partner's daily life, his/her anxieties, hopes and dreams. If positive answers are fewer than 10, the partners have to realize that they do not know each other well enough, or their map has got obsolete in the course of changes in their relationship. Such couples are in an acute need of action: they have to start communication in order to learn more about each other.

---

[247] Gottmann, J. M., Silver, N., p. 70.

Updating of Partner Maps

A mutual survey can be a first step in the direction of an up-to-date partner map. It is important that the partners listen to each other – that partners do not comment on what is said or even judge it and do not help each other in their answering of the questions.

In what follows, we outline two stages of the development of a partner map of Gottmann & Silver[248] which recognise securely-bound couples as natural and as comprehensible (readily), while non-securely-bound couples are expected to show a way to increase their level of emotional self-opening, to clarify the relationship definition within the partnership and to enhance mutual interrelatedness and with it the stability of the relationship.

Couples who engage in the coping process toward the development of a partner map and who pursue this process with self-discipline and mutual trust, will evolve in the direction of safe-bound couples; they can also gain a new gender role distribution for themselves through this. They pursue the route of increasing the sense of coherence of their partnership.

At the first stage, it is sufficient to provide a rough outline of the landscape of the partners. The following questions should be answered by the partners on a mutual basis:

- The most important people in the life of my partner
    - Friends
    - Possible friends
    - Opponents / rivals / adversaries
- Earlier major events in the life of my partner
    - Future events (What does my partner look forward to? What is he afraid of?)
    - What currently makes my partner stressed
    - What my partner is currently afraid of
    - What my partner hopes for and what he wants (for himself and for others)

Answering these questions on a mutual basis is a sensible way for providing a rough outline of the current life assessment. At the second stage, it's a matter of providing detailed versions of the partner maps. Gottman and Silver[249] formulate this second stage in the form of a series of partner exercises, as follows:

"The more you know about the inner world of your significant other, the more solid and fulfilling your partnership will be. This questionnaire will help you to get to know each other, and to share this knowledge about you with your partner. It's worth going through this exercise even if you and your partner feel that you can read each other like an open book. There is always more to learn about your significant other. Life changes us, and, for this reason, none of you will be the same person who made those marriage vows five / ten / fifty years ago.

---

248 Gottmann, J. M., Silver, N., pp. 74–80.
249 Gottmann, J. M., Silver, N., pp. 75–80.

Many of the questions in this exercise will be a challenge. Make sure that you have enough time and patience to do them justice. It's probably best that you leave this exercise up until a time in which you are doing nothing, are not expected to fulfill any appointments, are not expected to answer any phonecalls and do not need to care for any children (or others), and are undisturbed. However, you will probably not manage this exercise in a single meeting, and you should also not try this. Instead, divide it up, and work through everything together gradually.

Answer the questions in each exercise section as sincerely as possible. You don't need to answer every aspect of every single question – limit yourselves to the areas that are meaningful to your lives. Write your answers in your personal diary or exercise book. If writing things down is too much for you, then you can also simply record keywords; but the process of writing things down is very important to the success of the exercise. When you are finished, exchange your notebooks, and read together what you have written down. Discuss each others' entries, and what this additional knowledge means to your marriage and the deepening of your friendship.

My triumphs and my fights
What things in your life are you particularly proud of? Write about your personal triumphs; about times when everything went better than you dreamed; periods in which you successfully left all trials and difficulties behind you. These also include times of stress and hard times which you endured and overcame – small events which nevertheless may have been of major importance to you; events from childhood or your recent past; self-set challenges that you overcame; times in which you felt powerful; great moments and wins; wonderful friendships you gained; and so on.

How have these successes influenced your life? What influence have they had on your view of yourself and your abilities? How have you changed the goals and things to which you aspire?

What role does pride (i.e. being proud, being loved, praising others) play in your life? Did your parents show that they were proud of you when you were a child? And how did your parents show this? How have other people responded to your achievements?

Did your parents show you that they loved you? How? Was affection shown often and willingly in your family? If not, how has this influenced your marriage?

What role does pride play in your roles in your marriage? What role do your own aims play in your marriage? To what extent do you wish that your partner knows and understands these aspects about yourself, your past, your present and your plans for the future? To what extent do you show that you are proud of each other?

My injuries and heals
What difficult experiences or times have you lived through? Write about all serious personal difficulties and injuries that you have experienced; about your losses, disappointments, challenges and problems. You can include times of stress and hard times as well as periods of doubt, hopelessness and loneliness.

All deep-lying traumas which you have experienced as a child or as an adult, count here e.g. hurtful relationships, humiliating events, and even harassment, abuse and rape.

How did you survive these traumas? What lasting consequences have they had for you? How have you strengthened and healed yourself? How did you overcome your grief? How have you revived and restored yourself?

How have you protected yourself against such things happening again? How do you distance yourself?

To what extent have these injuries, and the manner in which you have recovered from them and taken measures to prevent them from happening again, influenced your marriage in the present day? What should your partner know about these aspects of you, and how much of it should they understand?

My feelings
When you were a child, how were the following feelings expressed in your family?
- Rage
- Sadness
- Fear
- Affection
- Mutual interest

During your childhood, did your family have to cope with any particular emotional problems e.g. aggression between parents, a depressed parent or a parent whose feelings were hurt in any way? What consequences has this had on your marriage and your other closer relationships (friendships, relationships with your parents, siblings or children)?

How do you personally think that one should express their feelings, in particular: rage, fear, sadness, pride and love? Is it hard for you to express any of these feelings or to have your partner express them? What is the cause behind it?

What differences are there between you and your partner when it comes to expressing feelings? What is the cause of these differences? What consequences have these differences had for you?

My life philosophy and my legacy
Imagine that you are at a cemetery, looking at your own gravestone. Write the words which you would like to see written there. Begin with: "Here lies..."

Write your own obituary. (It does not need to be short.) What should people think of your life, and how should you be remembered?

You have now come far enough that you can outline your life philosophy. What is the goal of your life? The purpose of it? What would you like to achieve? What are the greater struggles that you would like to survive through?

What legacy would you like to leave behind after your death?

Which key goals do you still need to achieve? This can be something you would like to accomplish, or a particular experience that you would like to have. Examples of smaller goals: learning how to play the banjo, climbing a mountain etc.

Who I want to become
Take a moment to think about what you have already written. We are all busy trying to be the person we want to be. In this struggle, we have to face demons and overcome them.

Describe the person that you want to become.
What can you do to become this person?
Which struggles have you already overcome to become this person?
What would you like to change about yourself? Which ones still lie ahead?
What would you like to change about yourself?
Which dreams have you still not made happen for yourself / developed?
How do you expect your life to look like in five years?
What is the story of the person that you would like to become?

All these exercises and questions will help you to get a greater personal insight and a more detailed partner-map of the life and world of your significant other. Getting to know your partner better and sharing the inner side of you with your partner is an on-going process which lasts a lifetime. So consider returning to these pages from time to time to keep your knowledge of each other up to date.

However, partner-maps are just the first step. It is not the case that happily married couples simply know each other. You build on this knowledge and expand it in a decisive way. And you don't just use your partner-maps to express your understanding of each other; it's also a time for showing your admiration and affection for each other."

Development of partner maps is the first dyadic coping process of stress reduction. It has three positive influences on partnership quality and stability:

- partners spend more time together,
- better quality of dyadic communication and
- long-term reduction of risk of psychical complaints.

Dyadic Coping acts as a buffer to reduce stress and improves partnership quality. Such dyadic coping is a communication process in which each partner can contribute to development of his dyadic self on his own responsibility and thus to accomplish a step toward the common growth, i.e. co-evolution. Common growth means continuous wrestling, mutual challenge and balancing of mutual resistance. However, it does not mean at all that one should surrender for the other or to give up the partnership, to be melted with the other or to sacrifice oneself. Partner maps are not aimed at melting the partners together. The maps let the partners come into being in a new form for each other again and again.

Emotional Attachment, Feelings and Love

Emotions are mostly short processes with a clearly outlined reference to the object, or a situation. Thence, it is not useful to extensively apply psychological emotion theories to the phenomenon of love, unless when concentrating on the phase of the first amorous feeling. In a narrower sense, emotions are only partial processes of "love" as a superior construct. The term of "feeling" seems to be more suitable to describe complexity of love. Feelings can be a generic term of many processes decisively influencing the partners' life: moods, attitudes and emotions. Moods are considered as non-intentional processes having a surviving modulating function of behaviour and experience.[250]

That means that events are valuated as pleasant or unpleasant depending on the mood they happened in and convergence or avoidance tendencies can be derived from them. In a good mood we come closer to life situations easier, and in a bad mood we mostly react negatively. That applies to emotions, too. Positive emotions usually lead to the wish to come closer, and negative ones go along with defensive and avoidant behaviour.

Emotion is the most subjective element of human consciousness since only the person himself can know whether he feels love, shame, thankfulness, or happiness. **At the same time, it is also the most objective part of the spirit**, since the feeling experienced by a person being in love, ashamed, scared or happy is more realistic for him than everything what he observes in the environment or learns by logics. The person gets into a paradox position.[251] Looking at others (quasi as a behavioural psychologist) he dismisses what they say and believes only what they do. But when he looks at himself he acts as a phenomenologist and takes his own inner feelings as more serious than events in the environment or concrete actions.

Besides genetically pre-programmed emotions people developed a variety of fine and tender, as well as spoiled feelings. Unlike other living beings, the person is capable of self-reflection. His self-reflective consciousness enables him to imitate or even to manipulate feelings. Feelings originally were used as signals to decoding the outer world. But in our society they are often separated from the object in the reality, and the person abandons himself for the sake of them. Since both married partners have more or less good self-reflecting ability they will always analyse or "re-feel" their own and the partner's emotions. At least, in our target group it is rather improbable that the partner can fake his/her feelings so long that the other will not notice that. However, psychotherapists detect again and again that one partner often tries to manipulate the other with feelings – whether wilful or not.

In a partnership oriented at equal values the power of feelings of one partner is balanced by the one of the other, and positive tender feelings will strengthen the

---

250 Engelen, E.-M., Erkenntnis und Liebe, Zur fundierten Rolle des Gefühls bei den Leistungen der Vernunft, Vandenhoeck & Ruprecht, Göttingen, 2003, pp. 164–182.
251 Csikszentmihalyi, M., Lebe gut, Wie Sie das Beste aus Ihrem Leben machen, dtv, Munich, 2001, p. 30.

emotional attachment. In different phases of life people wilfully or unconsciously pursue various and also contradicting aims: love, partnership, career, profession, children, etc. How they combine ways and actions to achieve these aims and what priorities they have depends on the individual biography interpretation and with their current life objectives. The latter directly influence meaning of emotional attraction and love for an individual and how the bring it into being and in which relationship constellation they „practice their love".[252]

Love is a very important subject for evaluation of emotional attachments, but in the framework of this book we will only try to depict a few of its most important concepts and theorems.

Alexandra Freund and Andreas Keil[253] tried to extend **the biologic dimension of love** related to changes in hormones and brain by the aspect of psychological research of **attachment theory**. They hold an opinion that love should primarily create and maintain a binding attachment which a sexual attraction makes a large contribution to. Although love has its attachment influence not only in couples but also between other family members the authors pay particular attention to **"passionate" or "romantic" love** described as a condition of intensive longing for the other person. The romantic and passionate love is distinguished from other kinds of love that it not only consists of sense of liking and togetherness but also of sexual attraction and activities. Sexual activities, too, contribute to the feeling of security and, thereby, to emotional attachment. So in many cultures the trustful co-operation of both parents heightens the survival chances of the descendants in their first years of life. That suggest the conclusion that sexual attraction first strengthens the attachment between the partners and that is good for children since they grow in a larger safety. However, in many romantic partnerships the mutual sexual attraction and frequency of sexual activities reduces in the course of time; that can also weaken the attachment and the probability of separation will grow. The high divorce rate in Germany demonstrate that partnership originally oriented at being maintained all life go broken after several years. But the majority of people stays together and says that they are satisfied with their marriage even when getting older. The attachment is not only caused by frequent sex. Especially in long continuing, other factors are of primary importance. As Freund and Keil[254] stated, reduction of sexual attraction is compensated by *"emotional love"* going along with physical proximity and trustfulness. An affectionate, emotionally-close and trustful relationship intensifies the emotional attachment and can contribute to a deep and firm attachment when sexual activities are not so intensive as before. It is interesting that such kind of relationship tends to arise in cases of long-term physical proximity – just the factor contributing to reduction of sexual attraction.[255]

---

252 Röttger-Rössler, B., Engelen, E.-M. (Publisher), Tell me about love, Kultur und Natur der Liebe, mentis Verlag, Paderborn, 2006, pp. 17–18.
253 Freund, A., Keil, A., Ein Grund zu bleiben, Liebe aus psychologisch-funktionaler Sicht, in: Tell me about love, pp. 165–184.
254 Freund, A., Keil, A., p. 166.
255 Diamond, L. M., What does sexual orientation orient? A behavioral model distinguishing romantic love

Diamond[256] describes a model in which sexual desire and romantic love can appear independently, but they can influence each other. Desire is governed by „sexual mating system" whose primary goal is reproduction. Romantic love is governed by attachment system and is aimed at a long-term relationship between two people. We know from experience that there can be sexual desire and "mating" without attachment (affairs, two-timing). People can also vice versa feel romantic love without sexual attraction (long-time partnerships).

Influence of both systems can run in both directions. Sexual desire can lead to amorous feeling, love and attachment. That is relatively undisputed and seems to be highly functional to ensure an optimal atmosphere in the family and enough resources especially for good growing of children. The opposite direction (from asexual love to sexual desire) seems to be unthinkable. However, it is obviously possible that friendship can turn into a relationship with sexual connotation. New researches on oxytocin as neurotransmitter seem to confirm this thesis. Oxytocin can be released in situations characterized by romantic love and lead to a high sexual arousal.

The focal function of positive feelings is that they extend the thinking & acting repertoire of partners and thus build long-term personal (psychical, intellectual and social) resources up. It is empirically proven that positive feelings go along with broad, flexible and integrative information processing and pleasant feelings (joy, satisfaction) lead to a larger action repertoire than negative ones, e.g. anxiety and fear. This is followed by the concept of a surviving positive mood toward the loved person. Therefore, love is a surviving disposition and a complex behavioural tendency to the loved person. This is a conception coming closer to our daily understanding of love.

In an evolution-psychological view, it is however reasonable to see love as feeling. Love feeling helps people enter long-term relations characterized by mutual trust and good-will and thus play an important role in living together. Empirical proofs that love and commitment are tightly linked to each other, originate inter alia from Gonzaga et al[257]. They have found out in young couples **that love subjectively heightens the feeling of being trusted and goes along with constructive solution of conflict at the behavioural level**. We have already identified constructive solution of conflict as an important predictor of satisfaction with the partnership and its longevity in all adult's. Love appears to be not only important commitment mechanism for long-term relationship but also an important (or perhaps the most important) Generalized Resistance Resource (GRR) in terms of Antonovsky's model. Partner loving each other see conflicts as comprehensive, manageable and meaningful.

Since the target group of this book is young managers with children in the nursery and primary school age, it is reasonable to point out one more correlation between

---

and sexual desire, in: Psychological Review, 110, pp. 173–192.
256 Diamond, L. M., p. 176.
257 Gonzaga, G. C. et al., Love and the commitment problem in romantic relations and friendships, in: Journal of Personality and Social Psychology, 81, 2001, pp. 493–503.

evolution-psychological and attachment theory approaches concerning love. New attachment theory researches assume that love relationships are strongly influenced by the patterns of the relation to a central caregiver in the early childhood. Such patterns become stable, cognitive representations or "internal working models". Hazan and Shaver[258] proved that the three attachment styles (secure, avoidant and anxious/ambivalent) prevailing in the childhood correspond with the styles of adults' romantic love. They assume that "internal working models" set in the early childhood are decisive for forming and experiencing of love when being adult and thus create relationship pattern stability. The child can successively explore the environment on his own only if he knows that the caregiver is close to him and security is provided. And only if the child is capable of independent interactions with his environment he gains an inner independence allowing him later a temporary separation from his caregiver.

Results of Shaver's and other's researches show that the form of emotional attachment of a small child to his caregiver is very important for love between adults and reproductive success. Love between parents ensures that the both are permanently available. The mechanism of emotional attachment between adults is a transfer[259] of an original highly active mechanism (attachment of the small child to his caregivers) served by other functions (attachment of parents to each other). Findings prove that mechanisms of the small child's attachment and of adults' romantic love are similar. Firstly, important cues contributing to a deep love relationship, e.g. closeness and mutual attention are also play their role in the attachment process of the small child to a caregiver. Such cues of a small child are feeling of being trusted and attention to the caregiver. **Secondly, oxytocin as a neurotransmitter is of primary importance both for a small child's attachment and for adults' romantic love.** Oxytocin is known as a hormone involved both in milk release during breastfeeding and in contractions during birth. Thereby it plays a central role in the attachment of the mother to the child. Oxytocin is a phylogenetic young hormone of the hypothalamus and closely connected to affective and learning processes. Oxytocin promotes development of emotional attachment, sexuality, pro-social activity and also learning. In situations of intimacy and sexuality an increasing release of oxytocin impedes stress and simplifies formation of new behavioural associations and memory contents. That can lead to an affectively positive coloration of memory contents associated with the partner. Thence these mechanisms can lead to keeping the caregiver or the partner in good memory. Due to repeating conditioning processes these factors go along with a positive evaluation of the partner's situation in the future course of relationship.[260]

It can be summarized that love is an attachment mechanism that allows in various ways to strengthen attachment between partners. Love goes along with positive emotions and moods. A person "exchanging" such positive feelings with a partner for a long time "learns" to be of a positive strengthening value himself. Love also

---

258 Hazan, C., Shaver, P. R., pp. 511–524.
259 Freund, A., Keil, A., p. 179.
260 Freund, A., Keil A., p. 180.

shields from alternative sexual partners especially in the first phase (infatuation). In the neuroendocrinological view, love is an appeal of attachment cue that can take effect on many levels. Such appeal is more than a mere emotional disposition. It includes complex biologic and psychical processes and behaviours. Therefore, neurobiological and evolution theory related investigation of this appeal system should include psychological aspects. **In terms of the salutogenic model, love is also a concept of mobilizing Resistant Resources that reduce stress and conflicts between the partners.** Love is an important force in the co-evolution of partners in the course of solving conflicts.

Love as a strengthening force has also to be seen as spiritual and philosophic issue. At the moment of orgasm the head is free of everything for some second, also free from any egoism. We break the limits of time and come into the timeless "Now" of blissful happiness.[261]

In tantric Buddhism, sexual unity is identical to the religious one. Such attitude is difficult for people grown in the Christian tradition. In the sexual surrender the person bodily and spiritually experiences how the limits of his ego go broken to allow for a unity with the other. In a sexual act, lovers can sometimes overcome their ego in ecstasies and become a part of a greater whole by giving up their will and mind self-control and getting united in a sensual orgy.[262] In this way, religion mystics describe experiences of a unity with God. However, Christian theologians do not see such merging with God as an important part of Christian religion. Despite all His closeness to a Christian, God always remains a concealed mystery of love.[263] Buber[264] criticizes the endeavour of such merging as escape from the world since the world constantly confronts the person with life torn asunder. In his opinion, such merging experiences in joy, ecstasies or a sexual act as a moment of blissful happiness where "I-You" knowledge goes down into the feeling of merging does not really exists in this world. According to Buber, this merging has nothing in common with real life. Instructions how to immerse in the true being do not lead to the practicable reality. **In the practicable reality there is no any unity ot being.**

However, Buber turns against the age spirit which speaks in favour of self-realization. "As I become I, I say Thou. All real living is meeting."[265]

According to Buber, a relationship starts from a category of human being and a soul model of the begot Thou. The self-awareness comes and disappears at the moment of meeting the loved partner. Buber always sees self-awareness only in the context of relationship, i.e. always related to Thou. Self-awareness needs Thou, but it is not Thou itself before it explodes the relationship. Then the "I" stands opposite to Thou. Henceforth the "I" can enter the relationship in its awareness. According

---

261 Anand, M., Tantra oder die Kunst der sexuellen Ekstase, Mosaik, Munich, 1995 (The Art of Sexual Ecstasy. The Path of Sacred Sexuality for Western Lovers, Tarcher, Los Angeles 1989).
262 Jellouschek, H., Wie Partnerschaft gelingt, Spielregeln der Liebe, Herder, Freiburg im Breisgau, 3rd edition 1999.
263 Kehl, M., Psychologie als religiöse Heilslehre, Selbstverwirklichung im New Age, in: Frielingsdorf, K., Kehl, M. (Publisher), Ganz und heil, Unterschiedliche Wege zur „Selbstverwirklichung", Echter, Würzburg, pp. 11–25.
264 Buber, M., Das dialogische Prinzip, Lambert Schneider, Heidelberg, 1973, 3. Auflage, pp. 85 f.
265 Buber, M., p. 15. u. p. 48.

to Buber, self-awareness does not make reality yet. All reality is a work in which I am involved but I cannot take it for my own. Self-liking is no reality. Involvement is no reality. The person in a relationship takes part in reality, i.e. in a being which does not consist in him only. He becomes aware of himself as one involved in the being (as co-being). So he wants a more and more absolute relationship, i.e. a complete involvement in the being. When contacted by Thou we are touched by our own life, too. **According to Buber, Thou which is not I of any both, maintains the marriage.** The loving person sees the other in their non-similarity, independence and self-being, however, they are here for me and I am here for them. Only that one who means the other oneself accepts the world in them and has a power to survive in this world.

Emotional Intelligence and Competence

Since the end of the 60s of the last century, psychologists have investigated the question how our mind detects and stores information using intelligence, but they ignored emotions. Today this cognitive model seems to be an obsolete and poor version of mind because it cannot explain the rush and force of feelings influencing the intellect. Only at the beginning of the new millennium psychologists began to pay attention to the fact that feeling is very important for thinking.[266] Gardner[267] concludes that an IQ test reflects only linguistic skills and mathematical abilities, so it can say how successful you can be at school or university, but it says almost nothing about other life phases which not relate to school education. Salovey enlarges the term of intelligence and tries to complete it by other things important for a successful life. So we realize that "personal" and "emotional" intelligence is decisive. Salovey gives a basic definition of emotional intelligence consisting of five fields:[268]

Those who are not able to recognise their own feelings, have surrendered to them. Knowing and understanding what others feel, and how to deal with it, is the basis of human understanding.

Peter Salovey
„Emotional Intelligence", p. 185

Knowing own emotions. Self-perception, i.e. recognition of a coming feeling is the basis of emotional intelligence. The ability to monitor your own feelings is decisive for psychological insight and understanding yourself. If you cannot recognize feelings you cannot control them. But if you are sure of your feelings you cope with life better and see more clearly what you really think of your own decisions, e.g. choosing a profession or a partner.

---

266 The Model of emotional intelligence was first introduced in Salovey, P. and Mayer, J. D., Emotional Intelligence, Imagination, Cognition and Personality, 9, USA, 1990, pp. 185 f.
267 Gardner, H., Multiple Intelligence, The Theory in Practice, New York, Basic Books, 1993.
268 Salovey, P., Mayer, J. D., p. 189.

Managing own emotions. To manage feelings and to make them adequate is a skill based on self-reflection. It is an ability to calm down and to ward off anxiety, melancholy and edginess. One who is not skilled in it struggles with his negative feelings all the time. A skilled one will recover from setbacks and conflicts of life much quicker.

Putting emotions into practice. To use emotions for your goals – or, as per Antonovsky, to see them meaningful – is important for our attention, self-motivation and skills, as well as for creativity. **Emotional self-control (to delay gratification and to suppress impulsivity) is a basis for every kind of success.**

Empathy. To know what others feel is another important ability for emotional self-reflection. This is the basis of knowledge of human nature. Empathy includes ability to distinguish between different emotions of other and of your own. An empathetic person recognizes concealed social signs of what the partner or a colleague needs or wishes. So he or she will be successful both as a spouse and as an executive.

Dealing with relationships. The art of relationship is also the art of dealing with the other's emotions. We call it **social competence**. This is the basis of being popular and of interpersonal effectiveness. If you master this skill you will be successful in everything what involves living and working together with others.

Some of these criteria of emotional intelligence formulated by Salovey, Mayer et al are already known from the salutogenic model of Antonovsky. We conjure up the main thesis of it: the sense of coherence (SOC) is a global orientation that expresses to what extent the person has a pervasive, enduring though dynamic feeling of confidence that:

- the stimuli deriving from one's internal and external environments in the course of living are structured, predictable and explicable;
- the resources are available to one to meet the demands posed by these stimuli;
- these demands are challenges which are worthy of efforts and commitment;
- the individual can solve emotional conflicts if they are comprehensible, manageable and meaningful.[269]

Antonovsky goes beyond self-set limitation to an individual and concludes that it is not possible to maintain a high SOC if one's own feelings and interpersonal relations are beyond the meaning boundary. However, he deals no longer with emotional interaction of people, but refers to future empirical researches. ***Insofar, researches on emotional intelligence, especially empathy and influence of relationships, are the first step towards forming a group sense of coherence.***

---

269 Antonovsky, A., Salutogenese, p. 36.

There is a logical difference between perception of own feelings and their active change, but one goes along with the other.

According to Mayer[270], there are characteristic styles of dealing with own emotions:

Careful.
> People of this type are aware of their own feelings and demonstrate a certain culture in dealing with their emotional life. Clearness of their emotions can support other personality attributes. They are autonomous, aware of their own limits, spiritually healthy and their attitude to life is usually positive. If they get into a bad mood they do not begin to brood and suffer and thus get out of such moods quicker. Their carefulness helps them in managing their emotions.

Overwhelmed.
> People of this type often feel flooded and overwhelmed by their emotions, helpless and unable to control their moods. They tend to rapid and violent changing moods and lose themselves in them instead of keeping a certain overview. They do not do anything to get out of a bad mood because they think they cannot influence their feelings

Suffering.
> People of this type mostly know their feelings, but they tend to simply accept their moods without trying to change them despite suffering from them. This is a typical pattern for depressive people who just resign and put up with their desperation.

Way of dealing with own emotions also depends of their intensity. Women feel positive and negative emotions stronger than men. Regardless of the gender, one who experiences his emotions more intensively has a richer emotion life. However, the key to emotional well-being is finally the ability to keep the burdening emotions at bay. That does not mean avoidance of negative emotions in order to be contented. The matter is to give negative feelings no chance to suppress all positive moods – the art to calm down. When normal bad moods (no morbid depressions) should be calmed down the person usually can only help himself alone. In this context, Aristotles's, advice to be only "adequately" angry is not a good one because what for one is adequate is not always adequate for the other; it can be everything from cold ignoring to rage explosion.

---

270 Mayer, J. D., Stevens, A., An emerging understanding of the reflective (Meta) Experience of Mood, unveröffentlicht, 1993, zitiert nach Goleman, D., Emotionale Intelligenz, Carl Hanser Verlag, Munich, Vienna, 1996, pp. 69–70.

Range and anger seem to be moods which are the most difficult to control. According to Zillmann[271], escalating rage is a sequence of provocations triggering a self-increasing reaction. **Each further rage triggering thought starts releasing of catecholamine driven by the brain amygdaloid nucleus. This strengthens hormonal force of previous release.** Before the first one subsides, the next one is already in coming, then the third one piles up and so on. Each wave eclipses the effect of the previous one so then the physiological irritation level of the body escalates. In this escalating process the thought coming later triggers a much stronger rage than the thought which was in the beginning of the escalation. At this point the people can no longer make it up and they cannot talk with each other. Their thoughts revolve around revenge in spite of consequences. According to Zillmann[272], such level of rage furthers an illusion of power and invulnerability, can provoke and ease aggression. A person in rage falls back upon primitive reactions because of lack of cognitive control.

How to intervene this process? At first, you can go into the rage triggering thought and put it into question. The earlier you intervene the rage cycle, the better the effect will be. You can even switch off the rage completely if calming information comes before the rage stimulus is followed. So you can tone the rage down by understanding. However, there is only a short opportunity for this de-escalation. It only works as long as the rage is not too strong. If rage is extreme, the person is no longer in the position to think clearly and dismisses all soothing. Another method to de-escalate the rage is to leave the partner for a while. During the calming down the person in rage can stop the drive of the escalating thought when seeking for diversion. But the calming-down does not help if the person keeps abandoning to the rage-triggering thought during this calming phase, since any of such thoughts is a small trigger of further cascades of rage. Diversion is only effective if it interrupts the rage-triggering thought.

The relaxing method alone is not sufficient. Whether the person is worried because of anxiety or falls in rage he has to fight the triggering thought by all means, otherwise he will get into an emotional escalation spiral again. Therefore, the next step is to critically deal with own suppositions. Are there any alternatives for my own behaviour? Which constructive step can I do now? Such combination of carefulness and healthy scepticism against one's own feelings seems to impede anxiety and anger.

The de-escalation process does not mean positive denying of negative thoughts. We do not mean the suppressing mechanism of people who obviously are so well-trained in shielding themselves against negative feelings that they do not ever notice negative things. Such people usually look quiet and calm, but in

---

271 Zillmann, D., Neutral Control of Angry Aggression, in: Wegener, D. M., Pennebaker, J. (Eds.), Handbook of Mental Control, New York, Guilford, 1993.
272 Zillmann, D., p. 235.

reality they are filled with physiological restlessness that they do not notice. This permanent pushing rage and anxiety to the back of the mind can be a strategy to survive in an unpleasant situation. The suppressors present themselves in a good light with an optimistic mood and deny being concerned by stress. As per Davidson[273], the increased physiologic irritation can be caused by lasting efforts to maintain positive feelings or to suppress or impede negative ones. He describes such "unshakability" as a kind of optimistic denying, i.e. a positive dissociation. Davidson says, if such suppression is not a posttraumatic stress coping but only equanimity "it seems to be a successful strategy of emotional self-regulation".

Emotional self-control, ability to delay gratification and to suppress impulsivity is a further ability of emotional intelligence.

An interesting research of Walter Mischel known as **Marshmallow Test**[274] shows how important is the skill of curbing emotions and delaying emotional stimuli. Four-year-old children were offered either to get a bonbon immediately or to get two bonbons after waiting a little. The brave kids got two marshmallows as a reward. Others who were more impulsive grabbed a bonbon in a second. The same children were examined again 12-14 years later. There were a significant emotional and social difference between the ones who grabbed the bonbon immediately and the ones who delayed the gratification. The ones who could resist the temptation already when they were four, showed a better social competence when they become adolescents. They were more assertive, self-confident and more in the position to cope with frustrations of life. When having stress they did not tend to collapse or to get nervous or distracted. They willingly took and respond challenges. In case of difficulties they did not gave up. They were self-assured, confident, trustworthy and reliable. One decade later they were still in the position to delay a gratification, to reach their goal. They developed a high sense of coherence.

What is a little visible in the early time develops later to a wide social and emotional competence. A variety of successful performance (keeping to diet or striving for a high position at job) is rooted in the ability to give a delay to a stimulus. This ability significantly contributes to intellectual performance without being depending on the IQ. In high probability, you can train your stimulus control and understanding of things required for social competence. Thus, emotional intelligence becomes a meta-skill. How good or bad you can use your other skills depends on this ability.[275]

Hope and optimism are very important for the degree of emotional intelligence learnable by a person in a partnership or at work. As per Snyder[276], hopeful people have similar abilities. They are able to motivate themselves and are convinced that

---

273 Davidson, R., in: Singer, J. L. (Publisher), Repression and Dissociation, University Press of Chicago, Chicago, 1990.
274 Shoda, Y., Mischel, W., Paeke, P. K., Predicting adolescent cognitive and self-regulatory competences from preschool delay of gratification, in: Development Psychology, 26, 6, 1990, pp. 978–986.
275 Goleman, D., p. 111.
276 Snyder, C. R. et al., The will and the ways, Development and validation of an individual-differences measure of hope, in: Journal of Personality and Social Psychology, 60, 4, 1991, p. 79.

they are imaginative enough to find ways of achieving aims or to change their aims if they become unachievable. They can also reasonably divide a large task in several smaller and easier ones.

Like hope, optimism means that you are sure that everything will take a turn to be better despite setbacks and disappointments. In the context of emotional intelligence, optimism is an attitude protecting people from falling in apathy, helplessness or depression in case of serious difficulties. Seligman[277] says, optimism is how you explain your successes and defeats. Optimists attribute a defeat to something what can be changed, so that next time they will be successful. Pessimists accept the blame for the defeat and ascribe it to a feature which they cannot change anything in. Such different explanations have a large influence on decision-making patterns. For instance, if an optimist loses his job he usually reacts pro-actively: he lays a plan out for a new job or asks a HR consultant for help and advice. He looks for new chances. A pessimist thinks that he cannot do anything against such a setback because he attributes it to his personal defect that he will lose out by again. For success, you need not only some talent, but also an ability to continue despite the defeat. What and how you think of yourself is very important for these abilities. Ability is not a rigid property. One's performance cannot be measured exactly since its scope is very wide. Self-confident people use professional and private conflict as opportunity to search for solutions and continue to do it despite risks.

Empathy is another important ability of emotional intelligence. Empathy is based on self-perception. The more clearly we deal with our own emotions the better we can explain feelings of others. The original psychical contact of any co-emotion is based on empathy (ability to adjust to others).

To detect feelings of others you have to know how to interpret nonverbal signals, i.e. how to "read" body language. Ability to read feelings on non-verbal clues is very useful. The advantages are obvious: one who is skilled in it is better adapted emotionally. He is more popular, extrovert and the others think he is sensitive. But if words what the person says do not correspond with his body language (posture, voice sound, gesticulation and other non-verbal signals) the emotional truth is not **what** he says but **how** he says that. Researchers of communication assume that an emotional message in European and Anglo-Saxon societies runs 90 per cent non-verbally. The other person perceives what the body language says, e.g. anxiety heard in the voice sound, annoyance signalized by gesture, etc. He does it almost always unconsciously without paying special attention to the message itself. He simply receives it and responds. Abilities allowing us to do it well are mostly learned unconsciously.[278]

Empathy is rooted in the early childhood. Development psychologists have found out that babies feel sympathy with others before they can perceive their independent existence. Few weeks after their birth, babies react on agitations of others so, as they would be concerned themselves, and cry when they see tears on anoth-

---

277 Seligman, M., Learned Optimism, Knopf, New York, 1991.
278 Goleman, D., p. 129.

er child. It is called **"motoric mimicry"**[279]. This early phase of empathy is a kind of physical imitation of the other's grief. Motoric mimicry disappears from the repertoire of small children when they become two and a half years old. In this age, they recognize that sorrows of the others are not the ones of their own. Thenceforth, the empathy of children is formed by their monitoring how adults react on sorrows of others. So they develop their own repertoire of empathic reactions. That runs in a continuous tacit emotional co-ordination, especially between the mother and the child. Daniel Stern[280] assumes that these innumerable co-ordinations sent by mothers every minute when they interact with their children are decisive for emotional expectations of adults to their relationships. He concludes that these emotional co-ordinations influence the child's emotional constitution even stronger than other more dramatic events in childhood. As per Stern, love relationship of an adult has something in common with inner co-ordination between mother and child – to feel the subjective condition of the other and his common desire communicated by non-verbal feeling of a deep emotional agreement. **In agreeing of careers (the focal approach of our issue) this important emotional imprint by the woman and mother of the child should be particularly taken into consideration.** As far as possible there should be enough time daily for an emotional conditioning of a child by his mother (and his father), and in this period of time should be no conflicts. If the emotional brain triggers a strong reaction (e.g. rage) in the body, neither empathy nor transfer of empathy is possible. Empathy needs a certain calmness and receptiveness in order to let the emotional brain accept subtle signals of another person and to imitate them.

When speaking of interaction between adults we do not mean co-ordination of moods. We mean **synchronisation of them**. The mood is usually transferred from the one who expresses his feelings stronger to the more passive one. Some people are very vulnerable for emotional infection. They are easier to appeal due to their sensitivity. Since they are easier moved by others' feelings they are more empathetic, however, exposed to emotional manipulation. To call the shots in emotional interaction is a certain sign of dominance. But on a deep and very personal level it means controlling emotional condition of the other. In personal encounters it is very usual that the one with a stronger expressivity (or power) involves the other in his emotions and takes him with. Such influence is based on carrying away the other's emotions.

On the other hand, the most intellectually gifted people can fail in relationships, partnership and job career because of lack of emotional and social competence. Others see them as arrogant and callous. One who possesses the **social skill to positively deal with relationships of others** can create and form them, mobilize and inspire others, can convince and influence them without manipulation and create a relaxed atmosphere in their environment. That also applies to situations when he does not obey "modelling rules" of his social environment: he is true to himself

---

279 Goleman, D., Empathie, Anfänge in der individuellen Entwicklung und ihre Neurologie, article in the New York Times, 28 March 1989.
280 Stern, D., The Interpersonal World of the Infant, Basic Books, New York, 1987, p. 30.

and acts in accordance with this convictions and values with no consideration of societal consequences. That means he has **emotional integrity**.

Family as a School of Feelings

Family life is the first school of emotional learning. In daily life with their parents, children learn what they ought to feel and how others react of their feelings. This school of feelings is not only what parents directly say or do with children, but also examples given by them in dealing with their own feelings that they exchange as man and woman. Children learn from their parents that in order to be happy you need the ability to take subordinate roles, to do without something in favour of the other and to find a way to self-discipline step by step. They learn that the happiness which follows a creative effort is more sustainable than the happiness which simply falls in one's lap – since the happiness of the effort is higher recognized by the parents and encourages others rather to imitation than to envy.

Bernhard Bueb[281] concludes: "**Happiness of an effort** is not the thing what today's young people think about when you talk about happiness. They often only know **happiness by animation** coming from outside. TV, Internet and PC are sources of happiness. Other sources are drugs, alcohol and cigarettes. Wealth ensures happiness, attractive and sexy bodies lead to erotic and sexual happiness. Compared with such kind of happiness the happiness of efforts seems to have no chance". Examples given by parents are very important for development of emotional intelligence of children. The way how the parents treat their children (whether with discipline or empathic understanding, or comfortable pre-tolerance or even indifference) has a decisive influence for the future emotional life of the child with deep and remaining imprints. That means that emotional intelligence of the parents alone is an enormous advantage for a child. Impressive lessons are given by parents when they show how they deal with feelings to each other. The child is in the position to recognize subtle emotional processes between the parents, too. **Children of emotionally intelligent parents show high affection to them and have less tension with them.** Moreover, they can better deal with their own feelings. They are not so often flustered and when they are sometimes excited they can quicker calm down. So they contribute themselves to a conflict-free family life. They are more popular among their classmates. Their teachers estimate them as socially skilled and less aggressive. Moreover, they are more attentive and learn better. At the same IQ lev-

Order is the foundation of human life and, therefore, all prospering growing as well: the order of familial togetherness; the rituals and the dependable daily routines; the protective shelter of the house; the regulating authority of parents; the order of values, virtues and manners.

The internal appropriation of these "orders" is what creates the morality of a person; it forms the guiding principle of their actions and provides stability in their life.

Bernhard Bueb
„Praise to Discipline", p. 93

---

281 Bueb, B., Lob der Disziplin, List Verlag, Berlin, 2006, pp. 42–43.

el, children who learned better social skills at home have better marks in reading and maths. As per Brazelton[282], "parents" "have to understand how their actions can contribute to create self-trust, curiosity and making learning enjoyable and understanding own limits". All of that make children more successful in their lives. The child should be self-confident and quick-witted. He should know what behaviour is expected from him and restrain stimuli to bad behaviour. He should be able to follow instructions and also to express his wishes and needs in order to have good relation with parents, brothers and other children.

An attitude toward the world in which conflicts are viewed as meaningful, understandable and manageable, provides the motivational and cognitive basis for behaviour with which problems caused by stressors are more likely to be resolved, compared to an attitude in which the world is viewed as cumbersome, chaotic and overwhelming.

Aaron Antonovsky
"Salutogenese", p. 137

Goleman[283] lists elementary skills which emotionally intelligent and competent parents can impart their children:

„1. **Self-confidence** is a feeling to control and to manage own body, behaviour and world; the child has a feeling that all what he does will be usually done successfully and adults will help him.

2. **Curiosity** is a belief that it is positive and enjoyable to discover something.

3. **Intentionality** is a desire and ability to achieve an effect and to be assertive in working on it. This is absolutely connected with a feeling of competence, i.e. a belief that you can something.

4. **Self-control** is the ability to control and to regulate own actions adequately to one's age (a feeling of inner control).

5. **Closeness** is the ability to involve yourself in others based on your feeling of understanding others and being understood by them.

6. **Communication ability** is a desire and ability to verbally exchange your ideas and feelings with others. This is connected with a feeling of trust in others and joy of being involved in them incl. adults.

7. **Readiness to co-operate** is the ability to co-ordinate own needs with the others' ones by joint acting."

The child's success in learning these skills and in using and deepening them in the course of his education depends mostly on the ability of parents to give the right **emotional example** and to actively transfer their emotional competence to their children, too.

---

282 Brazelton, T. B., Preface to: Heart Start, The Emotional Foundations of School Readiness, Nation Center for Clinical Infant Programs, 1992.
283 Goleman, D., p. 245.

Creating of a Common World

Since the beginning of the occidental philosophy we have known two main approaches of fulfil human possibilities. The first is **vita activa** – expression of own life by actions in the public, i.e. you have to pay attention to what happens in your social environment, to make decisions, to champion your convictions and to take a stand on it, even if it may endanger your own well-being. On the contrary, **vita contemplativa** influenced by the Christian philosophy became more important than the best form of existence: to find the greatest fulfilment in life by cogitation, praying and conversation with God. These two lifestyles were seen as irreconcilable differences: you cannot be the thinking and the acting one at the same time. As per today's researches in psychology, each person tends to one of these two styles, but it is assumed that he can be extrovert and introvert at the same time. Today it is supposed to be normal to dispose on the whole spectrum of inner and outer control.[284] It is not normal to live all your life only as a gregarious or only as a lonely person. Temperament and socialization push the person in one or another direction. One takes to the conditioning power of his environment and enjoys either being together with others or being alone, but usually not both. However, that would limit the entire range of all our possible experiences and our chances to enjoy life.

The merit of Aaron Antonovsky is that his salutogenic model overcomes this dichotomy between thinking and acting. In his model, connection between understanding and managing strengthens the sense of coherence, increases the ability to deal with conflicts and possibilities to solve conflicts. It is a precondition for enjoying life.

The most important approach for a well-working parent's alliance and common evolution manifests itself in the above-mentioned understanding and managing. Co-evolution in its narrower sense, i.e. only of a couple and not the partners' area of occupation, is aimed at creating a common world with ensured peace. The manifest personality is a function of a common and mapped-out dyadic coping process where one's behaviour results from other one's behaviour and of the greater whole. The relationship is no longer an end in itself. Togetherness alone is no longer enough for the partners. They orient their relationship at a third thing, i.e. their common future goal. The matter is no longer to come to know the partner or to be known by him. Rather, the partners set their common goal and their unique historical process from "I-Thou" experience. The partner is a pre-condition of recognizing this common goal and creating a common world which they both as I and You go down in. However, not only behaviour but also feeling and experience and even dream experience is co-influenced by the relationship. The one co-influences feeling, thinking and experiencing of the other. Each of them still remains the centre of his own energy, consciousness, own working-out and responsibility, but not independent from the partner. **Shares of the Self involved in the system of the "couple" are re-organized by a greater whole of the couple process.** In a marriage it can be

---

284 Csikszentmihalyi, M., p. 128.

large shares of the Self of the man and woman but not their whole Self. A person is only a part of his own relationship system. If a couple wants to create a common world, both partners have to integrate, to estimate and correlate their relationship systems into each other, especially private and professional ones. That will be repeated in the subject of coping concepts at job once more. We have already described conflicts arising when the partners invest different shares of their Self into the dyadic whole.

Conflict potential can be partly reduced by "over-summation" as it is called in the system theory. The Whole is something more and other than merely its summarized parts. The same applies to the partnership. The partners organize themselves as parts of the dyadic whole. Not so as they would be on their own. Both people at least partly orient their life structure at the common process. Jürg Willi[285] calls this unity as **dyadic Self**, i.e. such shares of the partner's personal Self that are integrated into the dyadic process and united to an overspread Self which is other than the personal Self of the partners. Common growth is possible when the partners perceive important experiences not independently but unitedly. Even if a common growth process includes both partners each of them often feels lonely deep down inside. He feels that the other cannot understand him completely. His yearning to be fully understood at least by one person cannot be completely fulfilled. No claim to happiness can be derived from the dyadic Self. Marriage is a decision to create a common world and a desire to realize oneself in it. If the partnership is only an end in itself and serves only ideal satisfaction of each one's needs or complete understanding and accepting each other, it will sooner or later lead to frustration. **But if the goal is a common mapped-out process requiring common growth by mutual challenge and stimuli, a full equivalence of characters would be really dangerous.**[286]

Co-evolution develops not from a full equivalence of the partner's characters but from suspense of their not-full-similarity. Partners should suit to each other but not be fully equal. Some non-similarity stimulates the common development and provokes permanent discovering each other. In a dynamic and developing partnership, such suspense has also some protective function. It prevents the partners of being totally and exclusively wrapped up in their togetherness. **On the other hand, co-evolution means that each of the both defines himself and thus limits himself. To create a common world means to "discover oneself" at the bounds set by relationship systems which the partners belong to and by the partner sharing the common living.**

The sense of coherence (SOC) plays an important role in development of the common world. As per Antonovsky, besides the individual's own feelings, direct social relationships (partnership and family) are also central subjects especially important

---

285 Willi, J., Koevolution, Die Kunst des gemeinsamen Wachsens, Rowohlt Taschenbuch Verlag, Reinbek bei Hamburg, 1989, p. 128.
286 Willi, J., Koevolution, p. 131.

for the sense of coherence. Antonovsky and Sourani[287] have proven in their research that families with a strong SOC more easily adapt themselves to tensions and better re-organize themselves after crisis, i.e. their common world is more stable. Bender and Lösel[288] examined in a research on "Protective Factors of Marriage Stability" whether individual sense of coherence correlates with relationship quality. They have found out that **not only the sense of coherence influences living together but also relationship experiences can influence the sense of coherence**. The salutogenic model of Antonovsky expressively considers such feedbacks. According to this research, there is no significant difference between the genders in this matter: women are even a little more satisfied with the marriage as men. At the same time, the experienced partnership quality highly correlates between the partners. The relatively similar perception of partnership quality by both partners reflects a social realty of the partnership and not only a construct of personality-dependent attitudes. This is a further step toward development of a dyadic sense of coherence. In other words: experiencing a long-lasting satisfactory partnership contributes to perception of meaning, structure and coping resources contained in the SOC. Results of the research also support the hypothesis that wives with high SOC are more ready to satisfactory development of the relationship than men with the same SOC. Such interpretation is also supported by the result showing that the woman's SOC stronger correlated with the man's satisfaction than vice versa (the man's SOC with the woman's satisfaction). Both mechanisms show that the woman's SOC has more influence than SOC of the man who is usually still more busy with his job than with his family. That especially applies to long-term relationships in which the woman is often only busy with the family and upbringing children for a long period of her life. However, it can be also seen in younger couples that men become more family-oriented after they get children. **There are different ways to create a common world. But we see that personal resources (good sense of coherence, emotional stability and positive self-concept of own competence of the both partners) have a positive function.**

Marriage can also have a spiritual meaning: internalized common life, a partnership culture with many symbols and rituals. They should provide meaning to the roles and goals connecting the partner and help them to understand to be a part of the family. Basically, each family is a certain **microculture**[289] with its customs, rituals and myths (stories that the partners tell each other and that explain or, perhaps, transfigure their feelings about what is their relationship and what does it mean to be a part of a group). As per Gottman, culture does not mean that the couple practices its life philosophy with each aspect eyeball to eyeball. Usually it is a mixture. The partner finds a way to respect dreams of the other even if he/she does not share

---

287 Antonovsky, A., Sourani, T., Family sense of coherence and family adaptation, in: Journal of Marriage and the Family, USA, 50, pp. 79–92.
288 Bender, D., Lösel, F., Kohärenzsinn und andere Persönlichkeitsmerkmale als protektive Faktoren der Ehestabilität, zitiert nach: Grau, J., Bierhoff, H.-W. (Publisher), Sozialpsychologie der Partnerschaft, Springer Verlag, Berlin, Heidelberg, 2003, pp. 410–424.
289 Gottman, J. M., Silver, N., The Seven Principles for Making Marriage Work, Random House Inc., New York, 1999, p. 288.

them. The culture jointly created by them contains dreams of them both. This culture is enough flexible to be modified when they both want to develop themselves.

Conclusion: resistance resources can be enlarged

A possible approach to solve conflicts between family and career is to strengthen the generalized resistant resources by development of a relationship. There are two process models of partnership development for that: attachment theory that describes different attachment styles of adults and differences in coping behaviour of people of different attachment types. Attachment styles of partners are only one side of the coin. The other side is gender roles orientation. The result is that feminine persons (both men and women) practice dyadic coping more often, but women with high femininity are less skilled in emotion-related stress communication than feminine men!

Emotional ties, feelings and love are important parameters of couples' development. Love subjectively increases the feeling of trust and goes along with constructive solving of conflicts at the behavioural level. In the salutogenic view, love is an effecting concept of mobilizing resistance resources, reducing stress and mitigation of conflicts between partners. The strengthening power of love has to be seen as spiritual thing even if unity of being does not really exist in the practiced realty.

Emotional intelligence and competence belong to co-evolution of partners. They have to know their emotions, manage them and put them into practice, as well as to possess empathy and ability to deal with the other's emotions. Emotional self-control and the ability to delay gratification and to suppress impulsivity are other important parts of emotional intelligence. One who can synchronize moods appearing in adults' interactions will be successful in dealing with relationships of others. He has emotional integrity. Children have to learn to distinguish between the happiness of animation and the happiness of efforts. Emotional example of parents is not enough for that. The parents should be in the position to transfer their emotional competence to the child. The superior goal is to develop a common world with ensured stable peace in it.

Changing Behaviour in the Relationship; Resources Input

According to our model, family partnership consists of two personalities integrated into a relationship. Both persons bring not only their biographies and experiences into this partnership but also their outlasting properties, i.e. their personalities.[290] That is why creation, development, success or fail of partnerships do not only depend on what the partners do (how they treat each other in daily life), but also on what kind of personalities they are. If the partner is optimistic, positive thinking and reliable,

---

290 Personality is the totality of all psychological features which persons of a population are consistently and durably are distinguished in.

or is moody, frightened, reserved and negative thinking? Such personal features are relatively constant. They influence both the person himself and the relationship. In other words: the individual personality makes the partnership's dynamics and can also be influenced and modified by partnership at the same time. That can lead to changes in the partner's behaviour.

We already discussed such mutual influences between personality and partnership, however, only from the dyadic point of view and not from the individual one. **Matching of partner's personalities can manifest itself in correspondence or complementarity.** So it can become visible whether partners' personalities are similar or not and how it changes in the course of family life. The dyadic viewpoint considers the fact that both partners are independent personalities on one hand, but depend on each other in their relationship on the other hand. Similarity plays a more important role in choosing a partner than non-similarity. Lykken and Tellegen[291] examined this correlation and have found out that the **most important fields of similarity are values and attitudes**, followed by intelligence and physical appearance and features. **Personality features were not so important.** Usually partners are not so similar in their personalities. But if to look at the similarity which is perceived by the partners and not at the actual one, you will come to quite another conclusion. We tend to overestimate our similarity and to project our self-image onto the partner.[292] It is surprising that this tendency is so strong – usually we suppose that partner who live together ought to know each other well. Perhaps, such a projection is a kind of psychological buffer that contributes to the partnership stabilization and higher satisfaction. When you think that your partner is so as you are and feels in the same way as you do, you feel more satisfied.

According to the central thesis of couple partnership researches, persons feel stronger attracted to partners who are similar to them in physical, psychical and social aspects.[293] **We come to the conclusion that similarity of values and attitudes is more important than similarity of personalities.** On the contrary, approaches of behavioural theory and couple partnership theory are focused on communication and interaction between the partners. The central assumption of these models is that the relationship quality and stability mostly depends on the partners' daily dealing with each other, their behaviour in conflict and crisis situations. So the partnership has functional interaction communication patterns that are good for it, as well as dysfunctional patterns that are bad for it. Daily disturbances can occur if one partner does match the ideal imagined by the other partner in one or more aspects; the other begins to try to change him/her in the desired direction. For instance, a dysfunctional pattern can be aversive behaviour and making to change by moaning, criticizing, shouting, love withdrawal etc. If

---

291 Lykken, D. T., Tellegen, A., Is human mating adventitious or the result of a lawful choice? A twin study of mate selection, in: Journal of Personality and Social Psychology, USA, 1993, 6, p. 556–568.
292 Watson, D., Hubbard, B., Wiese, D., Self-other agreement in personality and affectivity, The role acquaintanceship, trait visibility and assumed similarity, in: Journal of Personality and Social Psychology, USA, 2000, 78, pp. 546–558.
293 Mikula, G., Stroebe, W., Theorien und Determinanten der zwischenmenschlichen Anziehung, in: Amelang, M., Ahrens, H. J., Bierhoff, H. W. (Eds.), Attraktion und Liebe, Hogrefe, Göttingen, pp. 61 f.

such strategy may be successful for a short time, it can happen that such negative behaviour will be also used in other problem situations in the future. Durable suppressing of undesirable behaviour can be only achieved by continuous and more intensive questioning. The relationship becomes worse and worse. Gottman[294] has identified communication patterns of couples that endanger relationship quality and its development. According to his **cascade model**, there are several steps in a worsening relationship. Partners show certain characteristic behavioural patterns on each of these steps ("**four apocalyptic riders**"):

- Criticizing (reproaches, accusation, constant moaning)
- Contempt and disparagement (offences, pejorative, cynical and sarcastic remarks)
- Defence and resistance (self-justification, counter-reproaches, blame rejection)
- Stone-walling and blocking (resisting the communication, not listening to, ignoring the other)

Establishing of negative communication patterns can be avoided if there are enough positive patterns stabilizing the relationship. **As per Gottman[295], in a stable and satisfactory relationship the proportion of positive and negative patterns should be 5:1 (so-called Gottman's constant).** This was a basis for partner therapies and training courses which demonstrate very positive effects.

As per Gottman[296], besides changes in behaviour, changes in perception and in physiological processes also take place. All three levels influence each other. At the physiological level, negative interactions are accompanied by irritation processes leading to high blood pressure, muscles strain, release of stress hormones (e.g. cortisol) and increased subjective irritation. The kind and intensity of these physiological processes seem not to depend on the sex or duration and negativity of conflict discussions. The man's cardiovascular system seems to react stronger as the woman's one. That is why men usually react with withdrawal when their subjective over-irritation leads to a quarrel.[297] Moreover, physiological irritation processes influence cognitive procession of information. This is important for couples since selective perception, attribution and interpretation take place during arguing and rational behaviour control is reduced. Negative communication intensifies perception of negative stimuli, and the partners begin to blame each other in wrong behaviour and problems in their relationship. Finally, they see the entire relation history in a quite other way. If no personal resources are available to present contacts as

---

[294] Gottman, J. M., What predicts divorce? The relationship between marital processes and marital outcomes, Laurence Erlbaum Associates, Hillsdale, NJ, 1994.
[295] Gottman, J. M., The roles of conflict engagements, escalation and avoidance in marital interaction, A longitudinal view of five types of couples, in: Journal of Consulting and Clinical Psychology, 61, USA, 1993, pp. 6–15.
[296] Gottman, J. M., A theory of marital dissolution and stability, in: Journal of Family Psychology, 7, USA, 1993, pp. 57–75.
[297] Turgeon, L., Julien, D., Dion, E., Temporal linkage between wifes' pursuit and husbands' withdrawal during marital conflicts, in: Family Process, 37, USA, 1998, pp. 323–334.

conflicts comprehensible, manageable and meaningful, the partners usually break up with each other. How it can be avoided?

Founding a Dyadic Construct System

Based on above-mentioned personal resources, partners are in the position to **get accustomed** in their inner world created by them. We see it as a mutual behaviour development process driven by mutual knowledge, recognizing and understanding and by emotional attachment and feeling, as well as by emotional competence. This process should lead to the partnership stabilization. The partners create a partnership construct system containing guidelines and agreements of their relationship. They agree important binding rules, divide tasks, privileges and functions concerning living together, upbringing children, sexuality and also financial resources. This **dyadic construct system**[298] gives a scope of binding duties – so that rules once agreed need not be negotiated again and again. It determines the range of freedom and personal development in the partnership. Nobody says that all of us must live all our lives in the same way. It is only important that the partners find out what would be the most successful in their case. Therefore, the rules should be neither totally rigid nor changeable at each partner's discretion.

When construing their own world the partner quasi translate societal trends and examples into the language of their reality. Such trends are communicated in media non-stop. **That leads to intentional change in behaviour only if the partners are not only blindly imitate examples, but also examine by experiments what is useful and realizable for them**. Contacts with friends play a central role in this adaption process, since relatives and chosen friends mostly have similar (or, at least, compatible) construct systems. Meeting and contacting friends is a good help in finding your way in a whole host of options of behaviour and partnerships accepted by the society. Basically, it concerns all kinds and forms of co-habitation, especially family, children upbringing and division of earning money and housework. Speaking about solutions of other authoritative and respected people, the partners make their own dyadic world to the best-thinkable and best-felt one. **The partners search for "benchmarks" in behaviour of others in order to form their relationship and agree their behaviour based on those benchmarks.**

If they uncritically accept behavioural rules of opinion makers in their circle of friends (and in media) influenced by spirit of the age, they become mere multipliers of running societal modification processes and will be very dependent in changing their behaviour – without self-determination.

If they examine from a critical distance whether approaches of their social environment correspond with their individual and dyadic canon, they will be in a position to design their dyadic construct in their own way. **They will be recognized by others as "authentic"**, since their behaviour corresponds with their accepted values. They will develop a relation-stabilizing behaviour characterized by open

---

298 Willi, J., Was hält Paare zusammen?, Der Prozess des Zusammenlebens in psycho-ökologischer Sicht, Rowohlt Taschenbuch Verlag, Hamburg, 9th edition, 2004, p. 67.

communication. They will be able to listen to each other, to perceive different behaviour of the other one, to allow, accept and tolerate mutual influences, to overcome deadlocks by this behaviour and to generate positive partnership experience in daily life. If the couple has all resources described in the last chapter and uses them, their common development will result in a dyadic construct characterized by positive feelings, mutual support, humour and positive attitude towards life.

Since the 80s American trend researchers have reported on an extremely dominating dyadic construct. Young couples with small children reduce their family life to their own inner world created by themselves and isolate themselves from the rest of the world, especially from friends, relatives and also from media (mostly TV). Such dyadic construct is called **"cocooning"**[299]. The couple with their children (mostly not in school age yet) does not communicate with their social environment. In most cases, the man is the only one who is connected to the outer world – at his workplace (and only there). Women's social contacts of the external world are limited to necessary taking care of the family. Shopping in anonymized supermarkets and other forms of self-servicing does not bring any social contacts. Supporters of this dyadic construct (also known as "**homing**" – not so radical as "cocooning") think that so they have less stress and more control of their lifestyle. Such couples want to have their world of work, their own relationship and other relationships outside the family, their health and their soul under control. Even if there is no absolute inviolability, the couple expects, at least, less risk and more safety from such a lifestyle in the today's world getting more and more unsafe. This tendency became more and more "mainstream" in the USA after the terror outrage on 9/11. People began to flee from large cities. On the contrary, in German speaking countries, young families (not only singles) still tend to move to large cities. The reason is perhaps because the German speaking region has not been so endangered by terrorism yet. **Safety supposedly provided by cocooning has its price for dyadic constructs aimed at particular security.** Social researchers point out increasing loneliness of couples – not only due to reduction of social contacts but also between the partners because their life is not enriched by ideas and attitudes from their social environment. There is also a higher intolerance against other lifestyles seen as a danger for own well-being and decreasing of social encouragement of the partners.

Developing of Convergence Controlled by Behaviour

There are many ways to a successful partnership. However, personal resources described in the last chapter play an important role in satisfactory partnership. The question is which personal and social resources can contribute to coping with demands and stresses in the family and stabilizing this satisfaction. **Bender and Lösel**[300] **proved by their representative research on 105 married people in**

---

[299] "Cocooning" literally means encapsulation in a cocoon. The term was first time used by American market researcher Faith Popcorn and meant withdrawal into privacy.
[300] Bender, D., Lösel, F., Kohärenzsinn und andere Persönlichkeitsmerkmale als protektive Faktoren der

1998 that the sense of coherence (SOC) defined by Antonovsky is a central resource superior to all other personal resources. It determines cognitive, emotional and motivational processes in partnerships. The above-mentioned three components of the SOC (comprehensibility, manageability and meaningfulness) unite cognitive, emotional and motivational aspects. The more the individual perceives this world as ordered or organisable the easier it is for him to clarify the problems caused by a stressor. Believing in availability of resources supports choosing right coping strategies. The feeling that life itself and, thus, the coping with the current problem have meaning gives motivation to face up to conflicts. The SOC strongly depends on the feeling of meaningfulness. **Therefore, the SOC is an ability of determination. It mediates between stress resources created by stressors and individual resistant sources.** Due to repeating experience in the partnership, the three components of the SOC are usually interlaced with each other. Besides the individual's attitudes toward life, social relationships are also of central meaning for the SOC, as per Antonovsky. He also connects the SOC with the dyadic construct and the family construct resulting from that. It becomes visible that **families with strong SOC appear to be more capable of adaptation to problems and re-organization in crisis times**.[301] The SOC acts as a catalyst in establishing of social resistance resources (trust, control, binding, etc.). In case of normative changes (e.g. when the couple gets the first child), a strong SOC contributes to coping at the level of partnership. The above-mentioned research proved that the partner's self-concept and the sense of coherence demonstrate a stronger correlation with long-term marriage quality than all other examined personality traits. Partners who showed better rates in these individual features relatively had a better relationship. Therefore, not only the SOC influences living together but also vice versa: experiences in the partnership can influence SOC. As we already described above, Antonovsky's salutogenic model explicitly underlines such feedbacks. On the contrary, if both partners lack personal resources it will not be good for their relationship. Also vice versa: low SOC, no clear self-concept and lack of emotional stability make it difficult to cope with familiar problems (diminish resources). Without sufficient dyadic coping, the partners become less and less satisfied with their family life and, moreover, they personal resources can decrease.

The above-mentioned research of Bender and Lösel[302] has displayed that partners' personal resources protect the partnership quality. However it also displayed that comparable characteristics of relationship quality are based on different matching

The intensity of life reaches its climax when both partners share a corresponding willingness to develop, and where both have put forward something which can only take hold with the help of interaction.

Jürg Willi
"What holds couples together", p. 235

Ehequalität (aus dem Projekt „Protektive Faktoren der Ehestabilität"), quoted in: Grau, I., Bierhoff, H. W., Sozialpsychologie in der Partnerschaft, Springer Verlag, Berlin, Heidelberg, 2003, pp. 408 f.
301 Antonovsky, A., Sourani, T., Family sense of coherence and family adaptation, pp. 79–82.
302 Bender, D., Lösel, F., p. 424.

of personality traits. This result also demonstrates limits of this research. The research is rather a status report or a snap-shot without sufficient consideration of power of sense of coherence. High sense of coherence is not only defined by how comprehensible and meaningful is the conflict for the partners, but also how manageable it is for them. That means, **a high sense of coherence pushes for changes, development and influence**. The sense of coherence of the people living in dyadic constructs is the "***driver***" of their development readiness.

The core of a dyadic construct system cannot be derived from statistic property combinations. It is derivable from the event, i.e. from a one-time and non-recurring meeting of two people in a certain situation, with their desire, longing and hope at that moment. Not already existing things spark love but the desire to create something new, caused by the relationship. **Love can release bound things and mobilize the partner's deepest and concealed potential.** In the terms of our model of personal development, partners can cross thresholds to new development in the co-evolution process by influencing and responding to each other. "Intensity of love reaches its culmination when both partners see themselves ready for a mutually matching development and when both of them made something available what can only take its form by interaction," says Jürg Willi[303]: "You can better stimulate things in others, which stimulate you, too. You will better effectuate such things in others, which are effective in you. You will most likely announce an important personality development step to another person if the issue of this step already lives in you yourself." Such development readiness is decisive for a long-term relationship, **to enter the process of behaviour-controlled convergence**, to develop your dyadic construct and, thus, dyadic sense of coherence.

Perceiving, accepting, influencing and differentiating the behaviour in partnerships

In following, we will describe how partners influence each other. As already mentioned in description of individual and dyadic construct systems, partners can understand each other and interact only if their construct systems are compatible and mutual development readiness initiates a co-evolution process. This is the condition mutual influence. The key to positive development of relationship's behaviour is not how you deal with conflict but how you behave against the other partner without quarrel. Most of family disputations have no result. One tries many years to change the mind of the other, but with no success because most of conflicts are rooted in basic disagreement in lifestyle, personality and values, e.g. individual construct systems are not compatible. Typical approaches of conflict management will not work here. One way to come out of this dilemma is to consciously perceive and to accept the incompatibility of your construct systems causing conflicts, i.e. to learn to respect and to tolerate their different opinions.

Partners' expectations are often extremely close to the realms of possibilities of

---

303 Willi, J., Was hält Paare zusammen?, p. 235.

their partnership. **Nobody supports his partner out of pure altruism. Everyone also considers his own interests and benefits.** Nobody accepts his partner simply so as he is. It is often difficult to separate self-interest and other's interest if you do not regularly and mutually reflect your expectation critically – since your own identity is derived from identification with the partner and family. However, we know from socio-psychological researches that with increasing duration and satisfaction of a partnership, „egoism" change to „altruism", and a worsening partnership tends to be more egoistic than altruistic.[304] In a harmonious partnership, satisfaction of your partner is as important for you as your own one because you are directly concerned by your partner's self-contentment. It could be a good task to give some hold and confirmation to a person who has to struggle with life more than you, even if he will get more from that than you from him. For many people, to make the partner happy is a kind of love. In this respect, there is no more giving and taking because giving can be a form of taking and vice versa. Satisfaction with the partnership also includes individual satisfaction. The more harmonious the relationship the more individual interests will back away and are superposed by interests arising from the partnership.

In a severe conflict, partners often promptly react in quite other way – especially the one who physically gave more feels bitterness about "one-way-road" of his giving and investment. You can only avoid this bitterness by conscious compensation of giving and taking over longer periods in terms of above-mentioned "agreed career" and not making your self-contentment dependent on the partnership satisfaction alone. **The aim can be easier achieved by joint life planning accompanied by a running dyadic coping process.** This thesis is confirmed by Bodenmann's researches[305]. The more stress is eliminated dyadically the higher the life quality is esimated by the partners. If one takes up much more relationship space in the stress coping at the other's expense and the other does not withstand and gives up, the relationship will entirely degenerate because one partner deals no longer with the other partner on a par. The attitude aimed at maximizing of own self-asserting will be destructive for the relationship. For selfish reasons, self-interest ought to also satisfy third party interests, the demands of the partner. **Fairness balance** and **equivalence balance** immanent to the relationship should be adhered to.[306]

The matter of the fairness balance is **ethical principles** immanent to all families. They are demands on fairness, justice, reliability, trustworthy, mutual availability and personal involvement. Non-adherence to these principles can make one or another partner feeling guilty – fateful, wilful or unconsciously. When a stay-at-home wife supports the career of her husband, the latter can feel guilty against his wife. Sometimes men even feel as victims of their wives and pushed into careers overstressing them. We also know cases when the woman feels guilty because the

---

304 Kirchler, E., Reiter, L., Interaktion und Beziehungsdyamik in der Familie, in: Familienbericht 1989 des Österreichischen Bundesministeriums für Umwelt, Jugend und Familie, pp. 109–129.
305 Bodenmann, G., Stress und Coping bei Paaren, Hogrefe Verlag, p. 216.
306 Willi, J., Ko-evolution – die Kunst des gemeinsamen Wachsens, pp. 143 f.

man reduces his occupational involvement in order to take care of the family and to allow his wife a full professional self-realization. The fairness balance will be badly spoiled if one partner tries to give blame to the other by his involvement and derives a gratitude obligation from that. For a subjective feeling of fairness in an imbalanced situation, it is more important to recognize and appreciate the partner's credits than to balance guilt and credits objectively. Not the degree of help and support given to the partner is decisive but adequate involvement in him.

The matter of equivalence balance is to balance the self-esteem of the partners in the course of their relationship over and over again.[307] When choosing a partner, people usually intuitively consider equivalence and ally with partners with approximately the same self-esteem. In the course of long-term relationship, the balance of self-esteem can be disturbed: one can gain more self-esteem than the other. So one partner can give emotional support to the other one and allow him a career giving him more self-affirmation. In families with children, one partner can develop a much closer relation to children than the other and gain a central role on the family providing self-affirmation to him, whereas the other partner feels excluded from this field. The success of a long-term partnership depends on the possibility to compensate the career-related self-esteem of the one partner by the family-oriented self-esteem of the other one. To achieve that, both partners should consider their self-esteem fed from different sources as equivalent; the one should feel participating on the source of the other and not feel excluded. Such behaviour can be designed as **"equivalent participation in the partnership"**.

There is a correlation between fairness balance and equivalence balance. Self-esteem is strengthened both by feeling fairly treated and by recognition of own credits by the other partner.

Today's relationships contain relationship experience of the whole life.

Happy couples are not more clever or, from a physiological point of view, more ingenious than the others.

But they develop a certain kind of drive in their daily lives. This drive prevents the negative thoughts and feelings from getting the upper hand over the positive ones.

Their marriage is managed by emotional intelligence.

John M. Gottman
"Seven Secrets for a happy Marriage", p. 289

The result of the partner's interaction is always the sum of their push-and-pull of their corresponding development readiness and intentions. Although the partners' intentionality is influenced by their individual constructs, it is transformed into a process of mutual influence. Its result is very complex and difficult to diagnose. As per Jürg Willi[308], there are three basic influence behaviours:

Support: This kind of influence on personal development of the partner is wide-

---

307 Boszormenyi-Nagy, J., Krasner, B. R., Between Give and Take, A Clinical Guide to Contextual Therapy, Brunner, Mazel, New York, 1986.
308 Willi, J., Was hält Paare zusammen?, pp. 245 f.

ly accepted in our society. The matter is to give the partner much autonomy and self-responsibility, as well as to support and to confirm him in his development. However, such supporting is not altruistic. The partner intuitively supports the other one in such fields of development which are compatible with his own development goals, which further them or, at least, do not impede. For instance, supporting the partner in his career results in a higher social and economic status, and the other can take advantage of it. However, in such situations, one can feel left behind. One who is supported may feel constrained and fixed to a certain development course. If you support the partner in upbringing children, he/she will be capable of fulfilling this task, however, feel also more obliged to this. "The co-evolution vector is always what optimally helps the both ones in realization their life chances."[309] The supporter may start to feel predominant, but this feeling will disappear if the supported partner becomes coequal to him. On the contrary, subtle supporting of pathologic development readiness can be destructive, especially by heightening of anxiety and insecurity, as well as supporting in social isolation (cocooning), e.g. by escalation of the partner's mistrust against his social environment. That is destructive for the partner's development and the relation.

Limiting: Mutual setting of limits is absolutely necessary for a successful co-evolution in terms of behaviour-controlled convergence. In successful relationships, partners are in a critical suspense against each other and form each other by resistance. Limiting is a sensitive process of balancing tolerance and self-regard. **In this aspect, tolerance means to perceive and to accept other attitudes, but not to take over them. The own self-regard limits the tolerance against others acting or thinking in another way.**

Sometimes partners tend to avoid the other partner's limits by self-pity, laying back in the arm of the other, or illness. They think that the partner will get into it. Many destructive lifestyles, such as alcoholism, hypochondriac behaviour, depressive moods and uncontrolled rage are tolerated by the other partner because he/she likes to be a helper of a weaker one and, moreover, he is afraid that the partner breaks down if not unconditionally supported. Lack of resistance can also come from feeling guilty because of particular merits got by the other's help; he thinks that he owes something and must not resist. Limitations are especially destructive when they are intended to impede the partner's development which one feels endangered by, e.g. all forms of anxiety of change or of losing control. For instance, we realize again and again that mobility of applicants is limited by their partners and their impeding behaviour.

Challenging: We already mentioned above that the person have much more development potential than he can realize in all his life. A large part of this potential can be unfolded by the challenges from the partner. In harmonious relationships, partners require some things from each other by encouragement, by motivational

---

309 Willi, J., Was hält Paare zusammen?, pp. 245 f.

agreement or by sensitive asking, e.g. to wear attractive clothes, to groom oneself or keep oneself in a good physical condition. Challenging can be friendly, and it can be also driven by quarrel, rivalry and jealousness. Mutual stimuli to self-development do not only result from loving empathy, acceptance or supporting, but also from battles whose goals are to assert and to ensure self-respect.

Supporting, limiting and challenging are active forms of influence on a partner. Sometimes they miss their aim of developing behaviour-controlled convergence in the relationship because the partners feel themselves "cornered", and this provokes resistance. This process can end in an escalating spiral of challenge and resistance, if both partners have not developed mechanisms of "breaking away" in order to get out of it. We will mention it once more when discussing possible control mechanisms.

If in aspiring to develop a behaviour-controlled convergence, the partner has learnt to perceive, to accept and to influence the behaviour of the other, he will hit an unexpected limit. Two partners have the same inner and outer dwelling jointly created by them. However, each one sees this dwelling in other way. The same child, the same apartment, the same car, etc. are differently perceived and experienced by the wife and the husband. **The partners are often not aware of such differences in their perception and attaching importance to the things because they do not even consider the probability that someone can experience the same thing or event in quite other way as they do.** Usually they do not reflect and think that their personal point of view is the only one, right and true. Severe misunderstanding arises from this discrepancy in construing the own world. Jürg Willi dealt with this problem by family therapy. He developed a couples' therapy method called **"construct differentiation"**[310]. In therapy meetings, couples agree common portraying of facts and events experienced by them together. After that, they were asked on their beliefs effective for actions, as well as on guidelines and patterns behind them. In this way they learn how the other partner internally construed the event. The effect of this construct differentiation is that the partners better perceive themselves in their being different and learn to accept the paradox experience that such clear distinguishing internally brings them closer to each other. Partners learn that love does not mean to sacrifice your own construct system in favour of the partner but to try to understand the partner in his being different. „Non-similarity enriches your own construct system by the partner's views of life. Extending own possibilities to take part in other person's constructs, you expand the basis of your mutual understanding without giving up your own constructs."[311]

Differentiation of construct systems accompanied by a therapist is a promising method of better understanding and resulting actions between the partners.

When depicting personal resources for co-evolution we gave young couples of our target group the method of "partner maps" to improve their mutual understanding themselves.

---

310 Willi, J., Was hält Paare zusammen?, p. 331.
311 Willi, J., Was hält Paare zusammen?, p. 332.

Generation of Common Flow Experience

Individual construct systems and dyadic systems developed from them are called by us as **dwelling in which the partners construct their inner and outer world**. "I" and "We" arising from those construct systems includes all conditions, recognitions and experiences processed by the human consciousness. It contains all memories, actions and wishes, desires and pains. Information penetrates into our consciousness due to our habits, biologic and social directions or by our wilful paying **attention** to the things. Our attention chooses the most important information from all what is potentially available. You need attention in order to retrieve certain relations and links from your memory, to estimate events and then to make the right decision. A person capable of control his own consciousness is able to wilfully focus his attention on a certain task until it is fulfilled, without being distracted by other things. "Since our attention decides what happens or does not happen in our consciousness, and we need it to initiate other spiritual events (remember, think, feel and decide), it helps us in picturing us as a **psychical energy**."[312] The person's experience depends on how he uses his psychical energy, e.g. it depends on the structure and the kind of attention connected with his objectives and intentions. The total system of objectives containing the individual and dyadic construct is addressed when the person wants to change something. Psychical energy becomes cumbersome or even without any effect when **psychical disorder** troubles the consciousness and when information conflicting existing intentions blocks the person from following his intentions. Such disorder can be pain, fear, rage and jealousy. It coerces the person to direct his attention on undesirable objects. Depending on how important is the goal and how strongly it seems to be endangered, the person mobilizes his attention to switch off this danger. Always when some information disturbs the consciousness by endangering the goals, inner disorder or **psychical entropy** occurs, i.e. a disorganization of Self that diminish its effect. Long lasting phases of such entropy can weaken the person's self-esteem so that he is no longer in the position to control his attention and to follow his objectives.

Csikszentmihalyi[313] calls the opposite to psychical entropy as **optimal experience**. If information entering the consciousness corresponds with the person's objectives, the psychical energy will flow without spreading losses. There are situations in which we can freely steer our attention to achieve our personal goal. There is no disorder that has to be eliminated and no danger for the Self that has to be repelled. Csikszentmihalyi calls this short condition requiring high abilities and presenting high demands as **flow experience**[314] because the people interviewed by him felt themselves floating and carried by a wave – so they described this condition in its culmination. This status is the opposite of the psychical entropy and is called **psychical negentropy**. One who reaches this condition develops a strong and self-con-

---

312 Csikszentmihalyi, M., Flow – Das Geheimnis des Glücks, J. G. Cotta'sche Buchhandlung Nachfolger, Stuttgart, 1992, p. 53.
313 Csikszentmihalyi, M., Flow – das Geheimnis des Glücks, p. 61.
314 Csikszentmihalyi, M., Flow – das Geheimnis des Glücks, p. 62.

fident Self because he successfully invested more psychical energy into the objective which he had defined himself. Therefore, intentions, objectives and motivations are forms of appearance of psychic negentropy. They focus psychical energy, set priorities and bring consciousness in order. Intentions concentrate our psychical energy for a short time. Objectives are usually set for a long time. The highest extreme psychic entropy arises when action motive is based on the feeling that there is nothing to do else. Thence, both intrinsic motivation (want to do something) and also extrinsic motivation (have to do something) prefers a condition of acting "by chance" and without any goal to be concentrated on. To learn to deal with own objectives is an important step towards their achieving in daily life. You move between to opposites: extreme spontaneity and forcing control. The most successful will be that one who understands where his desires push him, sets his goals on all modesty and brings order in this consciousness without to causing much disorder in his social and material environment. Usually, the Flow begins when we fully employ our abilities to meet the challenge on the boundary of our possibilities. **Therefore, to get optimal experience, you need a good balance between your action ability and available possibilities to act.** If the high challenge fully corresponds with your high ability, you can be full taken up with activity. It will generate a feeling of hassle-free and untroublesome action. Sportsmen call it "to hit one's boundary", mystics call it ecstasy, and artists call it esthetical entrancement.

If you want personal control over the quality of your experiences, you have to learn how you can do it with pleasure, and do this day in, day out.

Mihaly Csikszentmihalyi
"Flow, the Mystery of Happiness", p. 40

That is primarily undivided and concentrated inner participation on flow experience that leads to an excellent life, and not so much the feeling of happiness. To feel happiness we need to focus on own inner condition and that would distract us from our current task. Only when the task is mastered, we feel thankfulness for an outstanding experience and are happy by hindsight. This happiness experienced by means of Flow is caused by us ourselves and not by somebody else. It increases complexity of consciousness and strengthens our growth.

How to generate flow experiences? You have to increase your demands on yourself. Exciting and control are very important for learning. Flow experiences actuate learning processes that allow for development of new requirements and skills at a higher level. According to Csikszentmihalyi[315], Flow can be generated by any kind of activity. If all relevant components are available, it will be possible **to improve the life quality by ensuring that clear objectives and abilities are in line with possibilities of action**. Using flow experiences you can personally control your experience quality. To learn it we first need to learn how to fill our daily experiences with **enjoyment**.

What is enjoyment? First of all, we should explain what does enjoyment really

---

315 Csikszentmihalyi, M., Lebe gut!, Klett-Cotta Deutscher Taschenbuch Verlag, Munich, 2001, p. 51.

mean. Csikszentmihalyi[316] was the first one who published the phenomenology of enjoyment. It was in 1990 – three years after Antonovsky[317] had published his salutogenic concept. **It was amazing how many parallels could be drawn from what one called "enjoyment" and what the other canned "sense of coherence"**. Csikszentmihalyi speaks about **eight components of enjoyment**. When people reflect on how it feels when their experience is most positive, they mention at least one, and often all following components. **Firstly**, enjoyment experience usually occurs when we are faced with a task we have a chance of completing. Antonovsky calls this component "manageability" and means that you have necessary resources to meet the challenge. **Secondly**, we must be able to concentrate on what we are doing. **Thirdly** and **fourthly**, such concentration is usually possible since the started task has clear goals and gives immediate feedback. Antonovsky calls this component "comprehensibility", i.e. the task is cognitively perceived as a meaningful one in form of ordered, consistent, structured and clear information which is also predictable (containing goals). **Fifthly**, one acts with a deep but effortless involvement that represses troubles and frustration of daily life from his awareness. This component can most likely be compared with Antonovsky's "meaningfulness": the task is seen as emotionally meaningful and as a positive challenge. **Sixthly**, enjoyable experiences allow you to exercise a sense of control over your action. The sixth component of Csikszentmihalyi can be compared with Antonovsky's manageability (available resources which can be controlled by the person himself or by other legitimated persons – his spouse, friends, colleagues, etc.). **Seventhly**, concern for the Self disappears, yet paradoxically the sense of Self emerges stronger after the **flow experience** is over. Antonovsky describes this process as "comprehensibility" making the stimuli predictable and arrangeable. This results in a sound ability to assess the reality. Such ability expresses the belief that „the things will be taken care of". This pervasive and enduring feeling of trust is called Sense Of Coherence by Antonovsky – as we described in Chapter 5. The sense of coherence gets stronger when all components ot **enjoyment** (as Csikszentmihalyi would say) are fulfilled. Moreover, there is one more component of enjoyment, the **eighth** one. Csikszentmihalyi determined that enjoyment alters the sense of duration of time. Hours pass by in minutes and minutes can stretch out to seem like hours. The combination of all these elements causes the sense of deep enjoyment that is so rewarding that you are ready to expend more energy in order simply to be able to feel it. Or, as formulated by Antonovsky, a strong sense of coherence makes demands to challenges which are worthwhile to expend more efforts and involvement.

But what does all of that mean for co-evolution of couples? How should they organize their resources to generate flow experience and to improve the sense of coherence? The first step toward improvement of life quality is **to organize daily activities so that they result in especially worthwhile experiences**. Regretfully,

---

316 Csikszentmihalyi, M., The Psychology of Optimal Experience, Harper, Row, New York, 1990.
317 Antonovsky, A., Unrevealing the Mystery of Health, How People manage Stress and stay well, Jossey-Bass Publishers, San Francisco, 1987.

we need to admit that due to peer-group pressure and power of habit many people cannot even distinguish which elements of their lives they really enjoy and which contribute to stress and depression. Writing a **diary** helps you to clarify different influences on your own and your partner's condition more systematically. As soon as it is clear which actions are highlights of the day, you can begin with experiments by increasing frequency of positive things and decreasing frequency of other ones.

Life quality improvement will be successful if we pay attention to what we do every day in interaction with others and recognize what feelings do the action, the place, the time and the partner cause in us. Creative people have a special ability to organize their lives so that everything what they do, where and with whom they do it enables them to achieve more. They find the right **diurnal rhythm** for them and their partners in with reasonable interchange of being alone and being together with the partner, children or other people. If we have to communicate with others during their being together, external demands structure our attention. Presence of others generates goals and gives feedback on all **interactions**. In intimate encounters of such kind, not only the level of demands but also the level of communication skills is sometimes very high. Insofar, such interactions have much in common with flow activities and require an orderly investment of psychical energy from us.

Our life quality significantly improves when we have people outside our families whom we can tell about our worries and who can support us emotionally. Emotional effect of **friendships** on the quality of our experience shows that to invest psychical energy into relationships with others is a good possibility of life improvement. However, for a real development, you need to find a person with fruitful attitude allowing animating talk. On the long run, it is more profitable (even though not so simple) to learn to be alone and even enjoy it, but not to devalue it with "being alone among others".

In a family, life quality strongly depends on enjoyment of interaction with relatives. However, people estimate their relatives very differently: they can be sincere and ready to help, challenging and demanding, or even endangering. They can make one happy or can be an unbearable burden. It significantly depends on how much psychic energy the family members invest into the mutual relationship, especially for other's goals.

Good co-evolution requires re-orienting of attention and re-positioning of goals. When two people begin a relationship they must accept certain constraints that each person alone did not have. Marriage means a radical and permanent **re-orientation of attentional habits**.[318] If one is unwilling to adjust personal goals when starting a relationship, then a lot of what subsequently happens in that relationship will produce disorder in the person's consciousness and lead to entropy because novel patterns of interaction will conflict with old patterns of expectation. When partners modify their personal goals they also modify their Self. Entering any relationship entails a **transformation of the self**.

---

318 Csikszentmihalyi, M., Flow – Das Geheimnis des Glücks, p. 233.

Until a few decades ago, families tended to stay together because parents and children were obliged to keep up the relationship for extrinsic reasons. Some of those reasons lost their bonding ability, as we mentioned above. The current "disintegration" of the family is the result of slow disappearance of external reasons for staying married. But **extrinsic reasons** are not the only ones why people live in families. It is often so that only family can provide good opportunities for enjoyment and inner growth. Such **intrinsic rewards** are no less important now than in the past; in fact, they are probably even more readily available today than before. The number of traditional families maintained for extrinsic reasons decreases; but there are more and more families maintained because partners find enjoyment in each other and develop a common sense of coherence. Of course, extrinsic reasons are still stronger than intrinsic ones (what may lead to a further fragmentation of family life). **But families that do persevere will be in a better position to help their members to develop an advanced Self than the families held together against their will are able to do.**

To provide "flow", a family has to have a goal for its existence. Extrinsic goals are not sufficient. Positive intrinsic goals are necessary to focus psychic energies of parents and children on common tasks. Usually, a family has very general and long-term goals: to build a house, to give children a good education or, perhaps, to implement religious way of living in secularized world. "For such goals to result in interactions that will help increase the complexity of its members, the family must be both ***differentiated*** and ***integrated***. Differentiation means that each person is encouraged to develop his or her unique traits, maximize personal skills and set individual goals. Integration, in contrast, guarantees that what happens to one person will affect all others."[319] **In an integrated family, each person's differentiated goals matter to all others.** In addition to long-term goals often called as "**setting**" of a family, there are also short-term ones that should ideally be ritualized. **Creation of common rituals** (having dinner together, family feasts, vacations and trips, common handcraft or sport activities or making music) **helps integrate differentiated individual goals as common objectives in the family**. Because each individual has goals that are to a certain extent divergent from those of all other members, the family needs permanent communication with agreed feedback rules. The most successful strategy keeping a family intact is to develop new activities in which challenges and abilities of all family members suit and complete each other. Also in children's upbringing, it is also necessary to improve the challenges and abilities. In the first years, most of parents enjoy development of their children's abilities rather spontaneously. Any ability of the child is an enjoyable challenge that the parents react on when extending the child's action opportunities. Parents adapt challenges and abilities between the child and the environment over and over again. If they can gradually extend freedom of action in an atmosphere of mutual trust, common flow experience will occur over and over again. In such a condition, all family members enjoy their belonging to a complex system that shapes individual con-

---

319 Csikszentmihalyi, M., Flow – Das Geheimnis des Glücks, p. 237.

sciousness of each one to a common goal. **However, unconditional acceptance of common goals is reasonable only if it is connected with stable attention.** Otherwise, all rituals will be only empty gestures and false-faced habits, i.e. almost pure desinterest.

Similar to Aaron Antonovsky, Richard Logan[320] made research on people who survive life-endangered situation. He has found out that they all deeply believed in their ability to manage their fates. They had no doubt that their own abilities would be enough to govern their fate. Such people are not centred on themselves. Their energy is not aimed at ruling their environment but at finding a way to harmoniously exist and function in it. Such attitude develops when a person does not feel himself being in opposite with his environment. He feels that he is a part of all what occurs and tries to do the best in the system where he has to operate. Strong but humble personalities are able to accept that their own goals are subordinate to a larger unity and that to be successful you have to play by other rules than you like. For sustainable flow experience, you have to be in the position to set goals, to deepen in your actions within the scope of existing action systems, to concentrate your attention on occurrences you want to manage and to learn to enjoy the gained experience. Order in the experience releases the energy driving your own development and evolution of the group (in our case, the family).

An attitude toward the world in which conflicts are viewed as meaningful, understandable and manageable, provides the motivational and cognitive basis for behaviour with which problems caused by stressors are more likely to be resolved, compared to an attitude in which the world is viewed as cumbersome, chaotic and overwhelming.

Aaron Antonovxky
Salutogenic Model, p. 137

Closeness and Distance

When we talk about partnership we assume that two persons have developed special dynamics, as well as a stable pattern in the course of time. Both partners bring their individual personalities, their time-outliving properties and their own life stories to the dyadic construct of partnership. As per Neyer[321] there is a partnership consisting of two personalities plus one relationship. He connects both viewpoints (individual and dyadic) in a dynamic and interactive attitude and assumes permanent reciprocity between the individual personalities of the partners and their common relationship.

This viewpoint allows portraying the conflict between emotional closeness and distance in a partnership. Reciprocity between the commitment style brought to the partnership and the current processes in the partnership has to be assumed, i.e. **that the attachment styles of partners can be influenced by their current**

---

320 Logan, R., The "flow experience" in solitary ordeals, in: Journal of Humanistic Psychology, 25 (4), USA, 1985, pp. 79–89.
321 Neyer, F. J., Persönlichkeit und Partnerschaft, zitiert aus: Grau, J., Bierhoff, H.-W. (Eds.), p. 167.

experience.[322] If we remember the attachment styles described in the penultimate chapter, we can conclude that the avoiding person tries to diminish emotional closeness in the partnership and to do not let it be at all. The anxious/ambivalent person tries to enlarge emotional closeness. However, it is important to distinguish between a secure and anxious/ambivalent partner. Acc. to Pistole[323], both of them seek closeness to their partner, but have different motives. While the secured one seeks closeness to create a good relationship, the anxious/ambivalent one tries to overcome his feeling of not being loved. Anxious persons suffer from lack of trust against the partner, whereas avoiding persons have not enough readiness to enter a long-term relationship (commitment).

To make it more understandable, we point out that partners of secured attachment style do not have many problems with conflicts. Both of them confidently deal with distance/ closeness conflict and maintain an adequate balance of closeness and distance. Avoidant and anxious partners behave quite in other way. Both of them are very contrast in their valuing of closeness and distance. The avoidant one tends to keep distance to his partner. The anxious one strives for strong closeness. The avoidant partner experiences just the engross he was afraid of and withdraws from his partner more and more. The anxious one thinks that his partner is loveless and rejecting. It is to expect that partners with unsecure attachment styles will increase their individual attachment style in their current partnership more and more and insist of their positions.

This relationship issue of closeness and autonomy seems to be more important for women than for men. Women express their need of closeness more often than men. Besides gender differences, empirical researches of Feeney[324] have confirmed that persons whose need of closeness is higher than the one of their partners are more anxious, and persons with lower need of closeness are more avoidant in their attachment.

How can the partners overcome feeling of lack of attention and trust, on one hand, and lack of self-disclosure and empathy, on the other hand? Therapists offer behaviour therapy measures. We think that many couples can find a solution for the closeness vs. distance conflict in a similar way as in coping with consequences of unconsciously running transaction processes, namely, by communicative learning to understand "closeness-vs.-distance" viewpoints of each other, to put oneself into feeling expectations of the other and to control and to order own expectations. **Sensitive dealing with the other's feelings without hurting him can offer a way of new modelling of the relationship from inside.**

---

322 Bowlby, J., Trennung, Fischer Verlag, Frankfurt am Main, 1976.
323 Pistole, C., Adult attachment styles, Some thoughts on closeness-distance struggles, in: Family Process, 33, USA, pp. 147–159.
324 Feeney, J. A., Issues of closeness and distance in dating relationships, Effects of sex and attachment style, Journal of Social and Personal Relationships, 16, USA, 1999, pp. 571–590.

Control of Commitment

Commitment in a partnership or family with children is the readiness of all members to make long-term plans of the relationship and enter binding agreements on it. One who enters a long-term relationship creates a common inner and outer world together with the partner. This world is however, limited to the corresponded development freedom of the both partners. It is limited to the area of mutual understanding and also limited by misunderstanding and wrong behaviour of the partners. One who once obligatorily committed himself to a partnership process cannot simply exit this process and go unscathed. Each partner will lose a little of his freedom of his own changing and modification. Each partner's potential is bound. It comes to a feeling of being caught, other-directed and influenced from outside – even if one had taken a large part in creation and shaping of this relationship. On the contrary, one who keeps oneself free and unbound does not create any obliging commitment in a partnership, and his self-realization remains without feedback – there is a lack of quality of a commonly created world. Jürg Willi[325] describes the dilemma of commitment and freedom as follows: "If you create a common sustainable and further-growing world together with your partner you will bind your potential within it, and if you keep yourself free and unbound you will create no common reality and commitment." It becomes visible in an orientation crisis, for example, when partners who decided to have a child long for freedom and new start, or partners who wilfully decided to be childless feel themselves as mere observers of life.

Schneider[326] offers a way out from this dilemma. He describes **basic requirements to be obligatorily regulated by the family partners**:

- Balanced proportion of autonomy and commitment between the partners or family members.
- Members' adequate dealing with congruency and incongruences in their existing self-perception and perception of others – dealing with the other and the ones who appear elsewise.
- Continuing confirmation of certain basic behavioural patterns of family members in result-oriented feedback conversations.
- Setting of limits of the family, primarily concerning individual or common contacts with environment at work and in leisure time.
- Task of a special definition of understanding relations between genders and roles, distribution of roles between spouses, as well as between parents and children and between occupational and family roles. In such distribution of roles, power and authority relations have to be clarified between the members – in the ideal case, not only for the current life period, but, as far as possible, for the future periods, as well.

Binding commitment of partners to their relationship gains a special quality since a relationship can be characterized as a social unity both highly conflict-endangered

---

325 Willi, J., Psychologie in der Liebe, Persönliche Entwicklung der Paarbeziehung, J. G. Cotta'sche Buchhandlung, Stuttgart, 2002, p. 54.
326 Schneider, W., Streitende Liebe, Zur Soziologie familialer Konflikte, Leske, Buderich, Opladen, 1994.

and conflict-resistant at the same time. Just because of inner unity of a marriage the tolerance can be high enough against inner contradictions also reflected in the commitments in order to avoid separation. On the other hand, just inner contradictions highly endanger a dyad based on inner unity. It can be summarized that commitments sustainably stabilize a couple only **if the made agreements are coherent**, i.e. **they shall be understood and perceived by the partners as an ordered, consistent, structured and clear communication process**. The agreements should be manageable for the partners. They should have enough resources available in order to contribute to fulfilment of commitments, e.g. concrete responsibilities of roles. Moreover, the partners have to be motivated to fulfil the commitments since they are meaningful for them and important for a satisfactory organization of the relationship. If these three criteria are fulfilled, the partners have a good chance to develop and to strengthen a dyadic sense of coherence using the commitments as tools.

The control mechanisms described above, the dilemma of closeness and distance, as well as commitments agreed by the couple to keep a harmonious balance of the relationship become an especially large challenge when the couple gets children. Upbringing a child brings the parents to more intensively deal with their life constructs, with their basic values and rules, and with their meaning and objective. They have to negotiate and to make an agreement on what would be the right solution, what psychic challenges are healthy for the child, what challenges he needs for his development and where they have to be limited. When searching for upbringing styles, partners construe their common world with more awareness than without child. Parents' self-discovery can be significantly stimulated by searching for a jointly construed world that the child demands from them. Babies and small children bring their parents to define themselves as man and woman. When going through puberty the child harshly criticizes the lifestyle and relationship of his parents, as well as veracity of their self-definition. This process has an important meaning both for the children and for their parents.

If a couple, before getting a child, has learned to develop its relationship in regular feedback and correction conversations, it can deal with conflicts flexibly and adequately and if it can understand and manage the running transactions then involving the child into the dyad will make a family relationship fulfilling all conditions of group sense of coherence. **If psychological processes in a couple are coherent, they can be also transferred from a dyad to a "triad", i.e. a family with a child.** That will be, at least, as long as the child is still in the primary school age, his adaption phase is not completed yet and he is still rather guided by feelings than by values. Intellectual adaption of adolescents and young adults to partnerships of their parents is an issue which does not belong to the present range of topics: our target group are families with children going to nursery or primary school.

Conclusion: A common inner world should be created

Matching of partner's personalities can be reflected in correspondence and complementarity. Similarity of values and attitudes is more important than similarity of personalities. Partners have to develop a dyadic construct system, i.e. adapt themselves as spouses and family with children in an inner world created by them. That leads to a wilful modification of behaviour in a relationship ensured by experiments and benchmarking processes and by experience that your own relationship is seen by others as an "authentic" one. The partners' sense of coherence is quasi a drive of their readiness to development. Love can mobilize the partners' inner and deepest potential. However, the partners never support each other from a pure altruism. They always consider their own interests and advantages. Satisfaction in the partnership is based on balance of giving and taking because satisfaction in the partnership also includes satisfaction of an individual. This objective can be achieved by working out a common life's plan. Doing that, the partners have to consider fairness and equivalence balance in their relationship since they want to participate in the relationship to equal parts. That can be achieved by supporting, limiting and challenging the partner. Partner's maps are a good method to improve mutual perception between partners. Moreover, development of couples can be done by common Flow Experience. Usually, flow is generated in situations when we completely utilize our skills to meet such a challenge (e.g. in sports) which closely hits our boundaries. Common flow experience of the couple is a particular highlight.

A good partnership begins from sustainable re-ordering of attention habits since entering a relationship means transformation of the Self. If it is accompanied by intrinsic rewards, the partners will find enjoyment in being together.

Recognizing and Monitoring of Control Mechanisms: Resilience, Transaction, Coherence

We described partnerships as interactive dyadic construct systems that can be controlled by using personal resources in coping processes. Antonovsky[327] pointed out that these processes are based on a complex pattern of modified relationships with their history and future. The actual action of coping with a stressor can raise new stressors since the coping requires modification of roles and mobilizing of potential resource not used before. Because stressors are omnipresent in the human world, Antonowsky concludes that we are permanently requested for coping. Partnerships evolution is a process of permanent **feedback and correction** – the most important control mechanisms in a partnership that are necessary for all development processes if one wants to keep the partnership stable. Further control mechanisms accrue from reciprocities between personality and partnership.

In adulthood, personal development is by no means finished and remains viv-

---

327 Antonovsky, A., Salutogenese – Zur Entmystifizierung der Gesundheit, p. 137.

id up to the middle adulthood. However, the personality is already so stable in the early adulthood that influences on partnership are strong enough. In the course of life, they will be stronger and stronger and even culminate. The personality becomes steadier with increasing stability of the environment. However, the older people are the less new experience they get.

Stabilization of personality and partnership are significantly furthered by **resilience**[328]. In individual personal development, **resilience means an ability to flexibly control your feelings adequately to the situation**. In a partnership, it means the ability of a couple to flexibly and adequately deal with stress and conflicts. So it is a further important control mechanism.

Matching between personality and partnership contributes to stabilizing of personalities of both partners and their relationship. It is the result of permanent reciprocities or **transactions** that act as long-lasting control mechanisms influencing the partnership by the partner's personality, namely in a double meaning: by possible positive and/or negative influence. Buss[329] distinguishes four basic kinds of transactions: **reactive**, **evocative**, **proactive** and **manipulative**. They also apply to transactions between personality and partnerships that are a special field of personal environment. Reactive transactions emerge when a partner interprets partnership experiences in keeping with his personality and self-concept. Evocative transactions appear when a partner causes other partner's reactions that fit with his personality. A proactive transaction is a result of actively searching for a partner who better fits with his personality. Manipulative transaction is when a partner tries to change and to manipulate the behaviour and the personality of the other. We illustrate it by following example of a negative influence:

In a quarrel, one person interprets the other's behaviour as dominant over and over again because such interpretation is compatible with his own role of victim (reactive transaction). Due to his personality disposition, he will behave as a victim in other quarrels, too, and thereby evoke dominant behaviour of the partner (evocative transaction). Perhaps, this person choose such a partner because he/she fits with this tendency (proactive transaction). Since they cause stress situations more or less wilfully and provokes the partner's outbursts of fury it will confirm his/her role of victim over and over again (manipulative transaction).

Such transactions can also have positive influence when they contribute to relationship quality. All transactions have in common that their influence is not short-term. They emerge from long see-saw between relative stabile personality features and attuned interaction patterns.

As we see at the example above, **transaction processes usually run unconsciously**. If both partners manage **to become aware of these processes**, to attentively understand them, to manage them together and to control, they will master the most important control mechanism of their relationship.

---

[328] Neyer, F. J., Persönlichkeit und Partnerschaft, zitiert aus: Grau, J., Bierhoff, H.-W. (Eds.), Sozialpsychologie in der Partnerschaft, Springer Verlag, Berlin, Heidelberg, 2003, p. 167.
[329] Buss, D. M., Selection, evocation and manipulation, in: Journal of Personality and Social Psychology, 53, USA, pp. 1214–1221.

Development of Culture of Constructive Controversy

In his shadow projection concept, C. G. Jung[330] says that reproaching each other is a projection of one's own shadow onto another person. By means of these projections, the person perceives what he demerges from his own consciousness. However, Jung makes a restriction that one can only project such aspects which really exist in the person receiving the projection. Vera Kast[331] criticized Jung's formulation in her book "Der Schatten in uns" ("The Shadow Within Us"). She called such formulation disastrous because it confirms the belief of the reproaching person that the other really has this shadow. In her opinion, it is not legitimate to ascribe another person his disturbing behaviour as his property. Ascribing a shadow is violating, and it would be felt by the partner as border violation because he did not ask the shadow-ascribing person to fathom shadows in him. Therefore, ascribing shadows is not constructive and objective critique. Ascribing shadows involves self-esteem of the criticized partner who is angry and offended.

> *Reproaching each other is a projection of one's own shadow onto another person. By means of these projections, the person perceives what he demerges from his own consciousness.*
>
> C. G. Jung
> "Return of the Soul"

Ascribing shadows is only possible if the partner has very resilient self-esteem and a strong Self that can cope with offending and charging him with a shadow. Acc. to Jürg Willi[332] reproaches that partners make to each other usually apply only in the light of counter-reproaches of the partner. It is decisive whether the partners use the counter-reproaches to devalue the reproaches directed on them or they show the ability to deal with reproaches seriously. It is a question of **culture of constructive controversy** whether one can deal with disturbing behaviour. There are many ways offered for avoiding escalation of mutual accusations.

The matter is to express constructive critique. You can rather listen to a reproach of a partner whose goodwill, respect and unselfishness you are trusted in. You have to feel that the criticizer does not want to accomplish his own disguised concern, and neither envy nor jealousy has caused his criticism. Critique has a constructive effect on a partner only if he is not criticized as an entire person, but only some of his attitudes or kinds of behaviour are criticized. It is not helpful to legitimate the reproach by pointing out similar critique from other related persons. A reproach should be only a note and not a threat. Love to a criticized person is visible in the freedom provided to him to decide himself what to do with the approach. So the criticized person will be in the position to deal with reproaches constructively; he will not feel devaluated with the critique or to be dominated and undervalued if he admits to this mistakes. So it will be easier for him to deal with reproaches without need of exculpating himself.

---

330 Jung, C. G., Die Wiederkehr der Seele, GW 16, Walter, Düsseldorf, 1971.
331 Kast, V., Der Schatten in uns, Die subversive Lebenskraft, Walter, Düsseldorf, 2003.
332 Willi, J., Psychologie der Liebe, p. 55.

According to Lewin[333], the partners' culture of constructive controversy becomes manifest at three levels:

(1) The **scope of needs of both partners** includes various and often contradictory needs to be satisfied in a partnership. The husband expects that his wife is a beloved, comrade, housewife, mother, co-upholder and representative of the family and in the society at the same time. The wife expects from her husband that he is beloved, comrade, upholder or co-upholder of the family and that he is a father and takes care of the house. Diverse tasks that the partner has to manage require distribution of roles. Such roles once agreed have to be re-adjusted or re-agreed for different periods of life over and over again, based on feedback conversations and positive culture of constructive controversy.

(2) **Space for free moving** is a condition for satisfaction of every family member. A family usually consists of few persons sharing the house, table and bed. That inevitably narrows possibilities of free moving for each individual. Any action of one family member inevitably interferes the space of another member to some extent. Allocation of spaces for free moving should be once clarified in the course of positive and constructive controversy and adapted to life conditions of the family again and again.

(3) **Membership of the partner in other groups** (family of origin, job environment, friends and acquaintances, religious communities, clubs and other societal unions). Family members shall decide on meaning their membership in the family compared to membership in other groups. The described field of conflicts between family and career is particularly prone to conflicts and needs a variety of interlaced agreements on actions and allocation of roles. It can be sustainably managed only by a positive culture of constructive controversy.

For all depicted levels of culture of constructive controversy in the family, it is necessary to define objectives and agree rules to achieve them:[334]

The important objective of the positive culture of constructive controversy is to work at (supposedly unsolvable) conflicts again and again. Couples who set certain demands on their partnership are usually more satisfied with it than the couples who scale down their expectations. Demands and wishes made by a partner on himself should also be discussed with the other partner. Such wishes can be dreams brought by the partner into the marriage. If such dreams are buried in the marriage, they will appear in another form again and lead to deadlock situations that you will need to overcome. To perceive and to respect the deepest personal hopes and dreams of the partner is a cornerstone in the positive culture of constructive controversy. To give space to your own wishes in a relationship it is reasonable to define minimum

---

333 Lewin, K., Die Lösung sozialer Konflikte, Christian, Bad Nauheim, 1953.
334 Gottman, J. M., Die 7 Geheimnisse der glücklichen Ehe, Econ Ullstein List Verlag, Munich, 2000, pp. 265 f.

requirements where one will not make compromises for the other. So you can find fields which can be managed so flexibly that an acceptable compromise can be found – even for a while. As we said above, marriage can have a spiritual dimension requiring inner common life, a family culture – full of symbols and rituals, roles and aims holding the partners together and giving their relationship a superior meaning. Basically, each couple and each family is a small micro-culture[335]. Like other cultures, a family has its **customs**, common habits and its **symbols** surrounding it to reflect the partners' values and believes, as well as its **rituals** celebrated in common feasting and expressing their commitment, as well as its **myths**, i.e. stories in which partners tell each other their feelings that they have as a part of a group. The microculture created in the family is the result of a positive culture of constructive controversy. This is a long, sometimes life-lasting process of joint treatment of these issues expressing convictions in the family. In the ideal case, a **"family style"** is generated. This style shows how the people express their admiration, recognition and emotional affection, how to deal with separation and meeting again and how to express thanks and, sometimes, humility. The family style can only be sustainable if it is organizationally embedded in daily, weekly and yearly rhythms, i.e. brings order into awareness and in behaviour of all participants – not be rigid unchangeable restrictions, but flexible and open for future changes.

---

335 Gottman, J. M., Die 7 Geheimnisse der glücklichen Ehe, p. 288.

Basics of Corporate Ethics

To clarify how to maintain a balance between family and career, we have to discuss the ethics of corporate behaviour. Human behaviour is influenced by the both ethical systems – family and work. Especially executive managers depend on the both ethical systems. Depending on which system they are more involved in (family or work), they are more family-oriented or business-oriented. However, there is still no balance between family and work.

What basics of corporate ethics can help us in localize executive managers in business ethics systems recognized by today's society? Is it possible to reliably connect these existing concepts with family ethics? To answer the first question, we refer to basics of Ulrich's economy serving the living and basics of Christian social studies. We know that there are many other concepts in the modern corporate ethics, also antagonistic ones. The second question (whether existing concepts of corporate ethics offer any approach of maintaining the balance between family and work) can be negated already now: we will discuss a new approach of a "Servant Leadership".

At first, we will describe basics of corporate ethics that already exist.

Today, in the beginning of the 21st century, socially recognized corporate ethics is a part of economy ethics that requires normative reference points of economy connected with human living. There are two different basic questions of life-serving economy: **the teleological one (question of meaning) and the deontological one (question of legitimacy)**.[336]

What kind of lifestyle our economic forms would be reasonable for? Today's society is a free society. An adequate answer shall be based on this freedom. However, freedom that can be really experienced needs a socio-economic foundation. In any lifestyle, elementary meaning of economy can be first found in securing of human basic needs: food, clothes, housing, health maintenance and education. They are general human needs. That is why modern industrial societies say that all people have the moral right for providing them all things necessary for living. Therefore, any work-sharing national economy is always a solidary association. Each national economy based on the division of labour should still be understood as a mutual alliance.[337] European national economies are now very advanced and high-developed. People's request for life's fulfilment is coming more and more to the fore. This life's fulfilment includes not only variety of goods, but also versatile and freely selectable cultural development opportunities of individuals and couples in career and family.[338] In social market economies, such striving for life's fulfilment often conflicts with market logics. As per Ulrich[339] in this competition of lifestyles, it is quite cer-

---

[336] Ulrich, P., Integrative Wirtschaftsethik, Grundlagen einer lebensdienlichen Ökonomie, Bern, Stuttgart, Vienna, 2001, pp. 203 f.
[337] Päpstlicher Rat für Gerechtigkeit und Frieden (Publisher), Kompendium der Soziallehre der Kirche, Freiburg im Breisgau, 2006, p. 250.
[338] Johannes Paul II., Enzyklika Centesimus annus Nr. 43.
[339] Ulrich, P., pp. 203f.

tain who will be the winner. The winner is a so-called "intra vitam" businessman, i.e. who invests all his energy into continuous improvement of his competitiveness and strengthening his position in the market. Both for an individual and a family, real freedom of practicing other styles of good living only consists in **"limitation of inherent necessity"**. This policy of limitation of inherent necessity is based on economic culture which is desired and accepted by the society.

The question of legitimacy is focused on economy-based rules of fair living together conflicting with the moral of the market and considers some conflicts. On the contrary, the work-sharing economy liberalism tunes those conflicts out. What can be a model for a legitimate economic system in a society of free people? What should be a framework for striving for commercial advancement? Such questions show economic ethics as a part of political philosophy and general ethics. The task of economic ethics is to point up the significant difference between civil liberties and market liberties and not to let the liberal order ideas be reduced to pure economic liberalism. Real freedom for everyone (independent of their buying power and their competitiveness in the market) is based not on a free market but on strong general civil rights.[340] As per Ulrich[341], facing growing orientation at competitiveness, we have to develop new **economic civil rights** that would improve the citizen's ability of self-reliant conduct of life and prevent them from being unable to secure their existence by their own efforts. Otherwise, the society would tend to disintegration, and it is not compatible with the basics of a „Decent Society"[342]. Such a society cannot be fair at all. Economic civil rights need **economic civil ethics** as a basis. According to this ethics, each individual would agree to only pursue such private goals which are compatible with legitimacy conditions of an orderly society of free citizen with equal rights. In this view, corporate ethics gains in importance. Today supranational companies can avoid constitutional bindings of some states. At the same time, there is no international framework order. In such a situation, it is necessary to demand on autonomous commitment of companies to the basics of business integrity in dealing with all stakeholders and of ethical responsibility for common welfare (corporate citizenship). **"Executive managers in large corporations have not only to care about yields of shareholders, but also about legitimate interests of their personnel and clients, as well as the entire society and environment."**[343] That can be achieved when each person as a dialog partner feels obliged to strive for the best argument consensus and to do everything in order to improve dialog circumstances of the real communication collective limited by inherent necessities.

All people strive for a good life. In a consuming society, economical success is essential for good life. Corporate ethics in terms of Christian values is aimed at successful

---

340 Zweites Vatikanisches Konzil, Pastorale Konstitution über die Kirche in der Welt von heute, Gaudium et spes.
341 Ulrich, P., p. 203f.
342 Margalit, A., Politik der Würde, Über Achtung und Verachtung, Berlin, 1997.
343 Marx, R., Das Kapital, Ein Plädoyer für den Menschen, Pattloch Verlag, Munich, 2008, p. 240.

development and fair limitation of human striving for self-interest. Christianity motivates people to strive for happiness based on virtuousness. In Aristotle's tradition, it would lead to a stable ethos moral which human acting is oriented at. However, we need first to create the right conditions for putting it into practice and to bring it in line with concrete societal conditions.

Corporate culture is strongly influenced by value systems and way of thinking of executive managers. Practical development of corporate culture needs certain ethical reflection, so that it would be possible to take responsibility of it. **"Corporate ethics can be defined as principle-oriented normative analysis, critics, and reasoning of corporate culture (values, way of thinking) that regulates strategic and operative acting in order to achieve corporate success in a morally responsible way."**[344]

Moral of the company is an object of corporate ethics. Corporate moral becomes apparent in the **corporate culture**. As per definition, corporate culture is a totality of moral concepts and way of thinking shaping the personnel's behaviour.[345] Ethical reflexion of moral concepts and ways of thinking in **an enterprise as a social system** needs to be understood and communicated. Such linguistic communicative consensus assumes understanding of meaning. Though the context of an **enterprise as an action system** is not solely created by making profits and the company's valorisation, it is formally and materially necessary to realize these operative and strategic business goals to communicate the meaning of this system. Companies can only make profits as long as they secure their viability. They can do it for a long time only if they create and communicate some meaning as efficient social systems.[346] We need corporate culture to communicate meaningful values that are systematically reflected and substantiated by corporate ethics and regulate and promote strategic and operative actions of the company.

A strong cultural work ethic translates into higher motivation, zeal and persistence – an emotional edge.

To the degree that our emotions interfere or enhance our ability to think and plan, to pursue training for a distant goal, to solve problems and the like, they define the limits of our capacity to use our innate mental abilities, and so determine how we do in life. And to the degree to which we are motivated by feelings of enthusiasm and pleasure in what we do – or even by an optimal degree of anxiety – they propel us to accomplishment.

It is in this sense that emotional intelligence is a master aptitude, a capacity that profoundly affects all other abilities, either facilitation or interfering with them..

Daniel Goleman
„Emotional Intelligence, p. 108

---

344 Rusche, T., Aspekte einer dialogbezogenen Unternehmensethik, in: Ethik und Wirtschaft im Dialog, EWD Band 4, Lit. Verlag, Münster, Hamburg, London, 2002, p. 242.
345 Pümpin, C., Kobi, J.-M., Wüthrich, H. A., Unternehmenskultur, in: Die Orientierung, Band 85, 1985, p. 8.
346 Johannes Paul II., Enzyklika Centesimus annus Nr. 32.

These meaningful values systems and ways of thinking shape Corporate Identity. The latter creates a „we"-feeling in employees. In the ideal case, this „we"-feeling would be transformed into a group's sense of coherence of the staff. However, the company's value system and ways of thinking should be recognizable and understandable for the employees, the company's goals should be manageable, i.e. achievable, and the staff should think that its own contribution to the social and action system of the company is meaningful. To make them think so, it is necessary not only to pay them fair salaries and to give them secured self-determination but also to let them experience the company's recognition of their efforts. The latter is very important since the social recognition in our modern working society is bound to one's workplace. There is no general recognition system that can be entered by everyone. The state seems to be no longer able to provide it to all its citizens.[347] That is why recognition by the company where one works becomes more and more important. When we discuss about social justice as a part of any recognition system, we always consider difficulties of participation or non-participation of the group members or the company personnel in recognition processes, i.e. inclusion or exclusion.[348] When citizen are excluded from social and business recognition system, fair salaries and transfer benefits from the state are not enough for securing a goof life. ***Social justice is not only social benefits from the government and the company but also considering of recognition dimensions by the company.***

These correlations of positive and negative corporate culture are shown in the table below: ***Recognition and Fairness in an Enterprise.***

Recognition processes	Examples of inclusion	Examples of exclusion
Culture	Cultural variety, diversity	Subcultures, ethnical conflicts
Communication	mutual esteem, integrity	Mobbing, discrimination, stigmatisation
Decision making	Involving in management processes	Instructions without substantiation
Success	Staking in company value growth, variable salaries	No staking in individual, team and company success
Chances	Personal development, career plans	No career opportunities at the company

Table 4: Recognition and Fairness in an Enterprise (own source)

---

347 Brink, A., Management und Anerkennung, in: Koslowski, P., Lütge, Ch. (Eds.), Wirtschaftsethik der Globalisierung, p. 141.
348 Brink, A., p. 142.

State policy has almost no influence in these fields. All responsibility has to be taken by the company management, i.e. by executive managers governing and shaping the company. If the company is only oriented at fulfilment of explicit working contracts (working times, scope of tasks in job descriptions periods on notice, etc.) and is neglectful of implicit matters (keeping promises, trust in agreements with employees), i.e. ignores ethic-existential recognition, its employees will be more and more excluded. It harms other groups of stakeholders and, finally, the company success.

In the business practice of German-speaking countries, the discussion on corporate ethics at well-known enterprises led to approaches that have become an integral part of business policy. Based on the company specific situational analysis of ethical strengths and weaknesses, those enterprises have worked out ethical norms as target values for the company management. A **Corporate Code of Ethics** considers the agreed norms as binding for everyone. When designing concrete ethical norms, all stakeholders are considered by portraying the business-relevant relations to concerned players, especially the company relations to

employees,

customers,

suppliers,

shareholders,

public institutions,

competitors,

natural environment.

Wording of the **Ethics Code** considers not only interests of all stakeholders but also fair and coherent compensation of interests between them. Ethical norms can only be fulfilled when they do not endanger individual stakeholders' responsibilities for company success. For instance, if an Ethics Code norm requires "candour and transparency" it may be applicable to employees (as claim holders) but not to the same extent for price negotiations with customers and suppliers, much less competitors.

To anchor an ethics code in a company, you need to design a corporate structure and organisation processes in terms of the ethics. In particular, executive managers and decision-makers should be convinced in necessity of the ethics code and demonstrate it in the practice. They have to ensure by their own behaviour and an appropriate organisation that the Ethics Code introduction is a pacemaker for moral orientation in the company. Only under this condition, the Ethics Code will have a chance to regulate the company's strategic and operative actions so that the company success is achieved by methods compatible with moral norms.

Hipp[349], a well-known manufacturer of baby and infant food was a pioneer of new corporate ethics in Germany. His **Ethics Charta** adopted in 1999 was an example for other famous enterprises. In his policy statement, Hipp sees the social market economy with its competition mechanism as a societally desirable and ethically legitimated economic system since it ensures respect of human dignity, contributes to wellbeing of everyone and allows acting within the framework of the Christian concept. For Hipp's business activity, the competition (under adherence to all restrictions of the framework

---

349 Hipp, C., Ethik-Charta 1999, in: Wertsteigerung durch Wertschöpfung, Tagungsband des Münchner Management Kolloquiums, Wildemann, H. (Publisher), Hofmann, Traunreut, 2007, pp. 447 f.

order) results in the moral obligation to long-term optimisation of earning power of the company. So Hipp contributes to social securing of competition by taxes and to stabilization of the society and democracy. To put this corporate ethics principle into practice, Hipp developed the ethics management concept allowing formulation of an ethics **management program** and **Ethics Charta** based on the quoted **Policy Statement**. The ethics management program prescribes procedural manners, i.e. it exactly regulates who in the company may or has to give thought to it, when and how. An Ethics Commission is designed as an institution dealing with all matters of the ethics management and processes openly or anonymously filed applications in accordance with a determined order. The Ethics Charta is finally a collection of all rules adopted by the **Ethics Commission** that should be used as references and guidelines for the Hipp's actions.

As shown on Hipp's example, such ethics management programs create immense instrumentalization pressure that especially small and midsized companies cannot withstand. It is very difficult to regulate all ethical behaviour with programs, codes and commissions and it could be too much for executive managers and other employees. Therefore, such role models should be completed by realization of recognition mechanisms, i.e. by a kind of intrinsic motivation of executive managers. Brink[350] suggests to create so-called **reflexion arenas** in which executive managers would be able to reflect their thinking and acting when being free from economic constraints to look for rational reasons. In this way, executive managers' perception of implicated agreements becomes more sensitive. Self-responsibility of executive managers also means increasing ethical contents and economic efficiency of management decisions. By recognition, participation, dignity and identification, strategic and normative personnel management are brought together again and become free of instrumentalization criticism which every ethics management is exposed to.[351]

However, this does not build a bridge between business ethics and family ethics. Both are still standing like iron blocks side by side. In the updated concepts of business ethics, there are still an "above and below" in business, i.e., a structure, as usually arranged hierarchically: there are instructors and executors in it. On the contrary, in families of well-trained and intellectually educated people (our target group), not hierarchy, but co-organizing and co-creating prevail.

As it will be shown below, a man can no longer establish himself in one world or the other, since the society, and thus also, the world of work, intervenes in the family by its new regulative measures. At least, it intensifies the ethical conflict between work and family, if the working world does not succeed to develop new ethical rules that match family ethics. The concept of "servant leadership" could be such a set of rules.

---

350 Brink, A., S. 158.
351 Die deutschen Bischöfe – Kommission für gesellschaftliche und soziale Fragen (Ed.), Mehr Beteiligungsgerechtigkeit, Beschäftigung erweitern, Arbeitslose integrieren, Zukunft sichern, Neun Gebote für die Wirtschafts- und Sozialpolitik, Bonn, 1998, pp. 6–7.

Pervasion of the Family by the Society – a Paradigm Change

Habisch[352] states in his preface of his series „Family-oriented Corporate Policy" that in the today's industrial and service society, our understanding of personal freedom is governed by separation of work and private life. He concludes that such separation divides human life in two parts – not only spatially (workplace vs. living apartment) but also temporally (working time vs. leisure) and even in questions of insurance. Since decades it has been recognized as a decisive achievement of a liberal society. Furthermore, he states that the central ethical idea of this separation was to protect the private living space of the employee from the employer's control and influence. The company was not permitted to interfere in family decisions of the employee. *As we know today, this strict separation of the family from the work turned up to be a "mental blockage"*[353] in finding solutions of the societal problems of family policy to be dealt with. Only in recent years, the persons responsible for family policy of the state began to increasingly influence enterprises and to develop life-phase-oriented personnel policy plans to support compatibility of family and career and to anchor it in company structures. This trend began in large companies first because they were the closest to the policy and could lead the way for others. In the meantime, this trend reached midsized companies. Even small enterprises amalgamated to common family supporting programs. The matter of these programs is tailor-made securing of day-care for children, family-friendly working conditions and efficient support of return into working life after pauses caused by child upbringing. In particular, the programs regulate flexible, family-friendly working times and efficient work organization providing introduction of mobile working norms, secure personnel and team development, promote professionalism of executive managers in controlling necessary transformation processes, offer children care facilities near the company (day-care and vacations care) and even support in taking care of older family members.

These basic societal trends deeply penetrate the core of current family traditions and increasingly interconnect the life areas which were separated in the past. Success (or failure) in one sphere of life will influence the success (or failure) in the other one.

Supporting in company daily life is often still difficult and there are still many unknown things, e.g. how to develop measures, how to overcome obstacles and how to find a solution for this area of conflict in practical co-operation of employees. Small and midsize enterprises often have no human resources to deal with these matters and no enough flexibility to organize their business processes in a fami-

---

352 Habisch, A. (Ed.), Familienorientierte Unternehmensstrategie, Beiträge zu einem zukunftsorientierten Programm, dnwe Schriftenreihe, Folge 1, Rainer Hampp Verlag, Munich, Mering, 1995, pp. 1–5.
353 Habisch, A. (Ed.), p. 1.

ly-friendly way. Neighbour co-operation models of non-competing enterprises of the same size show some solutions.

The mystery of all successfully implemented measures for balancing family and enterprise interests is **determination of the right intersection** from individual ranges of interest.

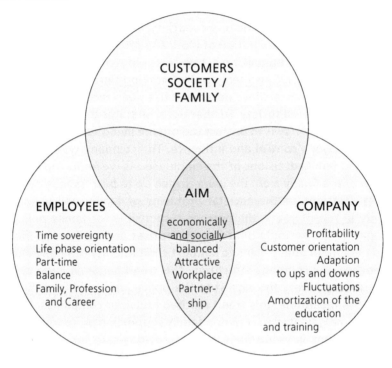

Table 5: Areas of Conflict: Work-Life (source: Fauth-Herkner[354])

Life-long full-time career biographies of men and women are put more and more in question due to economical and family circumstances and due to individualized human needs. The required possibility of working time changes during the career biography under family and further-education aspects gains more and more in importance. An increasing number of employees want variable creation of life phases both privately and at work. Not only employees without budget and leading competences but also first- and second line managers (in the future, also top-managers) express expectations of such kind. Decades ago, companies began to delegate responsibilities from the top positions to the lower ones. Nowadays, these democratisation processes begin to be reversed: a **wave of individualizing** from the bottom to the top significantly changed corporate structures and processes. Family fragmentation described in one of the previous chapters is now making its way through in enterprises: now the fragmentation process is entered by entire

---

354 Fauth-Herkner, A., Ergebnisse des Förderprojektes, Familienbewusste Arbeitswelt in Bayern, Bayer. Staatsministerium für Arbeit, Vereinigung der Bayer. Wirtschaft (Ed.), 2007, p. 10.

departments and the whole personnel. The traditional business process structures begin to dissociate in target- and project-related structures. **Transformation of values, demand on life-long learning and also on new understanding of allocated roles leads to withdrawal from normal labour relations, to designing new life plans and to life-phase-oriented agreed careers of men and women.** People want more and more to organize their lives in compliance with their individual needs so that there is also some space for other activities than work. So they generate life plans that we call **patchwork biographies**.

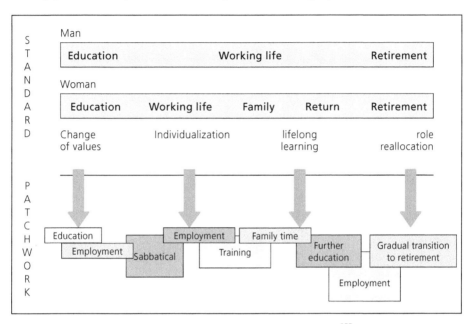

Table 6: From Standard Working Life to Patchwork Biography (source: Fauth-Herkner[355])

It can be foreseen that companies that consider such life plans of their personnel will win the battle for the best specialists. High-qualified specialists compare their working conditions with alternatives provided by other employers with particular criticism.[356]

Even the most sophisticated and family-friendly programs of the enterprises would not release the employees from the necessity of weighing their family needs against their career interests. However, the more they accept the offered family-friendly programs and participate in them the quicker the separation of family sphere from the world of work will disappear. The state and the enterprises offer family-friendly programs providing a social network of a new kind. If you want to use this social network you have to accept that the state and your company will exercise a higher influence on your family life than before. So the paradigm change is accomplished. One who does not want to accept the growing influence of the society

---

355 Fauth-Herkner, A., Ergebnisse des Förderprojektes, Familienbewusste Arbeitswelt in Bayern, Bayer. Staatsministerium für Arbeit, Vereinigung der Bayer. Wirtschaft (Ed.), 2007, p. 14.
356 Habisch, A. (Ed.), Familienorientierte Unternehmenspolitik, Schlusswort des Herausgebers, pp. 196–197.

on his family will have to step onto a thin line. He or she will only accept such family programs of the employer which leave the highest possible family autonomy and, at the same time, he resp. she will need to search for his/her own coping strategies at work that would be coherent for the both partners. When searching for them, he/she will surely find some support from Pius XI writing in his Encyclica "Quadragesimo anno": **"What an individual can do by his own initiative and forces must not be taken away from him and allocated to the society."**[357] In the following chapter, we will deal with the question how to find the right coping strategy.

---

[357] Pius XI., Enzyklika Quadragesimo anno, Nr. 79, in: Bundesverband der Katholischen Arbeitnehmer – Bewegung (Ed.), TKSL, Köln, 1982, pp. 91–152.

Coping Strategies at Work

In this chapter, we will discuss how to put the **gained family knowledge into the practice of the working world and career.** We pre-suppose that the human resources needed for couples further-development and the resources required for coping with conflicts of men and women at their work and career are almost the same, but with an only difference: In the view of an executive manager's career, using of resources is primarily oriented not at the dyadic construct system of the family but at the social construct system of the company which the executive manager makes his/her career in.

Unlike coping strategies in the family, the sense of coherence (SOC) at work is a special **connecting link** between all personal, organisational and social resources. The labour and organisation psychologists Martin Rimann and Ivars Udris[358] have examined 559 employees (265 women and 294 men) and found out that there is a significant correlation between the scope of activities (expression of the rank at the company) and the sense of coherence. They supposed that the SOC depends on the status at work and in the society (or on the person's business activity). To make possible correlations feasible, the activities of all questioned persons were coded with reference to many individual criteria. A code was a combination of the person's function in the company hierarchy and his status connected with it. His qualification level (education) and level of responsibility at the company were also taken into consideration.

Table 7 shows the correlation between the SOC and the position in the hierarchy:

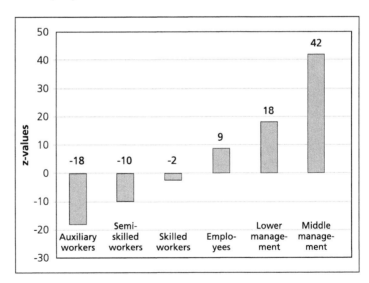

Source: Rimann, M. and Udris, I.

The variance analysis and mean comparison test results of Rimann and Udris are very significant. The middle management (our target group) showed the largest difference

---

358 Rimann, M., Udris, I., Kohärenzerleben (SOC), Zentraler Bestandteil von Gesundheit und Gesundheitsressource?, in: Handbuch der Salutogenese, Konzept und Praxis, Schüffel, W. et al. (Eds.), Ullstein Medical, 1988, pp. 359–360.

to other groups. Executive managers experience their own environment as highly coherent, and unskilled workers as least coherent. **Scopes of activities (control, decision-making and organization functions) and the sense of coherence are directly correlated to each other – it is almost a linear characteristic.** The results show that the correlation of personal, organizational and social resources is the decisive connecting link in a leadership model that connects requirements on professionalism, stresses, coping and health. This knowledge overcomes the limits of all what was said within the scope of salutogenic concept. Therefore, the sense of coherence (SOC) is not only a personality construct but also a resource. Experiencing the world as a coherent one is a resource of health and a component of health at the same time. **Coherence experience is a resource for health and, at the same time, an element of health.**[359]

Scope of Requirements on Executive Managers and Their Character Properties

One of the most important approaches for compatibility of family and career follows the **model of sequenced compatibility of family and labour activities**. As described above, it is oriented at chronological sequence of life phases: some of them are before the phase of occupation activity and some ones are after it. Consequently, there is a need of interrupting your occupation or withdrawing from it in order to meet the demands of your family. This model is more and more recognized by the society since the state and the enterprise supports it by a variety of measures.

On the contrary, the **model of simultaneous compatibility** is aimed on the possibility of simultaneous fulfilment of family and work demands. For the one who follows this model it is more difficult to agree family and work, especially when they manage other people. One who does not want to rely upon the form and content of the supporting measures from the state and the enterprise or upon other help from outside, has to look for help inside him/her. That begins with deepened thinking about the constitution conditions of modern life[360]. The first step is to **localize the own personality in the world of work**.[361] What does "vocation" mean? It is a work which you are called to due to your talent, addiction and skills. One who exercises a vocation does not only perform work of any kind but demonstrates his specific personal properties. For many people, vocation is an important possibility to identify themselves as personalities in today's system of values that is very much influenced by occupation. Your vocation allows your personality's localization in the working part of the society, provides you a feeling of sense of belonging as well as recognition and respect. You are called to your work if you do it well and with pleasure since you are really fit for these tasks – or, if to say in terms of Antonovsky's salutogenic criteria, you see your work

---

[359] Rimann, M., Udris, I., p. 364.
[360] Habisch, A. (Ed.), Familienorientierte Unternehmensstrategie, p. 191.
[361] Roth, J. R., p. 61.

as understandable, manageable and meaningful (what means "coherent"). In the view of career development and self-fulfilment, it is important to do the work which your skills and interests suit for. In this context, the right for freedom means that every citizen should have an opportunity to follow his skills and interests concerning work as far as possible. That means free choice of vocation, the right to strive for own happiness – not primarily to fulfil dreams and complete plans, but the right to follow the plans and to have dreams. Any limitation of freedom to follow own plans and to strive for own happiness would diminish aspects of autonomous self-determination and free will that are strongly connected with human dignity.

Another modern-life constitution condition of the equal rank is **localization of own personality in the smallest cell of the society, i.e. the family**. It also provides a feeling of belonging and recognition, however in another way than vocation. A person is a social being. In both fields (work and family), he defines himself through perception, recognition and respect by their co-beings. His occupation gives him a chance to gain recognition as a helpful colleague, professional expert, strong leader at work and as a caring partner, sympathetic husband and father in the family. **Evading the identification function of family and work and shifting the totality of his self-realization to activity fields outside the family and work will have bad consequences in the future.** His lack of motivation to work performance diminishes his chances to secure material subsistence of his family. If, because of lack of self-realization possibilities, the person is driven into making less performance at work and in the family than his own moral standards require, it will be degrading for him, in any case.

If we follow the model of simultaneous compatibility of family and work we have to look for personality-related demands, motives and competences suitable for initiating self-realization processes which would promote self-identification at work and in the family to the same extent. We will search for the above-mentioned "thin line", i.e. an **action corridor for coping with our family/work compatibility conflict**.

When defining the scope of demands on character properties of executive managers, we have to make difference between managing individual employees and managing entire teams of them. An individual employee has his own motives and his own way of self-realization. Managing a team means leading a group as a totality aimed at joint acting. When managing individual employees, you need to know how to

The dignity of a person does not depend on the income that they earn in their work. It depends on that person's ability to look for contacts and stable relationships in their daily work, and maintain them, and to define themselves through self-improvement and specialisation in a world of work characterised by free choice, and gain self-assurance through this. And, above all, it depends on the opportunities that are granted to that person to serve others through reasonable efforts as part of their moral obligation.

Steffen J. Roth
"Dignity, income and work in the social market economy", p. 74

design the employee's occupational environment so that he experiences pleasure in his efforts. But how can an executive manager motivate an individual to exert himself in working with pleasure? Felix von Cube [362] identifies three driving motives for working with pleasure: **flow, recognition and commitment**. The managing measures derived from them are called "**natural laws of leadership**". They are required for sustainable survival of the leaded team. Only if the employees are motivated you can manage the team successfully.

The **first driving motive** for desire to perform is **Flow Experience** de-scribed by Mihaly Csikszentmihalyi.[363] This motive was mentioned above as a possibility to bring about behaviour-controlled convergence in couple relationships. According to Csikszentmikhalyi, the flow is experienced in the same way as eating, sex or other sources of gratification that push on the person and lure him to make unknown things known and unsecure ones secure over and over again. At work, the flow is experienced only when you are exerting your skills and converting something unsecure into secure, i.e. "conquering the mountain with wounded fingers". When the drive to safety is satisfied you feel desire to bring efforts. This desire is characterized by its feeling during work performance itself, i.e. in "flowing".

Another performance motive is generated by the drive of aggression. It is the motivation force for any person's development of power. It is only ethically evaluated as a goal of aggression. Pushing one's own power in an enterprise means a higher rank, reputation and recognition. However, to gain recognition in a moral-compatible way, you have to perform well, even if an affluent society allows "buying" it in an immoral way. So the **second driving motive** for desire of performance is **recognition**. Achieving recognition by performance is the most human kind of aggressive satisfaction of drive.[364] Channelling the aggression by recognition of efforts is the best imaginable strategy to reduce harmful aggressive behaviour. People who perform well (at work or in family) and gain recognition for that are not the ones who use violence. In any case, recognition is a rank increase and always felt as a victory – directly or indirectly. And aggression is the drive to win and to be the victor. In a group of people, the meaning of aggression is to reach a higher rank, reputation, power and privileges connected with all of that. In the evolution history, direct, violent fighting was decisive for reaching this goal. In a civilized and democratic society, there is another method to be better than your competitors at work – i.e. your performance and efforts. The goal of aggression is the same as before, however, strategies to reach this goal have changed. As shown in today's discussion on managers' behaviour, people have found unhuman and immoral opportunities to get their ranks and privileges. Just because the person can also cream off something without adequate efforts, recognition is very important for performance. Only performance can be useful for a society, company or a group.

---

362 Cube, F. v., p. 75.
363 Csikszentmihalyi, M., Flow – Das Geheimnis des Glücks, p. 61–62.
364 Cube, F. v., p. 77.

Therefore, only performance can be a recognition criterion.

On the other hand, recognition as an action motive of managers is widely prohibited in our society. Instead of "recognition" definition, we tend to use "responsibility". Usually, more responsibility really means a higher rank in the hierarchy and, thereby, more recognition. Striving for recognition and promotion in the rank is still seen as "aggressive" up to now. And since aggression is usually associated with violence, the term is not politically correct and such striving is not admitted. Aggression drive is connected with the highest hypocrisy – even higher than sexual drive.[365]

The **third driving motive** for the desire of performance is **commitment**. One, who contributes to the common action of his group, team or family experiences not only recognition but also commitment. The feeling of commitment is an evolutionary gratification for the common action's selection advantage.[366] The common action is done by formation of a group. The latter needs an agreed division of labour. In the best of cases, there is enough freedom for self-organization of the group. The central criterion for the group's success is its members' motivation to individual efforts for reaching the goal of the group. The success is as strong as the mobilized motives of individual members and of the entire group. The mobilizing of motives is the original task of the manager who entrusts the group with challenges which contains insecurities and, therefore, can trigger flow experiences. Further motives pushing the common action of the group are advantages of the common action for the group's individuals and their desire of commitment to the group. Managers know that they can control the aggression potential of the managed groups by commitment. So the group remains harmonious as long as aggression and commitment can be kept in a dynamic balance.

The group's performance becomes higher when it is strengthened by personal commitment and sympathy relations between the members resulted from their common action. Sympathy to each other usually outreaching work relations and including even common leisure activities of colleagues' families promotes formation of a community and supports commitment to it. However, personal commitment will diminish since today's employees are often busy with project-related work in different group and in different places far away from each other. Because of that, the individual can rather identify himself with a community superior to his team, i.e. with a company as a totality. But how can an individual identify himself with a company as an anonym and unclear structure without knowing what does it really do? How can he/she be a

"Effort without pleasure is inhumane."

Should anyone get the idea of wanting to educate a "new human being", they should just let this idea slide. The idea of a new human being is but biological nonsense. The Marxists found this idea hard to swallow. No – the solution is neither "Pleasure without effort" nor "Effort without pleasure"; it can only be called "Effort with pleasure", "Pleasure with output".

Felix von Cube
„Pleasure with Output", p. 76

---

365 Cube, F. v., p. 90.
366 Cube, F. v., p. 78.

part of corporate identity? The answer is given by behavioural biology. **A human (and an animal, too) identifies himself with the ones who are of a higher rank**, i.e. with more successful ones. One can be proud of belonging to the enterprise which stands out with success, meaningfulness and power among the others. You take part in the victory of your community – that means **you are a victor, too**. That especially applies to employees who do not manage others. However, middle and high-level managers also identify themselves with their higher-ranking colleagues and their success. According to Cube,[367] commitment generated in such a way is not based on a real sympathy but on an aggression desire. The victor whom the group member identifies himself with needs not to be a large worldwide operating company. Midsized and small companies offering products for special niches can be also high-qualified and take leading position in the market in their field of industry.

Corporate culture can generate and maintain commitment only if it is supported by reliability, veracity and justness of the managers and if they fulfil their leadership tasks with a great deal of social competence, co-operation, fairness communicativeness and solidarity providing trust in them. They have to create a common ground and maintain it, to develop visions and to map goals, to put them into practice together with their team and, last but not least, ensure that people managed by them adhere to ethical norms. **Therefore, a skilled manager means the one possessing social skills on a high level.** To improve and to secure life quality of employees and economic success of the enterprise at the same time and to the same extent is their task which they cannot delegate to anybody else.

Such abilities of the managers is especially required in times of crisis when the company or a team is sometimes not a winner because of internal or external reasons and has to cope with losses. In the times when employees are demanded to additional work or even work without salary, it becomes visible whether their managers possess professionalism and social skills. The employees are committed to the company because their extraordinary efforts are recognized by the managers and the team and because the managers do the same and give the appropriate example.

The managers' action and the work of the employees will be more coherent if

Woe to you shepherds of Israel who only take care of yourselves!
Should not shepherds take care of the flock?
You eat the curds, clothe yourselves with the wool and slaughter the choice animals, but you do not take care of the flock
You have not strengthened the weak or healed the sick or bound up the injured. You have not brought back the strays or searched for the lost.
You have ruled them harshly and brutally.
[...]
I now consider these shepherds my enemies, and I will hold them responsible for what has happened to my flock.
I will take away their right to feed the flock, and I will stop them from feeding themselves.
I will rescue my flock from their mouths; the sheep will no longer be their prey.

Ezechiel 34, 2–10

---

367 Cube, F. v., p. 99.

they manage to communicate their own work and the team's work as a challenge and the kind and intensity of this challenge is adequate to their abilities and skills and all involved persons see this challenge as meaningful for them. Their sense of coherence will increase in the phase of a higher exertion, at least. Every time when the challenge and the abilities to meet it grows simultaneously, there is big chance to generate new flow experiences from an increased sense of coherence on a higher level of challenge.

Behavioural psychology calls these self-discovery processes "self-realization". If you release this term from metaphysically inspired wishful notions often connected with it, you will come to conclusion though not directly phased by Antonovsky, however, supporting his salutogenic concept. **In the context of described instinctive motivation, it is possible to reflect self-realization as one's own instinctive drives and thus to responsibly deal with the drives,**[368], which Antonovsky calls "self-efficacy" and "coherence". The decisive thing is not only the power of the manager and striving for keeping control over everything but a realistic and regenerating feeling of coping with demands of external and internal world and of possessing coping strategies suitable for that. Such coping strategy does not mean that you must cope with all your problems yourself. You can use help and support of your family. Your emotionality is not your weak point but your strong one. The most important is not your claiming for omnipotence but your flexible coping strategy paired with positive thinking of your own abilities and trusting in help of your wide social network,[369] including not only your family and work but also other areas. That is applicable both to male and female managers to the same extent. The division of power between men and women must be based on an adequate self-awareness of the both genders. **It means control over yourself and not control over others.** It is based on the power of relationship skills between the genders.

Researches of management consultancies have shown that the teams consisting of both men and women worked out better and more sustainable solutions than the teams consisting of men or women only. It is presupposed that there is no difference in professionalism of men and women. Differences between the genders are obviously not a real fact but a result from cognitive and emotional self-socialization supported by social and cultural factors. Of course, relationships between men and women are still governed by mutual notions and expectations, despite women's winning more and more positions in the management that were usually occupied by men before. However, the future relationships are no longer pre-programmed by the society. They will be shaped individually and personally. Everyone takes an exclusive responsibility for shaping one's own image of his personality, for choice of one's action repertoire, way of self-fulfilment and, therefore, for one's own imagination of masculinity and femininity.[370] Such understanding of self-fulfilment

---

368 Cube, F. v., p. 100.
369 Bründel, H., Hurrelmann, K., p. 177.
370 Hurrelmann, K., Alte und neue Bilder vom Mann und der Männlichkeit, Vortragstext, University Bielefeld, 1997.

Servant Leadership – Managers' Development as Personality Development

Servant Leadership[371] is a practical management philosophy based on understanding "serving" as a creative altruism and a responsibility to contribute for well-being of people and communities in the world. Servant Leadership is neither a concept nor a principle nor a technique but a **lifestyle** applying to all areas of life. In our context, such areas are especially work and family. Such lifestyle provides a trust basis for a personal and professional growth, efficient co-operation, self-responsibility and pushing energy.[372] Conventional leadership is focused on a question: How can I lead the people so that I can secure my personal goals and/or the goals of my company? Unlike that, serving leadership reverses this question: What can I do for others' personal development and reaching the common goals? This philosophy is centred on people and not on means. Servant leadership is based on serving and transforming force and not on the power of the management position.[373]

Conceptional Basics of Servant Leadership

The term of Servant Leadership was first used by the American author Robert K. Greenleaf in his essay „The Servant as Leader"[374] published in 1970. Today, 47 years later, this management philosophy began to make its way. In the list of „100 Best Companies To Work For" annually published in Fortune Magazine, more than a third of them are companies practicing Servant Leadership. Best leadership means outstandingly sustainable success. As per Greenleaf, "serving" is not a transferrable managing function but a natural lifestyle the person is steeped in. Servant Leadership is applicable to all people who deal with other people. It contains increasing serving and dedication to own growth and the growth of the others who, in some way, also serve and thus take the responsibility of their own lives. Servant Leadership regards qual-

History's Jesus of Nazareth, with or without his religious significance, was undoubtedly an executive: he continually checked the bond between himself and his disciples. He took their doubts seriously. He always made sure he had their consent and their willingness to follow him, or, as people would say today, their commitment. It is narrated several times that he asked them, "Are you with me?"

Reinhard K. Sprenger
„Servant Leadership", p. 72

---

371 Hereinafter we will use both terms as synonyms.
372 Schnorrenberg, L. J., Servant Leadership – die Führungskultur für das 21. Jahrhundert, in: Prinzipien dienender Unternehmensführung, Schnorrenberg u. a. (Ed.), Erich Schmidt Verlag, Berlin, 2007, p. 27.
373 Drucker, P. F., They're Not Employees, They're People, Harvard Business Review, USA, Februar, 2002.
374 Greenleaf, R. K., Führen ist Dienen – Dienen ist Führen, The Greenleaf Center of Servant Leadership, USA, 2005.

ities of a person, work and sense of community as a holistic entity und assumes spiritual understanding of identity, mission, vision and environment. Its goal is also to use the empowerment and social energy ethically and morally. In this respect, Servant Leadership is neither a new phenomenon nor a management concept, but a re-assessment of ancient rules of life – to give, to serve and to mean something for each other.

The Dilemma of Management

Why the lifestyle of Servant Leadership is so difficult to understand and to practice for many people, even if they recognized that it is the right lifestyle for them? The answer is obvious: our life is full of goal conflicts – as we already concluded above. **People's action conditions are affected by inconsistences, "plot holes" and insecurities.** We have to evermore choose between two alternatives that both seem to be attractive, but we often cannot estimate their consequences. All managers know this dilemma, and there is still no safe way out. To serve the employee is as much justifiable as to rule him, to support him, to take sanctions against him, to reward him or to punish. Both dismissing and promoting of employees belongs to management tasks. Management is full of such contradictions. A manager knows that both options are indispensable. Every day the manager is busy with finding a new balance and choosing between the alternatives what is more adequate to the situation or, at least, seems to be adequate. **"Decision" means his commitment to an action alternative whereas the future is unknown.** Choosing one alternative means excluding the other one, at the same time. So each decision contains some resistance that the manager has to overcome. One who side-steps this resistance is considered as weak-kneed. In many companies, it seems to be more important to demonstrate full-throated decidedness than to make really right decisions. It is a sign of lacking culture of management. Avoiding mistakes is often more valuable than a decision about the matter since a decision always means to choose one option and to lose another one at the same time. That also applies to career decisions of managers. They often know about consequences of the decision only after they have made it. There is a large temptation to justify the made decision and to bad-mouth the options that were provided. Psychologists call such behaviour **"post-decisional dissonance reduction"**[375].

The goal conflict between serving and ruling is also a dilemma of the management. A manager is primarily a representative of the company. In the case of conflicting interests, he has to defend the interests of the company first. The manager can do it clever and cautiously when acting with a cool head and maintaining balance. He can consider long and short-term consequences. But when conflicts cannot be solved he must decide. He will make himself guilty about one or another party, but just such inconsistences and pressure to take decisions are essential to be a manager. One who

---

375 Sprenger, R., Wer führt, ohne dass ihm die Menschen folgen, geht nur spazieren, in: Prinzipien dienender Unternehmensführung, Schnorrenberg, L. J., et al. (Eds.), p. 75.

wants to stay inculpable cannot be a manager. The manager is well advised when he considers interests of employees when making his decisions. He can even prioritize them. But sometimes he has to take decisions that the employees do not agree with. How to solve this dilemma?

Reinhold Sprenger[376] gives a pointed answer: "Many managers practice a very loyal "correction from the bottom". They begin to change from "either/or" to "both/and". They neither practice any value absolutely nor rely upon standard solutions. They are neither stuck in fixed principles nor satisfied with pettifogging contingence negations, e.g. guidelines. Such managers are real master of paradoxes. They avail themselves of mind artifice that quasi reconciles both interests with an "invisible hand" of Adam Smith, balances long and short-term things, tempers inadequate ones and moderates extremes. **They serve the capital by serving employees. But, of course, not only them both. They serve themselves, too.** At the same time, their manager careers are wonderfully developing along the way. Is that the main motivation? No, it would be still too egoistic. Let us rather impute nobleness to them."

The New Attitude of Servant Leadership

The core issues of Servant Leadership are centred on character properties of managers and the managed. There is a correlative relationship between them that is not based on mutual dependence. Servant Leadership acts with attentiveness and empathy. Both should be provided by the manager first. The manager has to be ready to give what he urgently needs himself: love, sympathy, recognition and commitment. All what others expect from him he has to expect from himself. As Schnorrenberg[377] said, the manager shall also "serve himself". He has to be ready to give more than he wants to earn himself. Moreover, he has to place his natural desire to win into service of others. Effective serving needs an ability to reflect, to search for meaning, to be honest and authentic, to guard your own borders and sometimes to relinquish your own wants. If the manager feels himself unfulfilled as a person it will be difficult for him to serve others, and he will be unfulfilled until he has not learned to serve himself. Our ability to serve is as high as we promote our own individualities. The best service we can offer to others is to be free of dependences – so we will be free to serve others unbiasedly.

Such an attitude places us exactly into the above-mentioned action corridor in order to manage conflicts at work as a manager and in the family as a partner, as well as to cope with conflicts between these two areas of life. **Servant Leadership is a method of mitigation of the conflict between family and career.**

---

376 Sprenger, R., p. 77.
377 Schnorrenberg, L. J., Servant Leadership, p. 30.

Key Elements of Servant Leadership

What are the key elements which can be used to undertake actions in the aforementioned action corridor?

Larry Spears[378], President of The Robert K. Greenleaf Center for Servant Leadership, Westfield, USA, regards the following ten elements as central to the development of a Servant Leader:

1. Listening

Communication and decision skills are expected of executives. These are the most important abilities of a Servant Leader. But it's not enough simply to address others. It is equally important to listen attentively i.e. to reflect what is said in an active and unbiased way, along with perception of what is not said (these messages are often emitted unconsciously). When we listen, we are already so often concerned with adopting a defensive stance, judging or discrediting what is said by the other person and formulating an appropriate response in advance. But are we actually able to accept the content of messages expressed to us in a personally neutral manner? The ability to listen to others attentively with interest, requires a certain kind of humilitty[379]: one which indicates that one doesn't know everything and is prepared to learn from others. An active listener tries to establish contact with the "inner voice"[380] of the other person, and to understand what their body language, attitude and way of thinking communicate. Listening, coupled with regular periods of reflection, is what essentially determines the growth of a Servant Leader.

2. Empathy

The Servant Leader endeavours to understand others and to "empathise" with them. Employees are people, and they need understanding and appreciation in order to be able to develop. People develop faster when they are accepted as they are i.e. when their need for recognition, affection and influence is satisfied. The most successful Servant Leaders are those who have learned to sense the feelings of others, and who encourage their staff to communicate with them at the emotional level – they are experienced, empathetic listeners.

3. Healing

According to Spears, learning to heal is a powerful force for the transformation and integration of people. One of the greatest strengths of Servant Leader is their ability to heal themselves and others from fears that makes us small and discouraged, and restore our broken confidence. "Once we are liberated from our own fear, our present will liberate others, even when we don't do anything", said Nelson Mandela[381] in his inaugural speech to the South African Parliament in 1994. When we transfer this idea to everyday management, we see that it is about enabling the potential and skills of those who are managed, to develop, and resolving their relationship conflicts. The American

---

378 Spears, L. C., Tracing the Past, Present and Future of Servant-Leadership, in: Focus on Leadership, The Greenleaf Center of Servant Leadership (Publisher), John Wiley & Sons, Inc., New York, 2002, pp. 4–8.
379 Schnorrenberg, L. J., Servant Leadership, p. 30.
380 Spears, L. C., p. 5.
381 Mandela, N., Antrittsrede 1994, own source.

management consultant Lance Secretan[382] says that managers should create a "sanctuary", a creative business culture in which spontaneity, dynamism, fun, humour, relief from fear of failure, incentives and mutual benevolence and cultured manners are the things that characterise the climate of collaboration in the company – a "to help make whole" climate which makes people whole again, as Spears[383] puts it.

4. Awareness

Awareness is the ability to direct one's attention to oneself and the surrounding environment, in order to receive information necessary for every management decision at an early stage. Only the right information will take one from awareness to knowing the truth. In the moment in which executives undertake an obligation to become aware of something, they proceed in a sometimes eerie way – often, they don't know in advance just what they may discover. Or, as Greenleaf[384] puts it, awareness is never a comforter; rather, it is the opposite: being something which makes one more concerned and stimulated. Competent managers are usually awake and with a fair amount of concern. They do not seek comfort when they become aware of something; rather, they develop their own inner serenity.

5. Persuasion

Another key criterion of Servant Leaders is their confidence in their own powers of persuasion, rather than in the authority granted them by the business organisation. A serving executive does not try to convince others through power and status, but by example and credibility. They try to convince others without forcing approval, and are able to establish consensus with those that are led. With power comes the threat of consequences – conviction creates trust and inspires the employees to follow and achieve their objectives themselves. Those who can inspire others reinforce the conviction of their employees with regard to their own innovative creativity.

6. Conceptualisation

Servant Leaders promote their ability "to dream big dreams", according to Greenleaf. To a Servant Leader, imagination is part of the central ethics of Serving Leadership. It is the ability to think and feel in overall contexts, and to rely on one's own imagination. In complex decision-making situations, it helps one to maintain their composure and to better consider developments in advance. Being able to think beyond one's goals for the day and arrive at longer-term conceptual thinking, requires discipline and experience. If we learn to use our imagination in an objective way, we can become able to make better decisions, find more creative solution options and be more successful in both our working life and our private life. Not just trusting your imagination but also allowing yourself to be guided by it, is partly a question of faith – a belief in something greater than ourselves.[385]

7. Foresight

The ability to see something in advance is closely linked to the term imagination. Foresight is a key skill which allows the serving executive to understand the lessons

---

382 Secretan, L., Soul-Management, Lichtenberg 1997.
383 Spears, L., C., p. 5.
384 Spears, L., C., p. 5.
385 Schnorrenberg, L. J., Servant Leadership, p. 32.

of the past and the realities of the present and to derive from them the consequences of forward-thinking decisions. The art of foresight is deeply rooted in what we label intuition and vision. It describes the ability of the Servant Leader to look beyond the boundaries of everyday operations and to develop a feeling for the bigger picture. Serving executives ask themselves questions about their visions and the courage necessary to make them a reality – with an intuitive force which may exceed their own imagination. True visions – those which come from within – cannot be understood without having an idea about the meaning of life. The next steps are, of course, deriving concrete aims and implementation strategies from one's personal vision.

8. Stewardship

The term Stewardship can only be transliterated in German language. It refers to the parables of Jesus in which he spoke of the good manager, who acted in a manner true to his service. Peter Block[386] defines the term Stewardship as "holding something in trust for another". Thus, this means the responsible conduct of the Servant Leader with the duties entrusted to them (inwardly) and for the benefit of society (outwardly). The company is a community of people and at the same time it is but a part of society. Responsible conduct with them is, above all else, part of the duty of the executive regarding serving the needs of others. From today's perspective, this conduct with those entrusted must be respectful of the environment and creative capacity, socially responsible, and compatible with the pursuit of peace and generation-friendly. Any such corporate culture which has already been experienced by the management, fosters a serving autonomy whereby, amidst all the actions that are undertaken, consideration of what one can do for others is still retained.

9. Commitment to the growth of people

Servant Leaders believe that their employees have an intrinsic value beyond their tangible work orders. This acknowledgement fosters their profound obligation of promoting the growth of each individual employee. They recognise the major responsibility of doing everything in their power to ensure the personal, professional and spiritual growth of all employees. In the scope of practical management, this may be achieved not just via staff development measures financed by the company, but also via the personal interest of the management in employees' ideas and suggestions and their participation in the decisions that are to be made. A serving executive will also be able to think beyond their own company and assisting employees who need to be dismissed for operational reasons, in finding a new position in another company. For leadership is about serious, responsible involvement in the lives of others.

10. Building Community

In high-tech industrial societies, large companies determine how people co-exist. Their hierarchical structures compel the employees to adopt compliant, adapted behaviours. Dependency factors and the pursuit of competitiveness leave little space for a serving, unselfish attitude. But knowledge is gaining ground in these industries as well, as our behaviour and our decisions can influence the lives of others, and we are the ones who should accept responsibility for it. A serving executive who is aware of this responsibility, knows that they cannot demand from others what they themselves are not prepared to furnish. This knowledge is able to reinforce executives' awareness of how to form a community among those for whom they are responsible. Serving executives are encouraged to bring the community (as a liveable form of cohabitation) closer to their employees, by showing them the ways of large-scale society which are based on the

---

386 Block, P., Stewardship and The Empowered Manager, USA, p. 7.

Servant Leaders' using their unlimited ability to form very specific community-based groups and use them to their, and others', advantage.

These ten key elements of Servant Leadership are neither an exhaustive list nor a clearly defined behavioural policy for arriving at the goal in a structured manner. Personal meaning, as well as substantive understanding, cannot be separated from the individuality of the observer, just as management cannot be separated from the character of the leader. They also represent no methodology for better quota achievement, but they are an important foundation for a leadership philosophy which is modern and responsible as far as people are concerned. They can also help to foster an understanding of the power and promise offered by this concept as an invitation and a challenge.

The New Type of Manager – Basic Trust instead of Primal Fear

C. G. Jung distinguishes between **"the primary and the secondary reality"**[387]. The primary reality is the conditionality of the human ego limited by its three dependences – time, space and individual biography. This reality includes the **primal fear** with all its consequences – also for dealing with people at work. The primal fear feeling just generates defensive mechanisms making the daily work of old-type managers especially difficult.

Leadership style of managers driven by the primal fear is manifested by following behavioural mechanisms from which such managers expect healing of their negative life feelings:[388]

- Defence from conflicts by contrived friendliness, extreme politeness and pseudo-harmonious way of conversation.
- Particularly rough and rejecting manner of communication manifesting inner hardening and discontentedness.
- Egoistic attitude in dealing with others; such attitude is visible in inability to listen or to percept feelings and needs of others – lack of empathy.
- Constrained and narcissistic tendencies in self-realization.
- Non-reflected and dependent relation to ideologies that can cause fanaticism and gang obedience.
- Self-righteousness and thinking that own behaviour is the norm for others.
- Holier-than-thou attitude and thinking that adherence to a norm is superior to respecting another person.
- No meaning in the own life concept what causes flight into leisure activities.

---

387 Jung, C. G., quoted in: Staehelin, B., Urvertrauen und zweite Wirklichkeit, Theologischer Verlag, Zürich, 1973.
388 Staehelin, B., Urvertrauen und zweite Wirklichkeit, Theologischer Verlag, Zürich, 1973.

- Possessive mentality leading to pre-occupation with material securities and generating enviousness and niggardliness.
- Self-esteem based exclusively on performance results; life feeling is governed by fear of failure and perfectionism.
- Rational critics rejection suppressing a critical self-reflection.
- Inability to verbalize personal emotions for others.

Of course, it is not so that a single person uses all of these mechanisms, but if you notice at least two of them about his management style you can be sure that the person is governed by fear. When the manager's metaphysical dimension is strongly clouded by primal fear it will leave almost inerasable mark on his personality. Such person can hardly be a good manager.[389]

According to Staehelin[390] the secondary reality is identical to the essence of basic trust. The elementary feeling of **basic trust** is an adequate form of experience of the secondary (emotional) reality. Managers who ground their life plans in basic trust exude confidence. As serving leaders, they are able to buoy up the managed people and to spiritually encourage them. We call them **managers of a new type**. Such managers have following properties:

- They are able to serve others.
- They are trusted in other managers who lead them.
- They understand daily life in the view of metaphysical impulses since they are aware of metaphysical affiliation.
- They have a constructive culture of communication allowing employees' experience of being cared of.
- They calmly deal with negative feelings of others.
- They have inner independence from material values.

Leo was one of our servants. This unaffected man had something so pleasing, so unobtrusively winning about him that everyone loved him.

I asked the servant Leo why it was that artists sometimes appeared to be only half-alive, while their creations seemed so irrefutably alive. Leo looked at me and said: "It is just the same with mothers. When they have borne their children and given them their milk and beauty and strength, they themselves become invisible and no one asks about them any more. Perhaps it is sad and yet also beautiful. The law ordains that it shall be so. The law of service. He who wishes to live long, must serve, but he who whished to rule does not live long."

"Then why do so many strive to rule?"
"Because they do not understand. There are few who are born to be masters; they remain happy and healthy. But all the others who have only become masters through endeavor, end in nothing."

"In what nothing, Leo?"
"For example, in the sanatoria."

Hermann Hesse
"Journey to the East", quoted in:
Suhrkamp Taschenbuch 750, 1st Edition,
Berlin, 1982, p.26, 33, 34.

---

389 Kirchner, B., Benedikt für Manager – die geistigen Grundlagen des Führens, Wiesbaden, 1994, pp. 13 f.
390 Staehelin, B., Urvertrauen und zweite Wirklichkeit, Theologischer Verlag, Zürich.

- They have far reaching understanding of life and death.
- They interpret fateful experiences positively.
- They are able to love (i.e. to accept others' needs)
- They responsibly deal with their own freedom and freedom of others.

The circle is closed. **The new manager's properties and attitudes are the coping resources in terms of Aaron Antonovsky's model.**[391] **They should be available to make a conflict or a decision comprehensible, manageable and meaningful.** The sense of coherence (SOC) defined by him exactly describes this main orientation in a manager's career. It expresses how extensive is your pervading, sustainable and still dynamic feeling of trust that conflicts resulting in management are structured, predictable and comprehensible when you have these resources and when requirements on the manager are challenges which are worth efforts and dedication to them.

---

391 Antonovsky, A., Salutogenese, Zur Entmystifizierung der Gesundheit, Deutsche Gesellschaft für Verhaltenstherapie, Tübingen, 1997, pp. 36.

8 History of the Future: Solution Approaches between Individualization and Collectiviation

At first, we shall make it clear: in this book, we do not want to give you an impression that we are going to create a new type of humans. Evolution history knows that genetic changes in human beings need long periods of time. That also applies to people's social behaviour. The latter has hardly changed significantly since the ancient human got his own consciousness – despite there were big changes in social constitutions that people created for themselves during the history of their culture from ancient high cultures till the today's industrial societies. Both in hierarchic and democratic states, individuals' social behaviour only imperceptibly wanders between two opposites – **individualization** vs. **collectivization**. Education and examples given by the society's opinion makers (top-managers in the economy, child carers in families, schools and media) push the individual in one or the other direction. The growing individualization particularly prevails because the value system of occidental Christianity continuously loses its meaning or is even only misused as an argumentative weapon against the supposed advancing Islamization of our society. **When a person begins to lose his believe, i.e. his metaphysical basis, there is a danger that he will be thrown back to his individual powerlessness and drifting without aims and orientation.**

How can we develop the history of the future of the human social behaviour in such a situation?

How can we develop behavioural and coping scenarios offering mitigation or solution of conflicts between family and career that concern many people and define their lives?

In previous chapters, we have formulated answers to these questions in different ways. Now we have to join all of them to a complex totality. **The theoretically and empirically secured clamp that connects all coping strategies described above is the salutogenic model of Aaron Antonovsky.** The core of this model is the Sense of Coherence (SOC). The SOC theorem provides a basis for using personal resources of the family partners for a positive change and development of their behaviour in their relationship. Furthermore, the SOC theorem is a strong basis for improving co-operation behaviour of managers geared to Servant Leadership. The matter of the both scenarios is co-evolution processes that mean simultaneous self-development, mutual stimulation and support, however, not the processes of merging the acting persons' behaviours.

In the present chapter, we will show that the process of searching for meaning and identity at work and in the family can even exceed individual sense of coherence and lead to a group sense of coherence. So we obtain an idea how to balance individualizing tendencies in our society with collective profit. **_Then we will interlock the concepts of co-operative leadership in the family and of the servant leadership at work with each other. Finally, we come to the mentioned complex and holistic approach which would depict the future of the history._**

Searching for Meaning and Identity at Work and in the Family as Holistic Co-Evolution Process

Each social group is hold together by two forms of energy: the material one (food, warmth, care of physical needs and money) and the spiritual energy of people dedicating their attention to the goals of others. If parents and children do not share their thoughts, feelings, activities, memories and dreams, their relationship will be kept only as long as it satisfies their material wishes and needs. As a spiritual entity, it will only exist on a very low and primitive level.[392]

The Impatient Society

The spiritual energy of the person governs his long-term behaviour. But how can he pursue long-term goals when living in our short thinking economy? How can he maintain loyalty and fulfil obligations towards the state, his company and his family when these institutions are threatening to break down and are subject to restructuring again and again? How can we determine what is really of long-lasting value, when living in an impatient society is only focused on the present moment? The competition and rivalry in our economy forces a lifestyle threatening to take away all securities from the people to let them "simply flounder"[393]. Since the children do not see an example of moral behaviour in the parents' occupation mothers and fathers have learned the horror of losing control over their children. Good quality of work has often nothing to do with moral values or a good character. Mothers' and fathers' social advancement is no longer an objective and valuable example that they could give their children. In the past the children regarded it as a matter of course. Nowadays it is no longer the case.

Short thinking of many enterprises impedes maturing of employees' confidence in their managers. The sense of community is especially shaken up when the company is sold. Even if a today's company is operated as a flexible and elastic network (not as a rigid command structure) its transfer to another owner will weaken the social relations inside it. In such a corporate culture, strong social bonds, e. g. loyalty have no longer so much meaning. *As concluded by John Kotter[394]* **loyalty can even be a trap in an economy in which business concepts, product design and advantages over the competitors, capital equipment and knowledge have shorter and shorter lifecycle.** Keeping distance and limited readiness to cooperation seem to be a better protection in the struggle with prevailing conditions than loyalty and willingness to help.

---

392 Csikszentmihalyi, M., Lebe gut, pp. 145 a. 146.
393 Sennett, R., Der flexible Mensch, Die Kultur des neuen Kapitalismus, Berliner Taschenbuch Verlag, Berlin, 2006, p. 22.
394 Kotter, J., The New Rules, Dutton, New York, 1995, pp. 81 a. 159.

Conflict between Character and Experience

So, our today's economical constitution is based on short-term objectives. This **time dimension** has even stronger influence on the person's emotional life at work and outside his workplace than high technologies and globalization. If we transfer this concept of the "flexible society" to the family, it will mean: remain mobile, do not enter binding relationships and do not make any sacrifices for others. In such a society, children see any obligations or bonds as abstract virtues that they can no longer perceive in their parents. Behaviour which promises success or at least survival in a world of work is aimed at short-term success and goals and cannot be a good contribution to the model of new roles allocation for parents. In today's realty, the parents have a reverse problem: how to protect the family relations from the behaviour characterizing the today's world of work, i.e. the behaviour based on short thinking, discussion rage and especially on lack of loyalty? **Instead of always changing economic values, the children's upbringing should pronounce commitment, reliability, loyalty and determination – however, these are virtues with a long-term effect.**

How can long-term goals be pursued in a short-winded society? How can you maintain sustainable social relations? How can you keep your identity in a society consisting of episodes and fragments?

Conditions of the today's economy have resulted in a **conflict between your character and your experience**. When experiencing times without coherence, you are in a danger of losing the ability to shape your character to a sustainably life story.[395] Many people seem to have lost the coherence between their characters and their experiences. The way out of this dilemma leads through development of a **group sense of coherence** to a **holistic co-evolution process** providing a new orientation of attitudes of the players at work and in families.

---

395 Sennett, R., p. 37.

Developing the Sense of Coherence in Groups

In his book "Health, Stress and Coping", Aaron Antonosvky always considers the sense of coherence (SOC) as a coping measure for individuals, however, he recognized that this concept of coping with conflicts is also applicable for groups: „The sense of coherence, as I suggested, is a concept that is applicable to groups as well as to individuals."[396] So a strong sense of coherence can characterize any social entity: a family, neighbourhood, a large city, a region or a country. **However, it is necessary to determine the group so that all members have the same philosophy of life. In this case, the philosophy will be an independent variable in moulding the SOC of individual members of the group.**

Group Consciousness and Group Vibes

According to Antonovsky, before you can speak about a group SOC as a resulting property of the group, you need a so-called **group consciousness**, i.e. an entirety of convictions and feelings that all group members have in common. The point of reference is the family, a small local community, a working team or a friends' circle, i.e. a primary group. According to our subject, we are dealing with two primary groups: a family and working team to be guided by a young manager. Shaping the group sense of coherence is again a question of time, i.e. you need to know how long an identified group can exist. A group's sense of coherence can grow in a relatively stable social context. That means, certain social conditions in the group shall exist for years. During these years, it can change its members, but it shall be still subjectively identified as a specific group. The group's sense of coherence grows from the members' collective behaviour embodied by myths, rituals, humour, language and ceremonies of the group. In a co-evolution process of common development close to each other, the group members agree their notions of comprehensibility, manageability and meaningfulness of conflicts that they experience together. The group's SOC gets stronger when its individual members begin to percept their personal sentiments as the group's ones **quasi as the group's vibes**[397]. On the other hand, the group's SOC can significantly contribute to development and modification of an individual's SOC. That especially applies to children and adolescents who are integrated into the family community. Development processes that we already discussed above show the importance of social environment. The latter transfers experiences which are decisive for formation of high or low SOC.

---

396 Antonovsky, A., Health, Stress and Coping, New Perspectives on Mental and Physical Well-Being, Jossey-Bass Inc., San Francisco, 1979, p. 132.
397 Antonovsky, A., Salutogenese, p. 159.

The Social Setting

In this connection, Antonovsky points out other mutual influences between the group and individual SOC. He determined that individual adults with stable SOC level are attracted by certain "social settings"[398] and that is not a mere coincidence. A person with strong SOC will more likely join a group that also has a strong SOC. That is an important finding for building of teams in enterprises. A coherently acting group is more in the position to attract coherently acting individuals. The same is applicable to families: coherently acting parents do not only better communicate their experiences to their children, but also become more attractive as a group for their children getting stronger and stronger in their SOC. Moreover, a group with strong SOC will more likely structure situations that would strengthen its members' SOC in the course of time.

To understand yourself, you have to be understood by the others.

To be understood by the others, you have to understand them.

quoted after:
Thomas Hora

Pearlin and Schooler[399] point out that there is a direct correlation between the group SOC and management of stressors. The authors stated examples from the world of work where many problems cannot solely be solved by individual coping. Such problems can rather be solved by intervention of the collective. The authors do not only mean stressors which individuals faced with and cannot do anything against it without engaging the group's resources, but also collective stressors and problems concerning the whole group. In such cases, the individual's SOC is much less important for releasing the tension than the group's SOC. Direct coping with collective stressors depends on what does the group do.

We have defined a group in the world of work as a team guided by a manager. On the contrary, a private group (a family) is usually defined as two persons with equal rights and rank upbringing one or more children. In Chapter 7, we have depicted coping strategies at work and in the family and have discussed the resources available and usable according to the today's state of knowledge. **Coping strategies at work and in the family overlapping in our depictions are however, not congruent, as we saw before.**

An important (or even the most important) approach for co-evolution of family and work would be found by trying to bring the both coping strategies closer to each other so that they intertwine. There are several ways that seem to be practicable to reach this aim:

---

398 Antonovsky, A., Salutogenese, p. 160.
399 Pearlin, L. J., Schooler, C., pp. 2–21.

Cooperative Leadership at Work

Leadership is typically understood as a merit afforded by an individual. Managers guide others, create and maintain luring visions, show ways and decide on strategies. They motivate and inspire their employees. However, the leadership needs basics of corporate ethics for its long-term success in an enterprise. It needs systems, structures and practical approaches mobilizing energies of all employees. Resources and abilities of a single manager are often not sufficient. In such cases, a cooperative leadership could be an alternative to an individual one.[400]

Such co-operative leadership requires two or more people participation in the power and join their forces to reach their common goals. It is a relationship in which people can act with equal rights. This kind of leadership is based on the prerequisite that the individuals behave as partners: they develop a common vision, set goals, solve problems and give meaning to their common work.

Conceptual Feasibility Prerequisites

Irrespective of whether the co-operative leadership concerns a team of two managers or entire project groups and departments or the whole company, there are some prerequisites that must be fulfilled to make this concept successful:

- It shall be ruled by **equation of power** between the individual players. Cooperative leadership will be disrupted if a person or a group invokes the power transferred to it by the company or seizes the power over others. Each individual should be able to develop this own personal power and may only use it for solutions which are profitable for everyone.
- There should be **common goals**. Individuals may have different opinions how to reach them, but they should agree on the goal's contents. They will surely face controversies and conflicts. However, they have to learn to accept them and to respect the other's opinion.
- There shall be a **common awareness of responsibility and accountability**. Everybody is responsible for his work and has to render an account of it to oneself and to others. In cooperative leadership, both the leader and the leaded persons are responsible for achieving the required results.
- Partnership requires **respect for the other.** Each person in the partnership has to be aware of the other persons' intrinsic worth and their dignity. Recognition and promotion of talents, abilities and energies offered by everybody of the team is a part of such cooperative leadership. To respect diversity of people surrounding requires means dealing with them with dignity and fairness.

---

[400] Moxley, R., Leadership as Partnership, in: Focus on Leadership, Spears, L., Lawrence, M. (Eds.), Wiley, J., Sons, Inc., New York, 2002, pp. 47 f.

- **Cooperative leadership is undividable.** "A little" of cooperative leadership in one or another issue would be absurd. This is the actual challenge. One who tries to limit it to one decision situation will realize that cooperative leadership is no longer possible in any other situation.

The Role of Individual in Cooperative Leadership

The reader should not get an impression that cooperative leadership can replace an individual as a leader. Quite the contrary: in the concept of cooperative leadership, the role of an individual gains in importance since this concept underlines importance of *all* individuals. Just because the cooperative leadership includes not only activity of a single individual, each employee's personality gets higher significance. The individual's role also grows within cooperative leadership due to resulting mutual dependence. Because one member of the team acts as a speaker, the other one as an organizer and the third one is in charge for a certain process, and all of them are dependent in their interaction, the cooperation gets stronger.

Long ago, the rules of cooperative leadership found their way into project management at many enterprises. However, they have become a kind of "subculture" only applicable for projects: as soon as a project is completed, the cooperative leadership collapses. There is still a lack of permanent and sustainable culture of cooperative leadership in the entire company. That requires changes in views of managers towards more independence in thinking and acting for themselves and their employees. The time of do-or-die managers once celebrated as heroes is up. If they do not start to accept the growing necessity of inner solidarity of all employees they will be lost in our today's world that equally values both individuals and collectives. The history of the future will slur over them.

Servant Leadership in Families – a Serving Family Leader

In chapter 7 we have defined the term of Servant Leadership as a practical management philosophy seeing serving as creative altruism. The philosophy means responsible behaviour towards this world and contribution to people's and communities' well-being. Servant Leadership is a lifestyle applying to all areas of life. Servant Leadership is applicable to all people who deal with other people. Servant Leadership is a trust basis for personal and professional growth. In families, cooperative leadership means efficient co-operation, self-responsibility and readiness for action. It is a holistic view of qualities of persons working together for family sustainment and promoting sense of collective. **Servant Leadership in the family includes a spiritual understanding of identity, vision, mission and shaping living together in a family and in the surrounding society.** But how do the family members (spouses and their children who are served) grow as personalities? Do they become healthier, more free and autonomous? Do they want to be Servant Leaders themselves? These questions underline that effective serving in the family requires quest for meaning, honesty, empathy, authenticity, watching own borders, ability to reflect and sometimes to relinquish own demands. However, that can be expected from adults in their family relation to each other, but not from children. When upbringing their children the parents ought to give them an example of honesty and empathy and limiting own inborn selfishness in favour of thoughtfulness to all others.

For fathers and mothers feeling themselves unfulfilled as persons, it is difficult to be at service to their partners and children. A person feels himself unfulfilled when he did not learn to serve himself. People who always think of themselves with times feel themselves unfree, lonesome inside and unhappy. As long they are only focused on claiming for own interests at all costs they find no peace with themselves and others.[401] The history of the future will slur over such people, too. However, a family member can develop the ability to serve others if he/she is aware of himself and able to serve himself to the same extent. They render a service to others by releasing themselves and their co-players from dependencies.

They will learn the core skills of Servant Leadership: active listening, empathy, healing, awareness, power of persuasion, imaginativeness, foresight, responsible dealing with others, promoting their growth and supporting the sense of community, recognizing them as resources and developing strong sense of coherence in the family. Such people are on their way to become **"family servant leaders"** for whom conflicts inside and outside the family are coherent in terms of Antonovsky's theory, i.e. they are comprehensible, manageable and can be meaningfully solved.

---

401 Schnorrenberg, L. J., Servant Leadership, p. 30.

The depicted coping strategies (cooperative leadership at work and servant leadership in families) overlap in the thing that we called **"serving ability"**. **This ability is the core essence for compatibility of family and work. Co-evolution of family and work can be successful only if the people remain integer in these both areas of life.** They maintain their leading style that does not forbid anything but provides space for the participants' own experiences. Such style of leadership does not govern but serves, does not judge but asks for insight, does not guide but looks about, does not conduct but explains, does not teach but shares experiences, does not instruct but informs, does not offend but respects and does not intrigue but acts candidly and veritably. People with integer leadership style will make the history of the future since they have corresponding coping strategies in family **and** at work.

Salutogenic Work-Life Balance

Co-evolution of the both existential areas of human life (family and work) is a long lasting communication process in which the players agree common conflict management behaviour and re-adjust it in case of changes again and again. By repeating or, if possible, ritualized feedback conversations, they have to ensure a balance between gratifications for activities at work and the gratifications from the family. **They can succeed in this matter only if the players pay a sustainable and not decreasing attention to the co-evolution process and its outer and inner conditions changing all the time.** In former times, the family was hold together by external ties of control by the society and internal ties of religious and ethical obligations. Now it is no longer the case. Contractual obligations had an advantage of making the relation predictable and saving energy by excluding other choices and necessity of regular negotiations. In the times when marriage was a contract for the rest of life, people did not need to permanently struggle for its maintaining. **Since everyone can decide personally whether he/she wants to stay in the family or not, the only way to save the family is to regularly supply spiritual energy to it.**[402]

Self-Management and Relationship Management

This new form of the family can only be kept stable if the partners offer intrinsic gratifications (i.e. entailed by stimuli inside the relationship). When any **flow** experience arises from the interaction inside the family both partners are interested in maintaining such a relationship and to promote it. However, families are still seen as a matter of course and only few people have learned to transform old-type relationships into new-type relationships that are hold up not because of external obligations but because of **enjoyment** and fun to maintain it.

Finding flow experiences in family relationships requires ability to serve your own Self, i.e. **effective self-management**, and serving others, i.e. **effective relationship management**. Serving yourself means shaping your own uniqueness from your available talents and experiences. Serving your inner Self means discovering your own identity to completely develop its potential and to use it for your own way. Serving and effective relationship management

A man should firstly recognize himself that conflict situations between him and other people are situated in his soul. Then he should try to overcome this conflict, to henceforward encounter his fellow human beings as a new and pacified person and enter new, converted relations to them.

The reason of all conflicts between my fellow human beings and me is that I do not say what I mean and that I do not do what I say.

Martin Buber
quoted after: Von Brück, M.,
Wie können wir leben?, p. 162.

---

402 Csikszentmihalyi, M., Lebe gut, p. 197.

arises from the knowledge that you have to accept other people as they are and that you cannot change them. For serving relationship management, it is important to be sometimes less self-centred and to convincingly let the others feel that you are interested in them as persons and not only in their achievements and that you value them as persons and trust them.

Self-management and relationship management in the family require a special kind of **flexibility**. In the nature, flexibility means both the ability of a tree to yield and to recover from the deformation. It is both a test and recovery of its shape. In the best case, the human behaviour should have the same ductility enabling it to adjust itself to changing conditions without being broken by them.[403] Edmund Leach, an anthropologist, has tried to divide all change experiences by humans in two types. The first kind of change is the one where we know that something changes but seems to have continuity with the things before. Another kind of changes means a crash due to action that changes our life irrevocably.[404] Flexible partners at work and in families shall specially monitor changes at their workplace and in their private life. If they imply the continuity with the past in their decisions and their actions they will be in the position to maintain and to improve their relationships. Any behaviour which denies the origin of the relationship's members means a risk of fiasco. **It is important to find the right degree of flexibility of your own and not to overstrain the other's flexibility.**

Salutogenic Health Management

At least by now, many a superficial observer would ask what kind of **health management** we need at work and in families in order to achieve a "**work-life balance**". If we speak about optimization of productivity in the family, many authors state health as a prerequisite for successful self- and relationship management. **Then the health management requires both relation prevention and behaviour prevention**, i.e. health promoting designing of working conditions at work and of life conditions at home, as well as people's readiness to behave healthy and promote health by their behaviour. In this argumentation, work life balance usually means that stresses at work and in the family are adequate to the person's potential performance. Then amplitudes of balance processes, i.e. rhythms of own life shaping are important variables of health. This approach supposes a more or less formal quantitative compensation of human stresses by releases. The solution would be to monitor your own stress level and the one of employees guided by you and to avoid overstress by consultation and support. However, such a solution is limited.

---

403 Sennet, R., p. 57.
404 Leach, E., Two Essays Concerning the Symbolic Representation of Time, in: Rethinking Anthropology, Atholone, London, 1968, pp. 124–136.

The salutogenic concept of Aaron Antonovsky[405] offers a more advanced solution. As mentioned in Chapter 5, he describes pathogenesis and salutogenesis as a complementary relation. His salutogenic orientation resulted in refusing the classification of people either healthy or ill and offering a multidimensional health/decease continuum instead of it. Instead of searching for stressors considered as illness causes in pathogenesis, he asks which factors are at least involved in the person's maintaining his position on the continuum or his moving to the healthy pole. That means, **he is focused on coping resources**. He does not regard stressors at work and in the family as something indecent that must be constantly reduced as far as possible. He considers them as omnipresent. Moreover, Antonovsky does not necessarily assume consequences of stressors as morbid. In his opinion, they often can be healthy depending on their character and successful release of the exertion. For Antonovsky, it is decisive whether the areas of life are subjectively important for the person involved. Beyond a doubt, family and work belong to the important ones.

In Chapter 7 we described coping resources and their use in families and at work. When using those resources people begin to see the stressors in the both areas of life and conflicts resulting from them as comprehensible, manageable and meaningful. They begin to generate strong sense of coherence (SOC) and maintain it in difficult situations concerning their own feelings, direct and interpersonal relationships, their own activities and existential questions at work and in the family (death, inevitable failure, personal mistakes). If you admit that these four areas are important in your life there will be still a question whether they are meaningful, i.e. whether they can be taken as challenges which are worth the energy input. Antonovsky[406] notes that this is not necessarily the matter of intrinsic satisfaction. It can be that a person has not so much pleasure with his work or housekeeping. But if he is convinced that his work is meaningful for his company, for supporting his family and kids and for promoting his career he can still achieve a high level of sense of coherence and thus move to the healthy pole of the healthy/decease continuum.

Conclusion: future development of the salutogenic model makes the rush hour of life controllable

The theoretically and empirically secured parenthesis, which binds all of the coping strategies that are presented, is the salutogenic model of Antonovsky. Using this model, we can, firstly, use resources of the partners in the family so that their relationship behaviour changes positively. Furthermore, the SOC theorem is a strong basis for improving co-operation behaviour of managers geared to Servant Leadership. If we then interlock the concepts of co-operative leadership in the family and of the servant leadership at work we will finally come to a holistic behavioural approach for solving conflicts between family and work.

---

405 Antonovsky, A., Salutogenese, p. 29.
406 Antonovsky, A., Salutogenese, p. 39.

We would suggest to transfer the principle of cooperative leadership in the family to the work, too and, in turn, to use the principle of servant leadership in the family, as well. The both of concepts are overlap in ability to serve. This ability is the core essence for compatibility of family and work. Co-evolution of family and work can be successful only if the people remain integer in these both areas of life.

Serving to one's own Self, efficient self-management in serving the others, efficient relationship management and clear monitoring of changes at work and in private life, as well as flexibility of a special kind are parameters of an enjoyable and spiritually healthy relationship.

So mitigation of impacts of stressors at work and in families by coping resources in terms of Antonovsky's model leads to controllability of the conflict between career and family orientation. The controllability of the conflict and its stability in different life periods depends on the ethics focused on serving behaviour of the members involved in the productivity of the family. Such ethics require behaviour based on veracity instead of manipulation, fair clarification of conflict instead of their suppression or fighting them by force and reconciliation of relationship instead of their breaking. The goal is to serve each other instead of fighting for power and to placing the other's interests before self-interest. So the rush hour of life will be manageable!

9 Summary and Forecast[407]

Over the last few decades, the struggle between men and women for equal opportunities in all socially relevant areas has strongly dominated European society. The conflict of goals between professional success and a harmonious family arrangement is at the core of this struggle, since an overwhelming number of people in our society are directly or indirectly concerned with this issue. Our marriage model is not the norm throughout the world, since societies of other cultures are far less focused on couples. **In our couple-centred society, work and relationships constitute happiness and contentment for people, if they remain together in a balanced relationship.** However, the social reality shows no sign of harmony. Instead, it is preoccupied with a complex and multi-dimensional net of conflicts, which appears in various forms at different phases of life and compel men and women to carry out certain arrangements within their dyadic construct system. The focal point of this discussion is "**agreement career**". This term means the phase in one's career in which gainful employment and parenthood – in particular, the responsibility for children who are not yet independent – overlap and should be matched. The core target group that is considered comprises younger male and female managers with 5-10 years of work experience and growing children at pre-school and primary school ages. In this phase of one's life and career, conflict arises between focusing on work and family. This is because both career progression and looking after growing children demand the greatest commitment. This situation is exacerbated if there are changes in the parents' value system and living conditions. A large number of working people in Germany cannot really identify themselves with their career goals. Instead, they have cultivated a cognitive dissonance between their objectives and identification. Frustration increases in the wake of the rising standards of living. People wish for more self-actualization, preferably away from their work and family. The level of frustration that people are exposed to or expose themselves increases. Despite a decline in work motivation, having a career is still a life goal of many young managers, as it provides recognition, income and power. **Managers should generate top performances in the two worlds of work and family. However, the rules of these worlds contrast each other.** What is seen as a "must" in the world of work – being resilient, tough and unsentimental – is misconstrued in a family context, where tenderness, warmth and empathy are desired. In addition, the mobility that is required at work leads to the "de-spatialization" of social relations.

---

407 Table 8: Schmidt, W., Process diagram, p. 207.

Tension caused by the dual burden of work and family grows, not only day after day but also, as shown above, night after night. If men or women choose one of these two worlds, they are dropped out of the patterns of success, which are adopted in other cultures. It is a close call between "burn-out" and a non-binding "social partnership". At work, existing hierarchies begin to dissolve because younger managers cannot demand subordination from their juniors and, at the same time, they refuse to obey their superiors. The change in our society's life conditions is characterized by the fact that the self-unfolding values, like emancipation, enjoyment, self-realization and independence, have replaced the previous prevailing duty and acceptance values such as obedience, readiness for acceptance, discipline and selflessness. Since family members' claims to power are also increasing, the family as a social group has become more fragile. On the other hand, the value and guidance system, which determines a manager's character, should be re-calibrated.

As a supplement to the formal concepts that the state and companies offer to cope with the conflict situation between work and family today, the present study provides an approach to a solution that is based on the **salutogenic model of A. Antonovsky**. We ask the question of how an individual (not a society) can appropriately and effectively get a grip on the existing conflict situation. The model is based on the statement that health and illness do not exclude each other. They are rather extreme poles on a continuum and can be imagined as a continuous movement on a line between two extremes – health and illness. This is why they are called a healthy/disease continuum. When facing interchanging protective and risk factors, a person is in the position to deal with critical life events or conflicts, to control his/her resources, to open up coping potentials and to develop a sense of coherence, meaningfulness, integrity and well-being. Through empirical investigations, Antonovsky proved that **healthy people have an intellectual-emotional global orientation, which he called the sense of coherence (SOC)**. This expresses the extent of a pervasive, enduring and dynamic feeling of trust: the person believes that the conflicts in which he has found himself in are structured, predictable and explicable, and that he has all of the resources available to meet the demands that are given by the conflict. He sees these demands as challenges that are worth his efforts and commitment. According to Antonovsky, a person possesses **generalized resistance resources** with which he can combat stressors. If we define the sense of coherence as a stable property, which is only characterized by social and cultural conditions and not by individual ones, **the salutogenic model can be transferred to our target group**. So we can first find a theoretical approach and then, several practical approaches. The theoretical approach leads us to conclude that a positive self-image, social support, the experience and consistency (in terms of the understanding of coherences) and the manageability of life demands (in terms of being neither overstressed nor unchallenged) prevent tensions from turning into stress. This can be achieved by **controlling the emotions** that determine one's self-esteem. This means making a **feeling of significance** emerging in the context of social recognition, i.e., participation in decision-making processes in a social environment. **Further important resistance resources are self-respect, identity and self-preservation.**

The practical approaches to solutions follow more leads. The illustrated co-evolution process shows a route through several coping scenarios. It describes complex and different but interdependent development systems that, in spite of disturbances, delays and malfunctions of the acting person, can, in an ideal scenario, lead to a long-lasting balance in the management of different relationship systems. The report is based on a viewpoint that is focused on the family. In our opinion, developing a conflict-free family as much as possible is a cornerstone for the further success of the economies of our macro-system. The goal is to work out family-friendly work relationships and not work-friendly families. In the context of our studies, co-evolution means the mutual influence on personal development of partners living together. The matter of these studies is the question of how a person develops his personality when living together with his partner and how they take paths that cannot be comprehended without taking each other into account. The more harmonious the relationship, the more the interests of the individual draw back and are overlain by the interests that develop from the partnership, without one being completely absorbed in the other. In this dyadically constructed world, on the one hand, social relationships are reproduced. On the other hand, being a private world, it sets itself apart from the outside world. This is because a person not only lives in the dyadic world but also, in other ones, e.g., in the world of work, he has to integrate contradictions and inconsistencies of these various construct systems into himself, since he is a member of these systems. With the salutogenic model, we can considerably reduce the conflicts between both microsystems – the world of the family and of work. We discuss the coping resources and coping processes that show the ways to make the conflict between work- and family orientation comprehensible, manageable and meaningful.

From an ethical viewpoint, the modern family is defined as an inter-generational personal life- and living community. This means parenthood, life partnership and personality. In the Christian sense, the family is to be understood as a bearer of social, personal and religious meanings: love, culture and education take centre stage. Here, children are coddled in love and, as such, can more easily learn the true order of reality. Therefore, in the Christian value system, marriages and families form an indivisible unity. **Family ethics are based on the Christian concept of a person, which understands a man as "being" and "co-being" with others – as an individual and, at the same time, as a social being.**

The family is undergoing an ethical-sociological change process, which is characterized by a further increasing individualization. In an extreme case, when family relations become more and more replaceable, only individual life stories of man and woman count in the family and outside of it. Former strong religious bonds in families lost their influence because of growing secularizing. **Today, a single person no longer recognizes himself as part of a large superior whole but increasingly as an individual.** He no longer lives in a consistent world but moves between different worlds such as between the highly specialized work world, public life and family. A consequence of the self-centring of a husband and wife is the increasing potential for conflict in the marriage, partnership and family. The question is, how can this spiral be broken? ***Spouses should continually search for individual solutions and negotiate with each other on how they can reconcile compulsions or ambitions concerning financial safety and career, and work with the desires and ideas concerning their partnership and family.***

The first step is to recognize that the best form of *self-actualization* will find its expression in human encounters, particularly in loving relationships. The coping concepts that are discussed here are based on all of the forms of self-actualization – through self-knowledge in encounters with others and in fulfilment, through one's own work and achievements. *The second step is dissolving former role allocations and reallocating them.* This can depend on the phase of life but, in general, will lead to a greater role variety for both men and women.

We are at a turning point when everyone is responsible for developing one's own personality, for choosing one's own action plan and, thereby, for imagination of masculinity and femininity. As soon as a child is born, both partners have to grow into their roles. These roles change again – in a "family career", in which the couple is adapted to the relationship with the child, to the differentiation between partner and parent roles and to a functional parental alliance. Differences in coping behaviours depend on the parents' relationship styles and their gender role orientation. The partners' maps can help them to better know, to recognize and to understand the other partner.

Emotional attachment, feelings and love are the main resources for coping with conflicts. Emotions are the most subjective elements of human consciousness. However, as well as genetically programmed emotions, they can be controlled through self-reflection. The various forms of love – from the passionate to the romantic – create an important binding force for the couple's relationship and, above all, in the case of conflict. The core function of positive feelings is to broaden the thought-action-repertoire of the partner and thus, to build up permanent personal (emotional, intellectual and social) resources. As a strengthening force, love should also be seen in the aspect of spirituality and philosophical contemplation.

All anger, all misery and all violence, he who is armed with Love conquers all fortune.

Michelangelo Buonarroti aka Michelangelo
"Dichtungen", p. 25.

Another coping resource of the same importance, which relates to family and work, is **emotional intelligence and competence**. Emotional intelligence is necessary to lead a successful life, in order to recognize and to know one's own emotions and thus, to be able to manage and utilize emotions. ***Emotional self-control – delaying gratification and suppressing impulsiveness – is the foundation of every kind of success.*** Other elements of emotional intelligence are **empathy** – knowing what others feel – and the art of dealing with the emotions of others, i.e. **social competence and emotional integrity**. Emotionally intelligent parents impart to their children self-confidence, curiosity, intentionality, self-control, attachment, the ability to communicate and willingness to cooperate.

With his salutogenic model, Antonovksy has shown the way between temperament and socialization and has overcome the dichotomy between thought and action. **The connection between understanding and managing increases the sense of coherence. It enhances the ability to deal with conflict and the possibility to solve it.** It is a prerequisite for the creation of a mutual world for partners.

The use of the resources created can lead to a change in relationship behaviour, to a convergence of values and attitudes, which is more important than similar traits of the two personalities. On the basis of personal resources, partners are in a position to establish themselves as a married couple and as a family with children in the inner world created by themselves – the **partners construct their own world together**. The sense of coherence thereby represents a superior resource, which participates in the cognitive, emotional and motivational processes in the couple's relationship. **The sense of coherence plays a catalyst role in the consolidation of social resistance resources – it is quasi a "driver" for the couple's willingness to self-development and entering together into a process of behaviour-driven convergence.** The partners head to perceiving and accepting different kinds of relationship behaviour. For selfish reasons, self-interest ought to also satisfy third party interests, the demands of the partner. Attention should be paid to the balance of fairness and equality, which is inherent in the relationship, i.e., an equal share in the relationship. The process of mutual influence is support, restriction and challenge.

If the partners, individually or together, fully utilize their abilities to meet a challenge that they can barely cope with, a "***flow-experience***" can emerge. This is a **state of uncertainty**, like the one of a sportsman who is not sure whether he can reach his goal. However, not only sportsmen experience this top form of dealing with own goals. Optimal experience pre-supposes a fine balance between one's own ability to act and ability to deal with existing possibilities – only under this prerequisition, we can control the quality of experiences. To let common goals lead to interaction, which strengthens the complexity of the family, the family **must be both differentiated and integrated at the same time**. In an integrated family, the differentiated goals of each member are important. Rituals create the necessary space for this. The individual's meekness and ability to be in submission determines the success of the family as a group.

By using resources, the couple's relationship behaviour should also positively change, so that **the control mechanisms are recognized and observed**. As stressors are omnipresent, we are permanently defied to cope. In this coping process, a couple's relationship develops in a state of continuous feedback and correction. The match between personality and partnership is the result of **continuous reciprocities** or **transactions** that function as **control mechanisms** over long periods of time. To make these transactions run purposefully, **control of the commitment** of all participants is necessary. There should be a willingness to plan relations long-term and to enter binding agreements with it. Such agreements should control the proportion between separation and togetherness, the dealing with congruencies and incongruencies, the mutual and individual external contact of the family member at work and in the family and the distribution of roles between work and family roles. **All of these rules should be coherent**, i.e., they should be perceived by the partners as an organized, consistent, structured and clear communication process. This also includes **a positive atmosphere of debate**, which takes into account the needs of the partners, their desire for free movement and their membership of other groups. This positive atmosphere also turns **common habits** into symbols, customs and rituals and is perhaps in a position to create myths.

The link to the vocational component of the shown co-evolution process attempts to establish today's business ethics, since each economy based on the division of labour should still be understood as a mutual alliance. The increase in the fullness of life (and not only in the volume of goods), in terms of independently selectable growth satisfaction opportunities, comes to the forefront. The economic rights that are desired by citizens require economic ethics as a basis according to which an individual agrees to only pursue such goals that are compatible with the legitimate regulations of an organized society of free and equal citizens. A company should be required to have an independent self-commitment to the principles of business integrity in its dealing with all stakeholders and to the ethical responsibility for the common good (corporate citizenship). The object of business ethics is the morality of companies, which manifests itself in the company culture. Meaningful value systems and mindsets lead to the formation of a company-specific identity (corporate identity), expressed in systems of recognition and participation. Not all company leaders have yet realized that not just the market mechanism control but recognition and fairness in business will be the determining success factors in the future.

However, this does not build a bridge between business ethics and family ethics. Both are still standing like iron blocks side by side. In the updated concepts of business ethics, there are still an "above and below" in business, i.e., a structure, as usually arranged hierarchically: there are instructors and executors in it. On the contrary, in families of well-trained and intellectually educated people (our target group), not hierarchy, but co-organizing and co-creating prevail.

A man can no longer establish himself in one world or the other, since the society, and thus also, the world of work, intervenes in the family by its new regulative measures. At least, it intensifies the ethical conflict between work and family, if the working world does not succeed to develop new ethical rules that match family ethics. The concept of "servant leadership" could be such a set of rules.

The core ethical idea, i.e., protection of the employee's personal living space from the control of and dependence on the company and the state, decreases more and more, since the family support notions of both the company and the state deeply penetrate into the heart of the previously familial self-image. **The family is visibly permeated by society.** On the other hand, companies are undergoing democratization processes. Decades ago, companies began to delegate responsibilities from the top positions to the lower ones. Now this democratization process seems to turn back, as a wave of individualization is changing company structures and processes from the bottom to the top. This leads to turning away from the normal working relationships and to the organization of new life layouts and to careers that are adjusted to phases of life, leading to patchwork life-stories. For someone who does not want society to increasingly influence his family, only family-social benefits from the state and company are acceptable which provide the highest family independence. He/she will begin to search for his own coping strategies at work.

In this investigation, the sense of coherence proves to be not only a personality construct but also, a resource. **Coherence experience is a resource for health and, at the same time, an element of health.** Approaches for the compatibility of work and family follow two guiding principles: the principle of sequential compatibility and the principle of simultaneous compatibility. If we, as presented above, follow the guiding principle of simultaneous compatibility, we have to search for personal requirements, instinctive motives and competences. These activate self-realization processes, which lead to a higher identification in both work and family. The instinctive motives are the described flow experience – the personal recognition, which is based on an aggressive instinct and attachment to the work group, providing the desire to achieve something. The professional competence of a manager is his/her qualified social competence, which means he/she has no control over others but does over his-/herself. This is consistent with the Christian virtues of wisdom, cleverness and moderation.

Managers' development as personality development leads us to the most important approach to solving conflicts in the world of work – the **"Servant Leadership"**. This is neither a concept nor a technique, but a lifestyle. The matter is the following: What can I do for others' personal development and reaching the common goals? Servant Leadership, as was developed by Robert Greenleaf in 1970, follows a holistic consideration of the qualities of people, work and a sense of community. This presupposes a spiritual understanding of identity, mission, vision and environment. With this approach, we find ourselves right in the individual "corridor of action", in order to, on the one hand, manage conflicts at work as a manager and, on the other hand, in the family, as a spouse. This approach enables us to cope with the conflicts between both areas of life. Servant leadership at work is the key to mitigating the tension between career and family. The core elements of servant leadership are described in detail. From these elements, a new type of manager can develop, who frees himself from his own primal fear and wins a new basic sense of trust, which strengthens his sense of coherence at work.

The social behaviour of individuals in our European societies moves between two poles – individualization and collectivization. How will it develop in the future? We combine our suggestions for solutions from the preceding chapters into a complex whole. The theoretically and empirically secured parenthesis, which binds all of the coping strategies that are presented, is the salutogenic model. To comprehend the finding of meaning and identity at work and in the family as an integrated co-evolution process, we should overcome the short-term thinking that characterizes our impatient society and thus, overcome the related conflict between character and experience. This is because the experience of an incoherent era threatens the ability of a person to shape his/her character into a sustainable life story.

The coming generations will successfully develop a group sense of coherence, if the respective group succeeds to achieve a joint vision of the world – namely, in the family and in the world of work. The group awareness that is required for this originates from a collective behaviour of group members, which finds its expression in myths, rituals, humour, speeches and ceremonies.

The coping strategies that we have been presented for both groups – the family and work team – overlap. However, they are not congruent with each other. The best approach for the co-evolution of work and family would be to make both coping strategies congruent (if it works). If we relate partnership management to the working world and servant leadership to the family, i.e., interweave both coping scenarios together, there are several paths towards this goal that seem to be practicable:

The first one describes the ***partnership management at work***. It requires two or three people who share power to pool their resources and strengths in order to reach their common goals. This method of management is based on individuals' behaving as partners, developing a common vision, setting goals and taking on responsibility together. Leadership in a partnership is indivisible; it should encompass all decision-making situations in business and cannot only be limited to project work.

The second describes **Servant Leadership in the family**. The actors of the family develop easement towards each other to the same extent as they learn to serve themselves. They will learn to recognize the core elements of servant leadership – active listening, empathy, awareness, persuasiveness, imagination, foresight and responsible dealings with others – as their resources. Thus, they will develop a stronger sense of coherence in the family. They are on the right way towards becoming a **"family servant leader", who recognizes the conflict within and outside of the family as comprehensible and manageable, as well as subject to a meaningful solution.**

The coping strategies presented here – partnership management at work and servant leadership in the family – are congruent with that what we have described as easement. The co-evolution of work and family can then succeed if the leadership in both spheres of life is with responsibility and integrity. This presupposes behaviour that is built on truthfulness, instead of manipulation. This behaviour resolves conflicts fairly, instead of suppressing them or violently fighting them out. It conciliates relationships instead of fighting for power and puts others' interests before their own ones. A noble goal? The target achievement begins with the first step!

It remains to be seen whether self-responsibility of the individual for solving conflict of the "Rush Hour of Life" can be permanently kept free from new social expectations, influences or even compulsions, which then postulate a new concept of humanity.

RUSH HOUR OF LIFE

Process diagram

Balance between work and family – Coevolution towards a more efficient and more family-aware behaviour

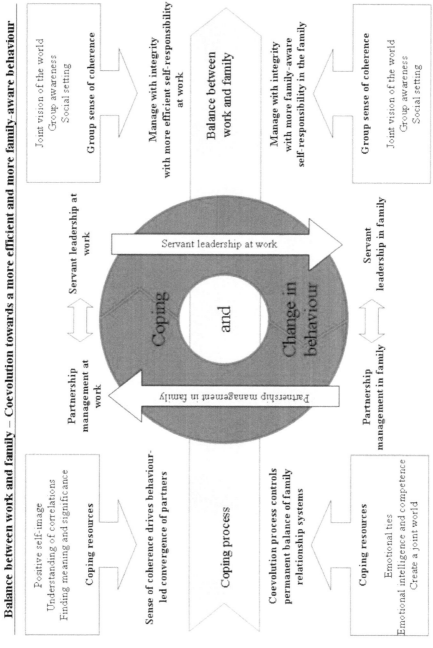

Table 8

Annex

Bibliography

A

- Adler, A., Praxis und Theorie der Individualpsychologie, Frankfurt, 2001

- Aldons, J., Family careers, Rethinking the developmental perspective, Sage, Thousands Oaks, CA, 1996

- Anand, M., Tantra oder die Kunst der sexuellen Ekstase, Mosaik, Munich, 1995, (The Art of Sexual Ecstasy, The Path of Sacred Sexuality for Western Lovers, Tarcher, Los Angeles, 1989)

- Antill, J. K., Sex role complementarity versus similarity in married couples, Journal of Personal and Social Psychology, 45, USA, 1983

- Antonovsky, A., Sourani, T., Family sense of coherence and family adaptation, Journal of Marriage and the Family, 50, USA

- Antonovsky, A., Health, Stress and Coping, New Perspectives on Mental and Physical WellBeing, Jossey-Bass Inc., San Francisco, 1979

- Antonovsky, A., Health, Stress and Coping, New Perspectives on Mental and Physical WellBeing, Jossey-Bass Publisher, San Francisco, 1985

- Antonovsky, A., „Salutogenese. Zur Entmystifizierung der Gesundheit, Deutsche erweiterte Ausgabe, Deutsche Gesellschaft für Verhaltenstherapie, Tübingen, 1997

- Antonovsky, A., Unrevealing the Mystery of Health, How People manage Stress and stay well, Jossey-Bass Publishers, San Francisco, 1987

- Antonovsky, A., Breakdown, A Needed Fourth Step in the Conceptual Armamentarium of Modern Medicine, Social Science and Medicine, USA, 1972

- Anzenbacher, A., (Publisher), Christliche Sozialethik. Einführung und Prinzipien, Paderborn, 1998

- Auer, M., Vereinbarungskarrieren, Eine karrieretheoretische Analyse des Verhältnisses von Erwerbsarbeit und Elternschaft, Die Deutsche Bibliothek, Hampp, Munich, 2002

B

- Bandura, A., Social foundations of thought and action, Prentice Hall, Englewood Cliffs, USA, 1986

- Bartholomew, K., Avoidance of intimacy, An attachment perspective, Journal of Social and Personal Relationship, 7, USA, 1990

- Beck, U., Risikogesellschaft, Auf dem Weg in eine andere Moderne, Frankfurt on the Main, 1986

- Beck, U., Was ist Globalisierung? Frankfurt, 1997.

- Becker, P., Minsel, B., Psychologie der seelischen Gesundheit, Vol. 2, Persönlichkeitspsychologische Grundlagen, Bedingungsanalysen und Fördermöglichkeiten, Hogrefe, Göttingen, 1986

- Beck-Gernsheim, E., Das ganz normale Chaos der Liebe, Frankfurt, 1990

- Beck-Gernsheim, E., Von der Liebe zur Beziehung? Veränderungen im Verhältnis von Mann und Frau in der individualisierten Gesellschaft, In Berger, J., (Publisher), Die Moderne-Kontinuitäten und Zäsuren, Göttingen, 1986

- Bem, S.L., Sex-role adaptability, One consequence of psychological androgyny, Journal of Personal and Social Psychology, 31, USA, 1975

- Bender, D., Lösel, F., Kohärenzsinn und andere Persönlichkeitsmerkmale als protektive Faktoren der Ehequalität (from the project „Protektive Faktoren der Ehestabilität"), quoted from Grau, I., Bierhoff, H.W., Sozialpsychologie in der Partnerschaft, Springer Verlag, Berlin, 2003

- Bengel, J., Strittmatter, R., Willmann, H., Was erhält den Menschen gesund? Antonovskys Modell der Salutogenese, Diskussionsstand und Stellenwert, BzgA, Cologne, 2001

- Berger, P. L., Kellner, H., Die Ehe und die Konstruktion der Wirklichkeit, Soziale Welt 15, 1965

- Berger-B., P.L., Berger-H., Kellner, Das Unbehagen in der Modernität, Frankfurt – New York, 1987

- Berkel, K., Konflikttraining. Konflikte verstehen und bewältigen, Berlin, 1995

- Bittman, M., Mahmud Rice, J., The rush hour: the character of leisure time and gender equity, Social Forces 79(1), p. 165-89, 2000. quoted after: 7th report on families, by the Federal Government of Germany, p. 34

- Block, P., Stewardship and The Empowered Manager, USA

- Bodenmann, G., Cina, A., Stress und Coping als Prädiktoren für Scheidung, Eine prospektive Fünf- Jahres-Langzeitstudie. Zeitschrift für Familienforschung, 12

- Bodenmann, G., Stress und Coping bei Paaren, Göttingen, Hogrefe-Verlag, Göttingen, 2000, quoted after Grau, I., Bierhoff, H.W., Sozialpsychologie in der Partnerschaft, Springer Verlag, 2003

- Bodenmann, Kehl, C., An integrative model of family competence, European Review of Applied Psychology, 47(2), 1997

- Bornemann, E., Die Zukunft der Liebe, Fischer Taschenbuch, 1997

- Bosch, G., Zukunft der Erwerbsarbeit, Frankfurt, New York, 1998

- Boszormenyi-Nagy, J., Krasner, B.R., Between Give and Take, A Clinical Guide to Contextual Therapy, Brunner, Mazel, New York, 1986

- Bowlby, J., Trennung, Fischer Verlag, Frankfurt on the Main, 1976

- Brazelton, T.B., Vorwort zu „Heart Start", The Emotional Foundations of School Readiness, Nation Center for Clinical Infant Programs, USA, 1992

- Brink, A., Management und Anerkennung, in Homann, K., Koslowski, P., Lütge, Ch., (Publisher), Wirtschaftsethik der Globalisierung, Mohr Siebeck, 2005

- Bronfenbrenner, U., Die Ökologie der menschlichen Entwicklung, Klett-Cotta, Stuttgart, 1981

- Bründel, H., Hurrelmann, K., Konkurrenz, Karriere, Kollaps, Männerforschung und der Abschied vom Mythos Mann, Kohlhammer, Stuttgart, 1999

- Buber, M., quoted after Von Brück, M., Wie können wir leben? Munich, 2002
- Buber, M., Das dialogische Prinzip, Lambert Schneider, Heidelberg, 1973, edition 3
- Bueb, B., Lob der Disziplin, List Verlag, Berlin , 2006
- Buonarroti, M., Dichtungen, übertragen von Heinrich Nelson, Eugen Diederichs Verlag, Jena, 1914
- Burisch, M., Das Burn-Out-Syndrom, Heidelberg, 1994
- Buss, D.M., Selection, evocation and manipulation, Journal of Personality and Social Psychology, 53, USA

C

- Cina, A., Dyadisches Coping bei verschiedenen Bindungstypen, Unveröffentliche Lizentiatsarbeit, Fribourg, Institut für Familienforschung und -beratung der Universität Fribourg, 1997
- Corell, W., Psychologie für Beruf und Familie, 18th edition, mvg- Verlag, Heidelberg , 2007
- Corell, W., Das Phänomen Konflikt in Psychologie für Beruf und Familie, Heidelberg, 2007
- Csikszentmihalyi, M., Flow - Das Geheimnis des Glücks, Cotta'sche Buchhandlung Nachfolger, Stuttgart, 1992
- Csikszentmihalyi, M., Lebe gut, Wie Sie das Beste aus Ihrem Leben machen, dtv, Munich, 2001
- Csikszentmihalyi, M., The Psychology of Optimal Experience, Harper, Row, New York, 1990
- Cube, F. v., Lust an der Leistung, Die Naturgesetze der Führung, Piper Verlag, Munich, 1998
- Czwalina, J., Walker, A., Karriere ohne Sinn, Gräfelfing, 1998

D

- Dahrendorf, R., Elemente einer Theorie des sozialen Konfliktes, in Gesellschaft und Freiheit, Munich, 1969
- Davidson, R., in Singer, J.L., (Ed.), Repression and Dissociation, University Press of Chicago, Chicago, 1990
- Dessler, G., Organisation und Management, A Contingency Approach, Englewood Cliffs, Prentice Hall, 1976
- Deutsch, M., Konfliktregelung, Munich, Basle, 1976
- Diamond, L.M., What does sexual orientation orient? A behavioural model distinguishing romantic love and sexual desire, Psychological Review, 110, USA
- Die deutschen Bischöfe - Kommission für gesellschaftliche und soziale Fragen, (Ed.), Mehr Beteiligungsgerechtigkeit, Beschäftigung erweitern, Arbeitslose integrieren, Zukunft sichern, Neun Gebote für die Wirtschafts- und Sozialpolitik, Bonn, 1998
- Drucker, P.F., They're Not Employees, They're People, Harvard Business Review, USA, February 2002

E

- Eagly, A. H., Sex differences in social behaviour, A social role interpretation, Hillsdale, NJ., 1987
- Engelen, E.-M., Erkenntnis und Liebe, Zur fundierten Rolle des Gefühls bei den Leistungen der Vernunft, Vandenhoeck, Ruprecht, Göttingen, 2003
- Erikson, E.H., Growth and crisis of the healthy personality, Psychological Issues 1, USA, 1959
- Erikson, E.H., Identität und Lebenszyklus, Suhrkamp, Frankfurt, 1973

F

- Fauth-Herkner, A., Ergebnisse des Förderprojektes, Familienbewusste Arbeitswelt in Bayern, Bayer. Staatsministerium für Arbeit, Vereinigung der Bayer. Wirtschaft, (Ed.), 2007
- Feeney, J., Noller, P., Adult attachment, Sage, Thousand Oaks, CA
- Feeney, J.A., Issues of closeness and distance in dating relationships, Effects of sex and attachment style, Journal of Social and Personal Relationships, 16, USA, 1999
- Frankl, V.E., Grundriss der Existenzanalyse und Logotherapie, Urban, Schwarzenberg, Munich, 1972, quoted in Riemeyer, J., Logotherapie Frankls,V., Eine Einführung in die sinnorientierte Psychotherapie, Quell, Guetersloh, 2002
- Freud, S., Die Traumdeutung, Frankfurt, 1961
- Freud, S., students' edition, volumes I to X and a supplementary volume, Fischer, Frankfurt on the Main, 1969 f.
- Freund, A., Keil, A., Ein Grund zu bleiben. Liebe aus psychologisch-funktionaler Sicht, in „Tell me about Love", Kultur und Natur der Liebe, Mentis, Paderborn, 2006
- Fromm, E., Haben oder Sein, Deutsche Verlags-Anstalt, Munich, 1976

G

- Gardner, H., Multiple Intelligence, The Theory in Practice, New York, Basic Books, 1993
- Glasersfeld, E.v., Einführung in den radikalen Konstruktivismus, in Watzlawick, (Ed.), "Die erfundene Wirklichkeit", Piper, Munich, 1984
- Glasl, F., Konfliktmanagement, Handbuch für Führungskräfte und Berater, Bern, Stuttgart, 1980
- Goeudevert, D., Die Herausforderungen der Zukunft, Management, Märkte, Motoren, Munich, 1990
- Goleman, D., Emotionale Intelligenz, Carl Hanser Verlag, Munich, Vienna, 1996
- Goleman, D., Empathie, Anfänge in der individuellen Entwicklung und ihre Neurologie, arcticle in New York Times, March 28th 1989
- Gonzaga, G., et al, Love and the commitment problem in romantic relations and friendships, Journal of Personality and Social Psychology, 81, USA, 2001

- Gottman, J.M., Silver, N., The Seven Principles for Making Marriage Work, Random House Inc., New York, 1999

- Gottman, J.M., Die 7 Geheimnisse der glücklichen Ehe, Econ Ullstein List Verlag, Munich, 2000

- Gottman, J.M., The roles of conflict engagements, escalation and avoidance in martial interaction, A longitudinal view of five types of couples, Journal of Consulting and Clinical Psychology, 61, USA, 1993

- Gottman, J.M, A theory of martial dissolution and stability, Journal of Family Psychology, 7, USA, 1993

- Gottman, J.M., What predicts divorce? The relationship between martial processes and martial outcomes, Laurence Erlbaum Associates, Hillsdale, N.J., 1994

- Gottmann, J.M., Silver, N., Die 7 Geheimnisse der glücklichen Ehe, Marion von Schröder Verlag, Munich, 1999

- Greenleaf, R. K., Führen ist Dienen- Dienen ist Führen, The Greenleaf Center of Servant Leadership, Wiley, J., Sons, New York, 2005

- Gruber, H.-G., Familie und christliche Ethik, Wissenschaftl. Buchgesellschaft, Darmstadt, 1995

H

- Habisch, A., (Ed.), Familienorientierte Unternehmensstrategie, Beiträge zu einem zukunftsorientierten Programm, dnwe Schriftenreihe, Folge 1, Rainer Hampp Verlag, Munich, Mering, 1995

- Habisch, A., (Ed.), Familienorientierte Unternehmenspolitik, Schlusswort des Herausgebers

- Hazan, C., Shaver, P.R., Romantic love conceptualized as an attachment process, Journal of Personality and Social Psychology, 52, USA

- Heckhausen, H., Motivation und Handeln, Lehrbuch der Motivationspsychologie, Springer Verlag, Berlin, 1980

- Hesse, H., Die Morgenlandfahrt, quoted after Suhrkamp Taschenbuch 750, first edition, Berlin, 1982

- Hibbard, J.H., Poe, C.R., The quality of social roles as predictors of morbidity and morality, Social Science and Medicine 36, USA, 1993

- Hipp, C., Ethik-Charta 1999, in Wertsteigerung durch Wertschöpfung, Tagungsband des Münchner Management Kolloquiums, Wildemann, H., (Ed.), Hofmann, Traunreut, 2007

- Hollstein, W., Die Männer, Vorwärts oder zurück? Deutsche Verlagsanstalt, Stuttgart, 1990

- Hora T., quoted after Raich, M., Die Philosophie von Ubuntu, in Servant Leadership, Schnorrenberg, L. J., (Ed.), Erich Schmidt Verlag, Berlin, 2000

- Hurrelmann, K., Alte und neue Bilder vom Mann und der Männlichkeit, Vortragstext, Fakultät der Gesundheitswissenschaften der Universität Bielefeld, 1997

- Hüther, G., Biologie der Angst, Wie aus Streß Gefühle werden, Vandenhoeck, Ruprecht, Göttingen, 2002

J

- James, W., The Principles of Psychology, Holt, Rinehart, Winston, New York, 1890, 2 vols., no date

- Jellouschek, H., Wie Partnerschaft gelingt - Spielregeln der Liebe, Herder, Freiburg im Breisgau, edition 3, 1999

- Jerusalem, M., Gesundheitspsychologie, Zur Mehrdimensionalität der Salutogenese, in Seelbach, H., Kugler, J., Neumann, W., (Eds.), Von der Krankheit zur Gesundheit, Huber, Bern, no date

- Johannes Paul II., Enzyklika Centesimus annus Nr. 43, no date

- Jung, C.G., quoted after Staehelin, B., Urvertrauen und zweite Wirklichkeit, Theologischer Verlag, Zurich, 1973

- Jung, C.G., Die Wiederkehr der Seele. GW 16, Walter, Düsseldorf, 1971

K

- Kast, V., Der Schatten in uns. Die subversive Lebenskraft, Walter, Düsseldorf, 2003

- Kehl, M., Psychologie als religiöse Heilslehre, Selbstverwirklichung im New Age, in Frielingsdorf, K., Kehl, M., (Eds.), Ganz und heil, Unterschiedliche Wege zur „Selbstverwirklichung", Echter, Würzburg, no date

- Kelly, G., die Psychologie der persönlichen Konstrukte, Jungfermann, Paderborn, 1986 Koupp, H., Ermutigung zum aufrechten Gang, dgvt-Verlag, 1997

- Kirchler, E., Reiter, L., Interaktion und Beziehungsdyamik in der Familie, in Family Report 1989 by the Federal Ministry of Environment, Youth and Family of Austria

- Kirchner, B., Benedikt für Manager - die geistigen Grundlagen des Führens, Wiesbaden, 1994

- Korff, W., Institutionstheorie, Die sittliche Struktur der gesellschaftlichen Lebensformen, In Handbuch der christlichen Ethik, Vol. 1, Basle, Vienna 1993

- Kotter, J., The New Rules, Dutton, New York, 1995

- Kurtz, H.-J., Konfliktbewältigung im Unternehmen, Köln, Dt. Inst.-Verlag, 1983

L

- Lamparter, U., Deneke F.W., Stuhr, U., Die „Hamburger Gesundheitsstudie" in Lamprecht, Johnen, Salutogenese, Ein neues Konzept in der Psychosomatik?, Kongressband, no date

- Larsson, G., Kallenberg, K.O., Sense of coherence, socio-economic conditions and health, European Journal of Public Health No. 6, no date

- Laubscher, M., Frau und Mann - Geschlechterdifferenzierung in Natur und Menschenwelt, in Schubert, V., (Ed.), Eos Verlag, St. Ottilien Archabbey, 1994

- Lazarus, R.S., Folkman, S., Stress, appraisal and coping, Springer, New York, 1984

- Lazarus, R.S., Launier, R., Streßbezogene Transaktionen zwischen Person und Umwelt, In, Nitsch, J., (Ed.), Streß, Huber, Bern, 1981

- Lazarus, R.S., Emotion and Adaption, Oxford University Press, London, 1991

- Leach, E., Two Essays Concerning the Symbolic Representation of Time, in Rethinking Anthropology, Atholone, London, 1968

- Lenz, H.-J., Männerbildung, Ansätze und Perspektiv in Möller, K., (Ed.), Nur Macher und Macho? Geschlechtsreflektierende Jungen- und Männerarbeit, Juventa, Weinheim, 1997

- Lewin, K., Die Lösung sozialer Konflikte, Christian, Bad Nauheim, 1953

- Lindberg, O., Childhood conditions, SOC, social class and adult ill health: exploring their theoretical and empirical relations, Social Science and Medicine, 44, USA, no date

- Logan, R., The „flow experience" in solitary ordeals, Journal of Humanistic Psychology, 25 (4), USA,1985

- Lorenz, R., Salutogenese, Grundwissen für Psychologen und Mediziner, Gesundheits- und Pflegewissenschaftler, Ernst Reinhardt Verlag, Munich, 2004

- Luhmann, N., Kopierte Existenz und Karriere zur Herstellung von Individualität, Frankfurt, 1994

- Lüscher, K., Die postmoderne Familie: Familiale Strategien und Familienpolitik in einer Übergangszeit, Constance, 1988

- Lüscher,K., Familie und Familienpolitik im Übergang zur Postmoderne, (publisher), Constance, 1990

- Lykken, D.T., Tellegen, A., Is human mating adventitious or the result of a lawful choice? A twin study of mate selection, Journal of Personality and Social Psychology, 6, USA, 1993

M

- Mandela, N., Antrittsrede 1994, own source, no date

- Margalit, A., Politik der Würde, Über Achtung und Verachtung, Berlin, 1997

- Maslow, A., Motivation and Personality, New York, Harper, 1954

- Matthias, H., Scheidungsursachen im Wandel, in Frauenforschung, 8, Bielefeld, 1990

- Mandry, Ch., Handbuch der Ethik, Düwell, M., Hübenthal, Ch., Werner, M.H., (Eds.), Verlag Metzler, Stuttgart, Weimar, 2002

- Marx, R., Das Kapital, Ein Plädoyer für den Menschen, Pattloch Verlag, Munich, 2008

- Mayer, J.D., Stevens, A., An emerging understanding of the reflective (Meta) Experience of Mood, not published, 1993, quoted after Goleman, D., Emotionale Intelligenz, Carl-Hanser Verlag, Munich, Vienna 1996

- Mentzos, S., Neurotische Konfliktverarbeitung, Einführung in die psychoanalytische Neurosenlehre unter Berücksichtigung neuer Perspektiven, Fischer, Frankfurt on the Main, 1997

- Mikula, G., Stroebe, W., Theorien und Determinanten der zwischenmenschlichen Anziehung, in Amelang, M., Ahrens, H.J., Bierhoff, H.W., (Eds.), Attraktion und Liebe, Hogrefe, Goettingen, no date

- Moxley, R., „Leadership as Partnership" in Focus on Leadership, Spears, L., Lawrence, M., (Publisher), John Wiley & Sons, Inc., New York, 2002

N

- Neyer, F.J., Persönlichkeit und Partnerschaft, zitiert aus Grau, I., Bierhoff, H.-W., (Publisher), Sozialpsychologie in der Partnerschaft, Springer-Verlag, Berlin, Heidelberg, 2003

- Nezu, A., Nezu, C.M., Psychological distress, problem solving and coping reactions, Sex role differences, Sex roles, 16, USA, 1987

- Nicholls, A.R., Polman, R.C.J. and Holt, N.L., The effects of individualized imagery interventions on golf performance and flow states, Athletic Insight: the Online Journal of Sport Psychology, 7(1), Issue Jan 6th 2006, from www.athleticinsight.com/Vol.7Iss1/ImageryGolfFlow.htm

O

- Ornstein, S., Making sense of careers, Journal of Management p. 243–267, Los Angeles, 1993

P

- Pakenham, K.J., Couple Coping and adjustment, Family Relations, 47, USA, no date

- Päpstlicher Rat für Gerechtigkeit und Frieden, (Ed.), Kompendium der Soziallehre der Kirche, Freiburg im Breisgau, 2006

- Pearlin, L.J., Schooler, C., The Structure of Coping, Journal of Health and Social Behaviour, 19, USA, 1978

- Perrez, M., Familienstress und Gesundheit, Familienleitbilder und Familienrealitäten, Leske, Budrich, 1997

- Petri, H., Geschwister-Liebe und Rivalität, Die längste Beziehung unseres Lebens, Kreuz Verlag, Zurich, 1994

- Petzhold, H.G., Steffan, A., Gesundheit, Krankheit, Diagnose- und Therapieverständnis in "Integrative Therapie", anniversary issue 2001

- Petzold, H.G., Integrative Therapie, Modelle, Theorien und Methoden für eine schulenübergreifende Psychotherapie, volumes 1–3, Jungfermann, Paderborn, 1993

- Pistole, C., Adult attachment styles, Some thoughts on closeness-distance struggles, Family Process, 33, USA, no date

- Pius XI., Enzyklika Quadragesimo anno, Nr. 79, In, Bundesverband der Katholischen Arbeitnehmer-Bewegung (Ed.), TKSL, Cologne, 1982

- Pümpin, C., Kobi, J.-M., Wüthrich, H.A., Unternehmenskultur, in: "Die Orientierung", volume 85, 1985

R

- Ratzinger, J., Zur Theologie der Ehe, in Krems, G., Mumm, R., (Publisher), Theologie der Ehe, Regensburg, Göttingen, 1969

- Revenson, T.A., Social support and martial coping with cronical illness, Annals of Behavioural Medicine, 16, USA, 1994

- Pakenham, K.J., Couple coping and adjustment... Family Relations, 47, USA, no date

- Rimann, M., Udris, I., Kohärenzerleben (SOC), Zentraler Bestandteil von Gesundheit und Gesundheitsressource? In Handbuch der Salutogenese, Konzept und Praxis, Schüffel, W., et al., (Eds.), Ullstein Medical, 1988

- Roth, S. J., Würde, Einkommen und Arbeit in der sozialen Marktwirtschaft, Roman Herzog Institut, Position 4, no date

- Röttger-Rössler, B., Engelen, E.-M., (Publisher), Tell me about love, Kultur und Natur der Liebe, mentis Verlag, 2006

- Rusche, T., Aspekte einer dialogbezogenen Unternehmensethik, in Ethik und Wirtschaft im Dialog, EWD Band 4, List Verlag, Münster, Hamburg, London, 2002

- Rüttiger, R., Transaktionsanalyse, Arbeitshefte zur Führungspsychologie, brochure 10, Heidelberg, 1980

- Rüttinger, B., Konflikt und Konfliktlösen, Neues Lernen - Studienbücher, Psychologie im Betrieb, 1980

S

- Sack, M., Lamprecht, F., Lässt sich der SOC durch Psychotherapie beeinflussen, in Salutogenese, ein neues Konzept in der Psychosomatik, VAS, 1997

- Salovey, P., Mayer, J.D., Emotional Intelligence, Imagination, Cognition and Personality, 9, USA, 1990

- Schelp, T., Karriere und persönliche Kompetenz, 1994

- Schenk, H., Freie Liebe – wilde Ehe, über die allmähliche Auflösung der Ehe durch die Liebe, Munich, 1988

- Schmidt, H.-L., Leben als Wagnis, Hilfe zur Bewährung und Bewährungshilfe, Festvortrag anlässlich des 25 jährigen Bestehens des Vereins, Förderung der Bewährungshilfe in Schwaben e.V., diritto Publikation, Eichstaett, 2003

- Schmitz, E., Hanke, G., Sinnerfahrung, innere Langeweile und die Modi der Stressverarbeitung, In, Integrative Therapie, Vol. 1, no date

- Schmitz, H., quoted after Lorenz, R., Salutogenese, Ernst Reinhardt Verlag, Munich, Basle, 2004

- Schneewind, K.A., Wunderer, E., Prozessmodelle der Partnerschaftsentwicklung, In, Sozialpsychologie der Partnerschaft, Grau, J., Bierhoff H.-W., (Eds.), Springer-Verlag, Berlin, 2003

- Schneewind, K.A., Graf, J., Gerhard, A.-K., (Eds.), Paarbeziehungen, Entwicklung und Intervention, no date

- Schneider, N., Limmer, R., Ruckdeschel, K., Familie und Beruf in der mobilen Gesellschaft, Frankfurt, 2002

- Schneider, W., Streitende Liebe, Zur Soziologie familialer Konflikte, Leske, Buderich, Opladen, 1994

- Schneider-Düker, M., Kohler, A., Die Erfassung von Geschlechtsrollen – Ergebnisse zur deutschen Neukonstruktion des Bem Sex-Role Inventory, Diagnostica, 34, 1988

- Schnorrenberg, L.J., Servant Leadership – die Führungskultur des 21. Jahrhunderts, in Servant Leadership, Prinzipien dienender Unternehmensführung, Hinterhuber H.H., Schnorrenberg, L.J. et al. (Eds.), Erich Schmidt Verlag, Berlin, 2007

- Schüffel, W., (Ed.), Handbuch der Salutogenese, Konzept und Praxis, Beitrag 3, Brucks, M., Wahl, W.-D., Schüffel, W., Ullstein Medical, 1998

- Schumacher, J., Gunzelmann, T., Brähler, E., „Deutsche Normierung der Sense of Coherence Scale von Antonovsky; appeared in Diagnostica, 46, 2000

- Schwarz, G., Gedanken zum Konfliktmanagement, Harvard Manager, H.1, USA, 1984 Secretan, L., Soul-Management, Lichtenberg 1997 Seligman, M., Learned Optimism, Knopf, New York, 1991

- Selye, H., Stress mein Leben, Erinnerungen eines Forschers, Kindler Verlag, Munich, 1979

- Sennett, R., Der flexible Mensch. Die Kultur des neuen Kapitalismus, Berliner Taschenbuch Verlag, Berlin, 2006

- Shaver, P.R., Collins, N., Clark, C.L., Attachment styles and internal working models of self

- Shoda, Y., Mischel, W., Paeke, P.K., Predicting adolescent cognitive and self-regulatory competences from preschool delay of gratification, Development Psychology, 26, 6, USA, 1990

- Siegrist, J., Selbstregulation, Emotion und Gesundheit – Versuch einer sozialwissenschaftlichen Grundlegung in Lamprecht, F., Johnen, R., Salutogenese, Kongressband VAS, Frankfurt, 1997

- Siegrist, J., Soziale Krisen und Gesundheit, Hogrefe, Göttingen, 1994

- Simonton, O.C., Simonton, M.S., Creighton, J., (Publisher), Wieder gesund werden, Eine Anleitung zur Aktivierung der Selbstheilungskräfte für Krebspatienten und ihre Angehörigen, Rowohlt, Reinbek near Hamburg, 1995

- Snyder, C.R. et al., The will and the ways: development and validation of an individual - differences measure of hope, Journal of Personality and Social Psychology, 60, 4, USA, 1991

- Spears, L.C., Tracing the Past, Present and Future of Servant-Leadership, In, Focus on Leadership, The Greenleaf Center of Servant-Leadership, (Publisher), John Wiley & Sons, Inc., New York, 2002

- Sprenger, R., Wer führt, ohne dass die Menschen folgen, geht nur spazieren, Servant Leadership, Prinzipien dienender Unternehmensführung, Erich Schmidt Verlag, Berlin, 2007

- Staehelin, B., Urvertrauen und zweite Wirklichkeit, Theologischer Verlag, Zurich, no date

- Statistisches Bundesamt, Leben in Deutschland, Haushalte, Familien und Gesundheit – Ergebnisse des Mikrozensus, 2005

- Stern, D., The Interpersonal World of the Infant, Basic Books, New York, 1987

T

- Thadden, E., Gesucht Fachkraft mit Familiensinn, Die Zeit, 45, Dossier, no date

- Tölke, A., Das Zusammenspiel von Familienentwicklung und Erwerbsverhalten von Frauen, Zeitschrift für Familienforschung 2, 1990

- Tournier, P., Aus Vereinsamung zur Gemeinschaft, Basle, no date

- Turgeon, L., Julien, D., Dion, E., Temporal linkage between wifes' pursuit and husbands' withdrawal during martial conflicts, Family Process, 37, USA, 1998

- Tyrell, H., Probleme einer Theorie der gesellschaftlichen Ausdifferenzierung der privatisierten modernen Kernfamilie, in: Zeitschrift für Soziologie 5, 1976

U

- Ulrich, P., Integrative Wirtschaftsethik, Grundlagen einer lebensdienlichen Ökonomie, Bern, Stuttgart, Vienna, 2001

W

- Watson, D., Hubbard, B., Wiese, D., Self-other agreement in personality and affectivity: The role acquaintanceship, trait visibility and assumed similarity, Journal of Personality and Social Psychology, 78, USA, 2000

- Weber, M., Wirtschaft und Gesellschaft, 1922 (posthum)

- Weimer, W., Credo - Warum die Rückkehr der Religion gut ist – Deutsche Verlagsanstalt, Munich, no date

- Wickler, W., extract from the preface to the German edition of "Das egoistische Gen" by Dawkins R., Spektrum Akademischer Verlag, Heidelberg, 2008

- Willi, J., Psychologie der Liebe, Rowohlt Taschenbuchverlag, Reinbek near Hamburg, 2002

- Willi, J., Ko-evolution – Die Kunst des gemeinsamen Wachsens – Rowohlt Verlag, Reinbek near Hamburg, 1985

- Willi, J., Wendepunkte im Lebenslauf, Klett-Cotta, Stuttgart, 2007

- Willi, J., Was hält Paare zusammen? Der Prozess des Zusammenlebens in psycho-ökologischer Sicht, Rowohlt Taschenbuch Verlag, Hamburg, 9th edition, 2004

- Willi, J., , Die Zweierbeziehung, Rowohlt Taschenbuch Verlag, Hamburg, Hamburg, 16th edition, 2004

Z

- Zillmann, D., Neutral Control of Angry Aggression, In, Wegener, D.M., Pennebaker, J., (Eds.), Handbook of Mental Control, Guilford, New York, 1993

- Zuschlag, B., Thielke, W., Konfliktsituationen im Alltag, Verlag f. Angewandte Psychologie, Göttingen, 1998

- Zweites Vatikanisches Konzil, Pastorale Konstitution über die Kirche in der Welt von heute, Gaudium et Spes, no date

List of tables

Table 1: Weighting of causes of conflict during the period from 1981 to 2009

Table 2: Corell, W. and own sources, The five basic motivations, 2014

Table 3: Sack, M., Lamprecht, F., Vergleich Behandlungsbeginn / Behandlungsende, Lässt sich der SOC durch Psychotherapie beeinflussen, in Salutogenese, ein neues Konzept in der Psychosomatik, VAS, 1997, p. 189, Table 4

Table 4: Schmidt, W., Recognition and Fairness in an Enterprise, 2009

Table 5: Fauth-Herkner, A., Spannungsfelder Work-Life, Ergebnisse des Förderprojektes, Familienbewusste Arbeitswelt in Bayern, Bayer. Staatsministerium für Arbeit, Vereinigung der Bayer. Wirtschaft, (Publisher), 2007, p.10

Table 6: Fauth-Herkner, A., Vom Standard- Erwerbsleben zur Patchwork- Biographie, Ergebnisse des Förderprojektes, Familienbewusste Arbeitswelt in Bayern, Bayer, Staatsministerium für Arbeit, Vereinigung der Bayer. Wirtschaft, (Ed.), 2007, p.14

Table 7: Rimann, M., Udris, I., Kohärenzerleben (SOC) und Hierarchieposition, Kohärenzerleben (SOC), Zentraler Bestandteil von Gesundheit und Gesundheitsressource? In: Handbuch der Salutogenese, Konzept und Praxis, Schüffel, W., et al., (Eds.), Ullstein Medical, 1988

Table 8: Schmidt, W., Process diagram – Balance between family and career, 2009